A Sum

A Summer in Skye

ALEXANDER SMITH

Edited by

William F. Laughlan

BIRLINN

This edition first published in 2012 by
Birlinn Limited
West Newington House
10 Newington Road
Edinburgh
EH9 1QS

www.birlinn.co.uk

First Published in 1865
by Alexander Strahan

British Library Cataloguing-in-Publication Data
A Catalogue record for this book is available from the British Library.

ISBN: 978 1 87474 438 2

Typeset by Hewer Text UK Ltd, Edinburgh
Printed and bound by Clays Ltd, St Ives plc

Contents

Editor's Note

A Summer in Skye is certainly a romance, yet it is firmly rooted in fact. Mr M'Ian of Ord has been identified as Charles Macdonald of Ord, Alexander Smith's father-in-law. The Landlord is Kenneth Macleod of Greshornish. Further information on both of these principals can be found in Otta F. Swire's excellent little book, *Skye – The Island and its legends* (OUP 1952). Charles Macdonald was the son and grandson of Jacobite 'outlaws' yet served the crown in every war he could find, from the West Indies via Ireland to Waterloo. Macleod (1809–69) returned to Skye after several years in India, planting tea and Indigo; bought Greshornish, Orbost and Skeabost when unable to purchase the family home of Gesto; suffered the loss of the girl he loved; planned and built the village of Edinbane and established its hospital; and was, in many senses, one of the dominant figures on Skye in his time.

If any readers have information concerning other individuals featured in the book, John Penruddock, Fellowes, Father M'Crimmon, the various shepherds and emigrants, pupils, cotters and landlords, or knows of, or has access, to paintings or photographs of these same people, I would be grateful for details.

W.F.L.

Introduction

A Summer in Skye was the product of happiness and contentment. Its place in the catalogue of Alexander Smith's work, firmly
locked into those later years when he had all but abandoned
poetry in favour of prose, ensured that it did not suffer by association with the controversies that blazed through his earlier phase
of fame, fortune and fallibility. And it was, in many ways, his
thanksgiving for the happiness of marriage to Flora, the Skye girl
who introduced him to her Island, her people and their legendary
past. *A Summer in Skye* is a distillation of seven summers, a prose
poem in which Alexander Smith explored his own soul as well
as the mist-wreathed mountains and the squall-rushed lochs, the
shadows of Fingal and Ossian and the Second Sight as well as the
flesh-and-blood inhabitants of the Island in his own time: M'Ian,
the Landlord, John Kelly, Lachlan Roy.

A vivacious, enthusiastic, full-blooded prose poem, a ramble
through the centuries, across moorlands and over the entire length
of the island, *A Summer in Skye* is filled with the breath of life
– Smith's own life – and perhaps it is his awareness of his own
mortality, when surrounded by the immortality of the mountains
and the ancient gods, that gives it a poignancy not often found in
books written about holiday haunts.

There is indeed something haunting about the book. It is rooted
in the character of Alexander Smith himself – the largely self-
taught son of a Kilmarnock lace-pattern-designer who followed
his father's trade but sensed that he had within himself something
to express and believed that poetry was the proper medium for

1

his sentiments. He began modestly enough, in his youth, writing for his own amusement; later, he summoned up the courage to submit a number of his poems to the Rev. George Gilfillan of Dundee, a renowned critic of the time. With the support and encouragement of Gilfillan, Smith's work began to appear in literary journals and to win an influential readership. In 1852 *A Life Drama* was published and the real-life drama of Alexander Smith was under way.

The collection of poems struck a responsive chord in the public imagination. Smith was hailed as 'a born singer,' 'a man of genius,' 'a finer poet than Keats,' 'the greatest poet Scotland has ever produced.' Heady stuff for a twenty-two-year-old lace-pattern-designer who had rarely ventured beyond the valley of the Clyde, who found himself the possessor of £100 with more to follow, who was sought after by literary Glasgow, Edinburgh, Lakeland and London. Fame and fortune brought immediate changes – Smith resigned his job and started for London with his friend John Nichol. He called on Harriet Martineau at Ambleside, on George Henry Lewes, Herbert Spencer and Arthur Helps, even Elizabeth Barrett Browning, who considered that he had 'noble stuff in him.'

He returned to Scotland, a guest much in demand. He spent a week at Inverary on the invitation of the Duke of Argyll and, later, visited Lord Dufferin in Ireland. But the money was running out and the famous poet had no desire to return to pattern-designing.

He already had contacts in the Glasgow newspaper world – with Hugh Macdonald, whose two books, *Rambles round Glasgow* and *Days at the Coast* had found considerable popularity in the West of Scotland and who was something of a mentor to the young poet. Macdonald, himself a former factory-worker turned journalist, amateur naturalist and occasional poet, was sub-editor of the *Glasgow Citizen* and, though a close friend, no admirer of Smith's work. 'It may be poetry,' he is reported as saying, 'I'm no sayin' it isna; the creetics say it's poetry, an' nae doot they suld ken;

but it's no my kind o' poetry. Just a blatter o' braw words, to my mind, an' bit whirly-whas, they ca' eemages!'

But Smith's reputation obtained for him the post as editor of Buchanan's *Glasgow Miscellany* until, in 1854, he became Secretary to Edinburgh University, which appointment he held until his death. He was still enjoying the critical favour won by *A Life Drama*, but his talents were about to be questioned.

A satire by Professor Aytoun, *Firmilian; or, the Student of Badajoz: A Spasmodic Tragedy*, was published that same year. It was aimed at the poetry of Bailey, Sydney Dobell and Alexander Smith and the epithet 'spasmodic' struck home.

In the following year, Smith and Dobell collaborated on *Sonnets on the Crimean War*, and in 1857 *City Poems* was published. The career which had started so promisingly, faltered. Indeed, it had begun too promisingly, success had been achieved too easily. Critics who had over-responded to *A Life Drama* now made amends by condemning *City Poems*. The murmur started by Aytoun grew in volume and it seemed as though nothing from Smith's pen would satisfy. He continued to work, however, to write, to socialize and enjoy the benefits of his life.

1857 was also the year of his marriage to Flora Macdonald, daughter of Charles Macdonald of Ord, and a blood-relative of the famous heroine of the same name, and that year saw the first of the annual vacations on the Island. Smith was captivated. The spirit of Skye, its mystic past, dramatic present, contrast of cultures – these forces combined to fill Smith with an awareness he had hardly dreamed of. There was something pagan in his response to the majesty of the mountains, to the loneliness of the sea-lochs, to the utter freedom to be experienced far from the constraints of Edinburgh. He loved Skye with his body and soul – absorbed the Island and made in part of himself. Sitting in his study at Wardie he had only to think of Duntulm to taste the salt spray, to hear the ocean's pounding roar, to lose himself in the mists whirling up from the broken shore.

Indeed Skye was becoming such an integral part of Smith that when in 1861 his next work, the epic poem *Edwin of Deira* was issued, two Skye poems, *Torquil and Oona* and *Blaavin* were included in the volume. But though it had been four years in the preparation. *Edwin* was to earn Smith just £15.5s. 3d and to bring a storm of protest about his head. That same year, Tennyson published *Idylls of the King* and when *Edwin* was issued shortly after, Smith was accused of, at the very least, imitation; at worst, downright plagiarism.

He took the advice of Professor Aytoun – a close friend, for all his 'spasmodic' taunts – and abandoned poetry as his principal medium. The collection of essays, *Dreamthorp*, was published in 1863 and was well received, as was *A Summer in Skye* in 1865 and *Alfred Hagart's Household*, serialised in *Good Words* and issued in book form in 1866. This last was his only novel, although he was planning a second when, in November 1866, he contracted typhoid fever, complicated with diphtheria, and died on January 5th 1867. He was buried in Edinburgh's Warriston Cemetery – to be joined just two months later by his beloved eldest daughter, Flora.

The story of Alexander Smith is, in many ways, so typical of the 19th century as to seem drawn from the pages of a novelette. It formed the basis of *Alfred Hagart's Household*, but the mixture of success and failure, literary feuding, a strong romantic interest, a youthful promise unfulfilled and then, seemingly, about to be realized, only to be dashed by sudden death, all set against strong scenic backgrounds – industrial Glasgow of the 1830s and '40s, academic Edinburgh, the untamed Western Isles – is the stuff of vivid, tear-jerking melodrama.

Yet Smith never saw himself as a hero – nor as a plagiarising villain. He was a modest man, fond of society but never the centre of the crowd; he gave an impression of always being somewhere else, usually in Skye. He excelled as an observer and it is in his observations that much of the real pleasure of *A Summer in Skye* lies.

The touch is gentle, for Smith is writing as much for his own pleasure as for the reader's. It is sincere and honest, and because of that it is, in a sense, timeless. Many summers make up the book, although principally it is that of 1864. But read today, it hardly seems as though a hundred and twenty years have elapsed. The facts say so. The trappings confirm it. The references to peat-huts and cotters, to dog-carts and M'Ian's military record set the book firmly in its period. But the mountains are unchanged, the legends still swirl around them with the white mists, it still rains on Skye and, above all, there are still people like M'Ian, the Landlord, Father M'Crimmon, John Kelly, Angus-with-the-dogs, Lachlan Roy, John Penruddock, the Tobacco-less Man, to be encountered on Skye.

Even briefly-met minor characters, the landlords of various inns, cart-drivers, ministers, travelling entertainers, all come alive in a few well-chosen words. But not just because Smith had the words, or the skill in using them – rather, because *A Summer in Skye* was, for him, an attempt to transcend time. Its beauty lies in its very spirituality – in Smith's subconscious awareness that his own life was to be curtailed. We are conscious of the irony, which he cannot have been, when he writes of M'Ian's longevity. For we know that Smith had only two more years to live.

But there is nothing gloomy about the book. Indeed, few books of the period are so full of colour and light gaiety. To Smith, Skye was a haven, a retreat, a breath of clean fresh air. He lived for his annual vacation and his enthusiasm for the island and its people, their customs, their foibles, leaps out of every page.

For this edition, I have re-arranged some sections of the original text and omitted others, to tighten-up the narrative – perhaps slightly at the expense of Smith's discursiveness – and make the book more accessible to the present day reader who will discover in *A Summer in Skye* what Alexander Smith intended for them: fun and pleasure. It is a book well worth reading again and again, worth taking to Loch Coruisk, to Dunvegan, to Duntulm, worth browsing through and dipping into. It may not qualify as a guidebook for the tourist, but as a guidebook for the lover of mountains, of surf, of moorland and river, for the lover of people as they were and as they are, for the lover of the poetry of eternal truths, *A Summer in Skye* is *the* book to read.

William F. Laughlan
Hawick
28 June 1983

Summer in Skye

SUMMER HAS LEAPED suddenly on Edinburgh like a tiger. The air is still and hot above the houses; but every now and then a breath of east wind startles me through the warm sunshine and passes on; yet, with this exception, the atmosphere is so close, so laden with a body of heat, that a thunderstorm would be almost welcome as a relief. Edinburgh, on her crags, held high towards the sun – too distant the sea to send cool breezes to street and square – is at this moment an uncomfortable dwelling-place. Beautiful as ever, of course – for nothing can be finer than the ridge of the Old Town etched on hot summer azure – but close, breathless, suffocating. Great volumes of white smoke surge out of the railway station; great choking puffs of dust issue from the houses and shops that are being gutted in Princes Street.

The Castle rock is gray; the trees are of a dingy olive; languid swells, arm-in-arm, promenade uneasily the heated pavement; water-carts everywhere dispense their treasures; and the only human being really to be envied in the city is the small boy who, with trousers tucked up and unheeding of maternal vengeance, marches cooling in the fringe of the ambulating shower-bath. Oh for one hour of heavy rain!

Thereafter would the heavens wear a clear and tender, instead of a dim and sultry hue. Then would the Castle rock brighten in colour and the trees and grassy slopes doff their dingy olives for the emeralds of April. Then would the streets be cooled and the dust be allayed. Then would the belts of city verdure, refreshed, pour forth gratitude in balmy smells; and Fife – low-lying across the Forth – break from its hot neutral tint into the greens, purples and yellows that of right belong to it. But rain won't come; and for weeks, perhaps, there will be nothing but hot sun above and hot street beneath; and for the respiration of poor human lungs an atmosphere of heated dust, tempered with east wind.

Moreover, I am tired and jaded. The whole man, body and soul, like sweet bells jangled, out of tune and harsh, is fagged with work, eaten up of impatience and haunted with visions of vacation. I babble o' green fields, like a very Falstaff; and my poor tired ears hum with sea-music like a couple of sea-shells. At last it comes, the 1st of August, and then – like an arrow from a Tartar's bow, like a bird from its cage, like a lover to his mistress – I am off; and before the wild scarlets of sunset die on the northern sea, I am in the silence of the hills, those eternal sun-dials that tell the hours to the shepherd and in my nostrils is the smell of peat-reek and in my throat the flavour of usquebaugh. Then come long floating summer days, so silent the wilderness, that I can hear my heart beat; then come long silent nights, the waves heard upon the shore, although *that* is a mile away, in which I snatch the 'fearful joy' of a ghost story, told by a shepherd or fisher, who believes in it as in his own existence. Then I behold sunset, not through the smoked glass of towns, but gloriously through the clearness of enkindled air. Then I make acquaintance with sunrise, which to a dweller in a city, who conforms to the usual proprieties, is about the rarest of this world's sights.

The month of August is to the year what Sunday is to the week. During that month a section of the working world rests. *Bradshaw* is consulted, portmanteaus are packaged, knapsacks are strapped on, steamboats and railway carriages are crammed and from Calais to Venice the tourist saunters and looks about him. It is absolutely necessary that the Briton should have, each year, one month's cessation from accustomed labour. He works hard, puts money in his purse and it is his whim, when August comes, by way of recreation, to stalk deer on Highland corries, to kill salmon in Norwegian fiords, to stand on the summit of Mont

Blanc and to perambulate the pavement of Madrid, Naples and St Petersburg.

Early in the month in which English tourists descend on the Continent in a shower of gold, it has been my custom, for several years back, to seek refuge in the Hebrides. I love Loch Snizort better than the Meditteranean and consider Duntulm more impressive than Drachenfels. I have never seen the Alps, but the Cuchullins content me. I confess to a strong affection for those remote regions.

Jaded and nervous with eleven months' labour or disappointment, *there* will a man find the medicine of silence and repose. Pleasant, after poring over books, to watch the cormorant at early morning flying with outstretched neck over the bright frith; pleasant, lying in some sunny hollow at noon, to hear the sheep bleating above; pleasant at evening to listen to wild stories of the isles told by a peat-fire; and pleasantest of all, lying awake at midnight, to catch, muffled by distance, the thunder of the northern sea and to think of all the ears the sound has filled.

In Skye I am free of my century; the present wheels away into silence and remoteness; I see the ranges of brown shields and hear the shoutings of the Bare Sarks; I walk into antiquity and see everything in the light of Ossian, as in the light of a mournful sunset. With a Norse murmur the blue Lochs come running in. The Island has not yet, to any considerable extent been overrun by the tourist and everything about me is remote and strange. I hear a foreign language; I am surrounded by Macleods, Macdonalds and Nicolsons; I come on gray stones standing upright on the moor – marking the site of a battle, or the burial-place of a chief. I listen to traditions of ancient skirmishes; I sit on ruins of ancient date, in which Ossian might have sung. The Loch yonder was darkened by the banner of King Haco. Prince Charles wandered over this heath, or slept in that cave. The country is thinly peopled and its solitude is felt as a burden. The precipices of the Storr lower grandly over the sea; the eagle has yet its eyrie on the ledges of the Cuchullins. The sound of the sea is continually in my ears; the silent armies of mists and vapours perpetually deploy; the wind is gusty on the moor; and ever and anon the jags of the hills are obscured by swirls of fiercely-blown rain. And more than all, the island is prevaded by a subtle spiritual atmosphere. It is as strange to the mind as it is to the eye. Old songs and traditions are the spiritual analogues of old castles and burying-places – and old songs and traditions there are in abundance.

There is a smell of the sea in the material air; and there is a ghostly something in the air of the imagination. There are prophesying voices amongst the hills of an evening. The raven that flits across my path is a weird thing – mayhap by the spell of some strong enchanter, a human soul is balefully imprisoned in the hearse-like carcass. I hear the stream and the voice of the kelpie in it. I breathe again the air of old story-books; but they are northern, not eastern ones.

To what better place then, can the tired man go? There I will find refreshment and repose. There the wind blows out on me from another century. My bourne is the island of which Douglas dreamed on the morning of Otterburn; but even to *it* I will not unnecessarily hurry, but will look on many places on my way. You have to go to London; but unless your business is urgent, you are a fool to go thither like a parcel in the night train and miss York and Peterborough.

The Highlands can be enjoyed in the utmost simplicity; and the best preparations are – money to a moderate extent in my pocket, a knapsack containing a spare shirt and a toothbrush and a courage that does not fear to breast the steep of the hill and to encounter the pelting of a Highland shower. No man knows a country till he has walked through it; he then tastes the sweets and the bitters of it. He beholds its grand and important points and all the subtler and concealed beauties that lie out of the beaten track. Then, O reader, in the most glorious of the months, the very crown and summit of the fruit year, hanging in equal poise between summer and autumn, leave London or Edinburgh, or whatever city your lot may happen to be cast in and accompany me on my wanderings. Our course will lead us by ancient battle-fields, by castles standing in hearing of the surge; by the bases of mighty mountains, along the wanderings of hollow glens; and if the weather holds, we may see the keen ridges of Blaavin and the Cuchullin hills; listen to a legend as old as Ossian, while sitting on the broken stair of the castle of Duntulm, beaten for centuries by the salt flake and the wind; and in the pauses of ghostly talk in the long autumn nights, when the rain is on the hills, we may hear – more wonderful than any legend, carrying us away to misty regions and half-forgotten times – the music which haunted the Berserkers of old, the thunder of the northern sea!

The chain of islands on the western coast of Scotland, extending from Bute in the throat of the Clyde, beloved of invalids, onward to St. Kilda, looking through a cloud of gannets toward the polar night, was originally an appanage of the crown of Norway. In the dawn of history there is a noise of Norsemen around the islands, as there is today a noise of sea-birds. Old Norwegian castles, perched on the bold Skye headlands, yet moulder in hearing of the surge. The sea-rovers come no longer in their dark galleys, but hill and dale wear ancient names that sigh to the Norway pine. The Skye headlands of Trotternish, Greshornish and Vaternish, look northward to Norway headlands that wear the same or similar names; The names of many of the islands, Arran, Gigha, Mull, Tyree, Skye, Raasay, Lewes and others are, in their original form, Norwegian and not Gaelic. The Hebrides have received a Norse baptism.

Situated as these islands are between Norway and Scotland, the Norseman found them convenient stepping-stones, or resting-places, on his way to the richer southern lands. There he erected temporary strongholds and founded settlements and in course of time a mixed race was the result of alliances between the song of the Norseman and the daughter of the Celt. To this day in the islands the Norse element is distinctly visible – not only in old castles, the names of places, but in the faces and entire mental build of the people. Claims of pure Scandinavian descent are put forward by many of the old families. Wandering up and down the islands you encounter faces that possess no Celtic characteristics; which carry the imagination to 'Noroway ower the faem;' people with cool calm blue eyes and hair yellow as the dawn; who are resolute and persistent, slow in pulse and speech; and who differ from the explosive Celtic element surrounding them as the iron headland differs from the fierce surge that washes it, or a block of marble from the heated palm pressed against it.

The Hebrideans are a mixed race; in them the Norseman and the Celt are combined and here and there is a dash of Spanish blood which makes brown the cheek and darkens the eye. This southern admixture may have come about through old trading relations with the Peninsula – perhaps the wrecked Armada may have had something to do with it. For many a gallant ship of the Spanish Armada was wrecked on the shores of the Western Islands, on the retreat to Spain; and a gun taken from one of these, it is said, lies at Dunstaffnage Castle.

The Highlander stands alone amongst the British people. For generations his land was shut against civilisation by mountain and forest and intricate pass. While the large drama of Scottish history was being played out in the Lowlands, he was busy in his mists with narrow clan-fights and revenges. While the southern Scot owed allegiance to the Jameses, he was subject to Lords of the Isles and to Duncans and Donalds innumerable.

The Highlander was and is still, so far as circumstances permit, a proud, loving, punctillious being: full of loyalty, careful of social distinctions; with a bared head of his chief, a jealous eye for his equal, an armed heel for his inferior. He loved the valley in which he was born, the hills on the horizon of his childhood; his sense of family relationships was strong and around him widening rings of cousinship extended to the very verge of the clan. The Isles-man is a Highlander of the Highlanders; modern life took longer in reaching him and his weeping climate, his misty wreaths and vapours and the silence of his moory environments, naturally continued to act upon and shape his character. He is song-loving and out of the natural phenomena of his mountain region – his mist and raincloud, wan sea-setting of the moon, stars glancing through rifts of vapour, blowing wind and broken rainbows – he has drawn his poetry and his superstition. His mists give him the shroud high on the living heart, the sea-foam gives him an image of the whiteness of the breasts of his girls and the broken rainbow of their blushes. To a great extent his climate has made him what he is. He is a child of the mist and you may discover in his music the monotony of the brown moor, the seethe of the wave on the rock, the sigh of the wind in the long grasses of the deserted churchyard.

The Highlands are now open to all the influences of civilisation. The inhabitants wear breeches and speak English even as we. Old gentlemen peruse their *Times* with spectacles on nose. Young ladies knit and practise music and wear crinoline. But the old descent and breeding are visible through all modern disguises; and your Highlander at Oxford or Cambridge – discoverable not only by his rocky countenance, but by some dash of wild blood, or eccentricity, or enthusiasm, or logical twist and turn of thought – is as much a child of the mist as his ancestor who, three centuries ago, was called a 'wilde man' or a 'red shanks;' who could, if need were, live on a little oatmeal, sleep in snow and, with one hand on the stirrup, keep pace with the swiftest horse, let the rider spur never so fiercely.

It is the Isles, however and particularly amongst the old Islemen, that the Highland character is, at this day, to be found in its purity. There, in the dwelling of the proprietor, or still more in that of the large sheep farmer – who is of as good blood as the laird himself – you find the hospitality, the prejudice, the generosity, the pride of birth, the delight in ancient traditions, which smack of the antique time. Love of wandering and pride in military life, have been characteristic of all the old families. The pen is alien to their fingers, but they have wielded the sword industriously. They have had representatives in every Peninsular and Indian battlefield; India has been the chosen field of their activity and the Island of Skye has itself given to the British and Indian armies at least a dozen generals. And lads, to whom the profession of arms has been shut, have gone to plant indigo in Bengal or coffee in Ceylon and have returned with gray hairs to the island to spend their money there and to make the stony soil a little greener; and during their thirty years of absence Gaelic did not moulder on their tongues, nor did their fingers forget their cunning with the pipes. The palm did not obliterate the memory of the birch; nor the slow up-swelling of the tepid wave and its long roar of frothy thunder on the flat red sands at Madras, the coasts of their childhood and the smell and smoke of burning kelp.

The important names in Skye are Macdonald and Macleod. Both are of great antiquity and it is as difficult to discover the source of either in history as it is to discover the source of the Nile in the deserts of Central Africa. Macdonald is of pure Celtic origin, it is understood; Macleod was originally a Norseman. Macdonald was the Lord of the Isles and more than once crossed swords with Scottish kings. Time has stripped him of royalty and the present representative of the family is a Baron merely. He sits in his modern castle of Armadale amid pleasant larch plantations, with the figure of Somerlid – the half-mythical founder of his race – in the large window of his hall. The two families inter-married often and quarrelled oftener. They put wedding rings on each other's fingers and dirks into each other's hearts. Of the two, Macleod had the darker origin; and around his name there lingers a darker poetry. Macdonald sits in his new castle in sunny Sleat with a southern outlook – Macleod retains his old eyrie at Dunvegan, with its drawbridge and dungeons. At night he can hear the sea beating on the base of his rock. His 'maidens' are wet with the sea foam. His mountain 'tables' are shrouded with the mists of the Atlantic. He has a fairy flag in his possession. The rocks and mountains around him wear his name as of old did his clansmen. 'Macleod's country,' the people yet call the northern portion of the island.

In Skye song and tradition, Macdonald is like the green strath with milkmaids milking kine in the fold at sunset, with fishers singing songs as they mend brown nets on the shore. Macleod, on the other hand, is of darker and drearier import – like a wild rocky spire of Quirang or Storr, dimmed with the flying vapour and familiar with the voice of the blast and the wing of the raven.

The Western Islands lie mainly out of the region of Scottish history and yet by Scottish history they are curiously touched at intervals, Skye more particularly so. In 1263 when King Haco set out on his great expedition against Scotland with one hundred ships and twenty thousand men, the multitude of his sails darkened the Skye lochs. He passed through the Kyles, breathed for a little while at Kerrera and then swept down on the Ayrshire coast, where King Alexander awaited him and where the battle of Largs was fought. After the battle Haco, greviously tormented by tempests, sailed for Norway, where he died. This was the last invasion of the Northmen and a few years after, the islands were formally ceded to Scotland.

Although ceded, however, they could scarcely be said to be ruled by the Scottish kings. After the termination of the Norway government, the Hebrides were swayed by the Macdonalds, who called themselves Lords of the Isles. These chieftains waxed powerful and they more than once led the long-haired Isles-men into Scotland, where they murdered, burned and ravaged without mercy. The Macdonald dynasty, or quasi-dynasty, existed till 1536, when the last Lord of the Isles died without an heir and where there was no shoulder on which the mantle of his authority could fall.

Although the Lords of the Isles exercised virtual sovereignty in the Hebrides, the Jameses made many attempts to break their power and bring them into subjection. James I penetrated into the Highlands and assembled a Parliament at Inverness in 1427. He enticed many of the chiefs to his court and seized, imprisoned and executed several of the more powerful. Those who escaped with their lives were forced to deliver up hostages. In fact, the Scottish kings looked upon the Highlanders very much as they looked upon the Borderers; in moments of fitful energy they broke on the Highlands just as they broke upon Ettrick and Liddesdale and hanged and executed right and left.

One of the Acts of Parliament of James IV declared that the Highlands and Islands had become savage for want of a proper administration of justice; and James made a voyage to the Islands in 1536, about the time that the last Lord of the Isles died, when many of the chiefs were captured and carried away. The Jameses were now kings of the Highlands and Islands, but they were only kings in a nominal sense. Every chief regarded himself as a sort of independent prince. The Highland chieftains appeared at Holyrood, it is true; but they drew dirks and shed blood in the presence; they were wanting in reverence for the sceptre; they brought their own feuds with them to the Scottish court and, when James VI attempted to dissolve these feuds in the wine cup, he met with but indifferent success. So slight was lawful authority in 1589 that the Island of the Lewes was granted by the crown to a body of Fife gentlemen, if they would but take and hold possession – just as the lands of the rebellious Maoris might be granted to the colonists at the present day.

Then came the death of Elizabeth and the accession of James to the English throne; and the time was fast approaching when the Highlander would become a more important personage than ever; when the claymore would make its mark in British history.

At first sight it is a matter of wonder that the clans should ever have become Jacobite. They were in nowise indebted to the house of Stuart. With the Scottish kings the Highlands and Islands were almost continually at war. When a James came amongst the northern chieftains he carried an ample death-warrant in his face. The presents he brought were the prison key, the hangman's rope, the axe of the executioner. When the power departed from the Lords of the Isles, the clans regarded the king who sat in Holyrood as their nominal superior; but they were not amenable to any central law; each had its own chief – was self-contained, self-governed and busy with its own private revenges and forays. When the Lowland farmer was busy with his crops, the clansman walked his misty mountains very much as his fathers did centuries before; and his hand was as familiar with the hilt of his broadsword as the hand of the Lothian farmer with the plough-shaft. The Lowlander had become industrious and commercial; the Highlander still loved the skirmish and the raid. The Lowlands had become rich in towns, in money, in goods; the Highlands were rich only in swordsmen.

When Charles's troubles with his Parliament began, the valour of the Highlands was wasting itself; and Montrose was the first man who saw how that valour could be utilised. Himself a feudal chief and full of feudal feeling, when he raised the banner of the king he appealed to the ancient animosities of the clans. His arch-foe was Argyll; he knew that Campbell was a widely-hated name; and that hate he made his recruiting sergeant.

He bribed the chiefs, but his bribe was revenge. The mountaineers flocked to his standard; but they came to serve themselves rather than to serve Charles. The defeat of Argyll might be a good thing for the king; but for that they had little concern – it was the sweetest of private revenges and righted a century of wrongs. The Macdonalds of Sleat fought under the great Marquis at Inverlochy; but the Skye shepherd considers only that his forefathers had a grand slaying of their hereditary enemies – he has no idea that the interest of the king was at all involved in the matter.

While the battle was proceeding, Blind Allan sat on the castle walls with a little boy beside him; the boy related how the battle went and the bard wove the incidents into extemporaneous song – full of scorn and taunts when the retreat of Argyll in his galley is described – full of exultation when the bonnets of fifteen hundred dead Campbells are seen floating in the Lochy – and Blind Allan's song you can hear repeated in Skye at this day.

When the splendid career of Montrose came to an end at Philiphaugh, the clansmen who won his battles for him were no more adherents of the king than they had been centuries before:

but then they had gratified hatred; they had had ample opportunities for plunder; the chiefs had gained a new importance; they had been assured of the royal gratitude and remembrance; and if they received but scant supplies of royal gold, they were promised argosies. By fighting under Montrose they were in a sense committed to the cause of the king; and when at a later date Claverhouse again raised the royal standard, that argument was successfully used. They had already served the house of Stuart; they had gained victories in its behalf: the king would not always be in adversity; the time would come when he would be able to reward his friends; having put their hands to the plough it would be folly to turn back.

And so a second time the clans rose and at Killiecrankie an avalanche of kilted men broke the royal lines and in a quarter of an hour a disciplined army was in ruins and the bed of the Garry choked with corpses. By this time the Stuart cause had gained a footing in the Highlands, mainly from the fact that the clans had twice fought in its behalf.

Then a dark whisper of the massacre of Glencoe passed through the glens – and the clansmen believed that the princes *they* served would not have violated every claim of hospitality and shot them down so on their own hearthstones. All this confirmed the growing feeling of attachment to the king across the water.

When the Earl of Mar rose in 1715, Macdonald of Sleat joined him with his men; and being sent out to drive away a party of the enemy who had appeared on a neighbouring height, opened the battle of Sheriffmuir.

In 1745, when Prince Charles landed in Knoydart, he sent letters to Macdonald and Macleod in Skye soliciting their aid. Between them they could have brought 2,000 claymores into the field; and had the prince brought a foreign force with him, they might have complied with his request. As it was, they hesitated and finally resolved to range themselves on the side of the government. Not a man from Sleat fought under the prince.

The other great branches of the Macdonald family, Clanranald, Keppoch and Glengarry, joined him however; and Keppoch at Culloden, when he found that his men were broken and would not rally at the call of their chief, charged the English lines alone and was brought down by a musket bullet.

The Skye gentlemen did not rise at the call of the prince, but when his cause was utterly lost, a Skye lady came to his aid and rendered him essential service. Neither at this time, nor afterwards, did Flora Macdonald consider herself a heroine; and she is noticeable to this day in history, walking demurely with the white rose in her bosom.

When the prince met Miss Macdonald in Benbecula, he was in circumstances sufficiently desperate. The lady had expressed an anxious desire to see Charles; and at their meeting, which took place in a hut belonging to her brother, it struck Captain O'Neil, an officer attached to the prince at that moment the sole companion of his wanderings, that she might carry Charles with her to Skye in the disguise of her maid-servant. Miss Macdonald consented. She procured a six-oared boat and when she and her companions entered the hovel in which the prince lay, they found him engaged in roasting for dinner with a wooden spit the heart, liver and kidneys of a sheep. They were full of compassion, of course; but the prince, who possessed the wit as well as the courage of his family, turned his misfortunes into jests. The party sat down to dinner not uncareless of state. Flora sat on the right hand and Lady Clanranald, one of her companions, on the left hand of the prince. They talked of St James's as they sat at their rude repast; and stretching out hands of hope, warmed themselves at the fire of the future.

After dinner, Charles equipped himself in the attire of a maidservant. His dress consisted of a flowered linen gown, a light-coloured quilted petticoat, a white apron and a mantle of dun camlet, made after the Irish fashion, with a hood. They supped on the sea-shore, parted with Lady Clanranald and sailed in the evening with a fair wind; but they had not rowed above a league when a storm arose and Charles had to support the spirits of his companions by singing songs and making merry speeches. They came in sight of the pale Skye headlands in the morning and, as they coasted along the shore, they were fired on by a party of Macleod militia. While the bullets were falling around, the prince and Flora lay down in the bottom of the boat. The militia were probably indifferent marksmen; at all events no-one was hurt.

After coasting along for a space, they landed at Mugstot, the seat of Sir Alexander Macdonald. Lady Macdonald was a daughter of the Earl of Eglinton and an avowed Jacobite; and as it was known that Sir Alexander was at Fort Augustus with the Duke of Cumberland, they had no scruple in seeking protection. Charles was left in the boat and Flora went forward to apprise Lady Macdonald of their arrival; however, there was a Captain Macleod, an officer of the militia, in the house and after consultation between Flora, Lady Macdonald and Kingsburgh – Sir Alexander's factor – it was agreed that Skye was unsafe and that Charles should proceed at once to Raasay, taking up his residence at Kingsburgh by the way.

Taking with him wine and provisions, Kingsburgh went out in search of the prince. He searched for a considerable while without finding him and was about to return to the house when, at some little distance, he observed a scurry amongst a flock of sheep. He approached the spot when, all at once, the prince started out upon him, a large knotted stick in his fist.

'I am Macdonald of Kingsburgh,' said the factor, 'come to serve your highness.'

'It is well,' said Charles, saluting him.

While Charles and Kingsburgh made their way towards Kingsburgh House, the ladies at Mugstot were in sad perplexity on account of the presence of the captain of militia. As Kingsburgh had not returned, they could only hope that he had succeeded in finding the prince and in removing him from that dangerous neighbourhood. Meanwhile dinner was announced and the captain politely handed in the ladies. He drank his wine, paid Miss Macdonald his most graceful compliments, for a captain – if even of militia only – can never, in justice to his cloth, be indifferent to the fair.

He talked of the prince, as a matter of course – the prince being the main topic of conversation in the Islands at the period – perhaps expressed a strong desire to catch him. All this the ladies had to endure.

After dinner, Flora rose at once, but a look from Lady Macdonald induced her to remain for yet a little. Still the gallant captain's talk flowed on and *he* must be deceived at any cost. At last Miss Flora was moved with the most filial feelings. She was anxious, she said, to be with her mother, to stay and comfort her in these troublous times. She must really be going. She would not listen to entreaty; her apology was accepted at last, but only on the condition that she should return soon to Mugstot and make a longer stay. The ladies embraced each other and then Miss Macdonald mounted and, attended by several servants, rode after Prince Charles, who was now some distance on the road to Kingsburgh. Lady Macdonald returned to the captain, than whom seldom has one – whether of the line or the militia – been more cleverly hoodwinked.

Miss Macdonald's party, when she rode after the prince and Kingsburgh, consisted of Neil McEachan, who acted as guide and Mrs Macdonald of Kingsburgh, who was attended by a male and female servant. They overtook the prince and Mrs Macdonald, who had never seen him before, was anxious to obtain a peep at his countenance. This Charles carefully avoided. Mrs Macdonald's maid, noticing the uncouth appearance of the tall female figure, whispered to Miss Flora that she had 'never seen such an impudent-looking woman as the one with whom Kingsburgh was talking,' and expressed her belief that the stranger was either an Irishwoman or a man in woman's clothes.

Miss Flora whispered in reply, that she was right in her conjecture – that the amazon was really an Irishwoman, that she knew her, having seen her before.

The abigail then exclaimed, 'Bless me, what long strides the jade takes and how awkwardly she manages her clothes!'

Miss Macdonald, wishing to put an end to this conversation, urged the party to a trot. The pedestrians then struck across the hills and reached Kingsburgh House about eleven o'clock – the equestrians arriving soon after.

When they arrived there was some difficulty about supper, Mrs Macdonald having retired to rest. When her husband told her that the prince was in her house, she got up immediately and, under her direction, the board was spread. The viands were eggs, butter and cheese. Charles supped heartily and, after drinking a few glasses of wine and smoking a pipe of tobacco, went to bed. Next morning there was a discussion as to the clothes he should wear; Kingsburgh, fearing that his disguise should become known, urged Charles to wear a Highland dress, to which he gladly agreed. But as there were sharp eyes of servants about, it was arranged that, to prevent suspicion, he should leave the house in the same clothes in which he had come and that he should dress on the road.

When he had dressed himself in his feminine garments and come into the sitting-room, Charles noticed that the ladies were whispering together eagerly, casting looks on him the while. He desired to know the subject of conversation and was informed by Mrs Macdonald that they wished a lock of his hair. The prince consented at once and, laying down his head in Miss Flora's lap, a lock of yellow hair was shorn off – to be treasured as the dearest of family relics and guarded as jealously as good fame. Some silken threads of that same lock of hair I have myself seen. My friend, Mr M'Ian – with whom I shall stay this summer – has some of it in a ring, which will probably be buried with him. After the hair was cut off, Kingsburgh presented the prince with a new pair of shoes and the old ones – through which the toes protruded – were put aside and considered as only less sacred than the shred of hair. They were afterwards bought by a Jacobite gentleman for twenty guineas – the highest recorded price ever paid for that article.

Kingsburgh, Flora and the prince then started for Portree, Kingsburgh carrying the Highland dress under his arm. After walking a short distance Charles entered a wood and changed into a tartan short coat and waistcoat, with philabeg and hose, a plaid and a wig and bonnet. Here Kingsburgh parted from the prince and returned home. Conducted by a guide, Charles then started across the hills, while Miss Flora galloped along the common road to Portree to see how the land lay and to become acquainted with the rumours stirring in the country.

There was considerable difficulty in getting the prince out of Skye; a Portree crew could not be trusted, as on their return they might blab the whereabouts of the fugitive. Two friends of the prince, brothers, dragged a small boat across a mile of boggy ground to the sea-shore and, though it was utterly unseaworthy, nothing fearing got it launched and rowed across to Raasay.

When the news came out that the prince was at hand, Young Raasay, who had not been out in the rebellion and his cousin, Malcolm Macleod, who had been, procured a strong boat and, with two oarsmen whom they had sworm to secrecy, pulled across to Skye. They landed about half a mile from Portree and Malcolm Macleod, accompanied by one of the men, went towards the inn, where he found the prince and Miss Macdonald talking and joking with the people in the inn, who had no suspicion of his rank. Macleod returned to the boat to await the prince's coming; but it rained heavily and Charles spoke of waiting where he was all night. His guide implored the prince to go off at once and he at last agreed, after smoking a pipe of tobacco. He smoked his pipe, bade farewell to Miss Macdonald, repaid her a small sum which he had borrowed, gave her his miniature and expressed the hope that he should yet welcome her at St James's.

Early in the dawn of the July morning, with four shirts, a bottle of brandy tied to one side of his belt, a bottle of whisky tied to the other and a cold fowl done up in a pocket-handkerchief, he went, under the direction of the guide, to the rocky shore where the boat had so long been waiting. In a few hours they reached Raasay.

In Raasay the prince did not remain long. He returned to Skye, abode for a space in Strath, dwelling in strange places and wearing many disguises – finally, through the aid of the chief of the Mackinnons, he reached the mainland. By this time it had become known to the government that the prince had been wandering about the island and Malcolm Macleod, Kingsburgh and Miss Macdonald were apprehended.

Miss Macdonald was at first confined in Dunstaffnage Castle and was afterwards conveyed to London. Her imprisonment does not seem to have been severe and she was liberated, it is said, at the special request of Frederick, Prince of Wales. In 1750 Flora married Allan Macdonald, son of Kingsburgh and on the death of his father in 1772 the young couple went to live on the farm. Here they received Dr Johnson and Boswell. Shortly after, the family went to America and in 1775 Kingsburgh joined the Royal Highland Emigrant Regiment, afterwards served in Canada and finally returned to Skye on half-pay. Flora had seven children, five sons and two daughters – the sons, after the old Skye fashion, becoming soldiers and the daughters, the wives of soldiers. She died in 1790 and was buried in the churchyard of Kilmuir.

To the discredit of the Skye gentlemen – in many of whom her blood flows – the grave is in a state of utter disrepair. When I last saw it it was covered with a rank growth of nettles. These are untouched. The tourist will deface tombstones and carry away chips from a broken bust, but a nettle the boldest or the most enthusiastic will hardly pluck and convey from even the most celebrated grave. A line must be drawn somewhere and vandalism draws the line at nettles – it will not sting its own fingers for the world.

After the departure of the prince the arrival of Dr Johnson was the next great event in Hebridean history. The doctor came and looked about him and went back to London and wrote his book. Thereafter there was plenty of war; and the Isles-men became soldiers, fighting in India, America and the Peninsula. The tartans waved through the smoke of every British battle and there were no such desperate bayonet charges as those which rushed to the yell of the bagpipe.

Then Scott came into the Highlands with the whole world of tourists at his back. Then up through Skye came Dr John M'Culloch – caustic, censorious, epigrammatic – and dire was the rage occasioned by the publication of his letters – the rage of men especially who had shown him hospitality and rendered him services and who got their style of talk mimicked and their household procedures laughed at for their pains.

Then came evictions, emigrations and the potato failure. Everything is getting prosaic as we approach the present time. Then my friend Mr Hutcheson established his magnificent fleet of Highland steamers. While I write the iron horse is at Dingwall and he will soon be at Kyleakin – through which strait King Haco sailed seven centuries ago. In a couple of years or thereby Portree will be distant twenty-four hours from London – that time the tourist will take in coming, that time the black-faced mutton will take in going.

Wandering up and down the Western Islands, one is brought into contact with Ossian and is launched into a sea of perplexities as to the genuineness of Macpherson's translations. That fine poems should have been composed in the Highlands so many centuries ago and that these should have existed through that immense period of time in the memories and on the tongues of the common people is sufficiently startling. On the other hand, the theory that Macpherson, whose literary efforts when he did not pretend to translate are extremely poor and meagre, should have, by sheer force of imagination, created poems confessedly full of fine things, with strong local colouring, not without a weird sense of remoteness, with heroes shadowy as if seen through Celtic mists is, if possible, more startling than their claim of antiquity. If Macpherson created Ossian, he was an athlete who made one surprising leap and was palsied ever afterwards; a marksman who made a centre at his first shot and who never afterwards could hit the target.

It is well enough known that the Highlanders, like all half-civilised nations, had their legends and their minstrelsy; that they were fond of reciting poems and runes; and that the person who retained on his memory the greatest number of tales and songs brightened the gatherings round the ancient peat-fires. And it is astonishing how much legendary material a single memory may retain. There was the boy of the Island of Skye who, between twelve and fifteen years of age, could repeat from one to two hundred Gaelic poems, differing in length and in number of verses; learned from an old man about eighty years of age who sang them for years to his father when he went to bed at night and in the spring and winter before he rose in the morning. The old Highlander who repeated for the late Dr Stuart, minister of Luss, without hesitation and with the utmost rapidity, over three successive days and during several hours each day, many thousands of lines of ancient poetry – and would have continued his repititions much longer if the doctor had required him to do so.

Without a doubt there was a vast quantity of poetic material existing in the islands and it can be seen at a glance that the Ossianic poems were not forgeries – at all events Macpherson did not forge them. Even in the English translation, to a great extent, the sentiments, the habits, the modes of thought described are entirely primeval; in reading it we seem to breathe the morning air of the world.

The personal existence of Ossian is, I suppose, as doubtful as the personal existence of Homer; and if he ever lived, he is great, like Homer, through his tributaries. Ossian drew into himself every lyrical runnel, he augmented himself in every way, he drained centuries of their songs; and living an oral and gipsy life, handed down from generation to generation, without being committed to writing and having their outlines determinately fixed, the authorship of these songs becomes vested in a multitude, every reciter having more or less to do with it. For centuries the floating legendary material was reshaped, added to and altered by the changing spirit and emotion of the Celt.

In these poems not only do character and habit smack of the primeval time, but there is an extraordinary truth of local colouring. In Ossian, the skies are cloudy, there is a tumult of waves on the shore, the wind sings in the pine. This truth of local colouring is a strong argument in proof of authenticity. I do believe that Ossian lived and Fingal sung; and, more than this, it is my belief that these misty phantasmal Ossianic fragments, with their car-borne heroes that come and go like clouds on the wind, their frequent apparitions, the 'stars dim-twinkling through their forms,' their maidens fair and pale as lunar rainbows are, in their own literary place, worthy of every recognition.

If you think the poems exaggerated, go out at Sligachan and see what wild work the pencil of moonlight makes on a mass of shifting vapour. Does *that* seem nature or a madman's dream? Look at the billowy clouds rolling off the brow of Blaavin, all golden and on fire with the rising sun! Grim and fierce and dreary as the night-wind is the strain, for not with rose and nightingale had the old bard to do; but with the thistle waving on the ruin, the upright stones that mark the burying-places of heroes, weeping female faces white as sea-foam in the moon, the breeze mourning alone in the desert, the battles and friendships of his far-off youth and the flight of the 'dark-brown years.'

These poems are wonderful transcripts of Hebridean scenery, as full of mists as the Hebridean glens themselves.

It is not to be supposed that the Ossianic legends are repeated often now around the island peat-fires; but many are told resembling in essentials Norse sagas. As the northern nations have a common flora, so they have a common legendary literature. Supernaturalism belongs to their tales as the aurora borealis belongs to their skies. Those stories I have heard in Skye and many others, springing from the same roots, I have had related to me in the Lowlands and in Ireland. They are full of witches and wizards; of great wild giants crying out, 'Hiv! Haw Hoagraich!

It is a drink of thy blood that quenches my thirst this night;' of wonderful castles with turrets and banqueting halls; of magic spells and the souls of men and women imprisoned in shapes of beast and bird.

In these stories all times and conditions of life are curiously mixed and this mixture shows the passage of the story from tongue to tongue through generations. In a ballad, the presence of an anachronism, the cropping out of a comparatively modern touch of manners or detail of dress, does not in the least invalidate the claim of the ballad to antiquity – provided it can be proved that before being committed to writing it had led an oral existence. Every ballad existing in the popular memory takes the colour of the periods through which it has lived, just as a stream takes the colour of the different soils through which it flows.

In the old Highland stories to which I allude, the wildest anachronisms are of the most frequent occurrence; with the most utter scorn of historical accuracy all the periods are jumbled together; they resemble the dance on the outside stage of a booth at a country fair before the performances begin, in which a mailed crusader, a barmaid and a modern 'swell' meet and mingle and cross hands with the most perfect familiarity and absence from surprise.

Many of these stories, even when they are imperfect in themselves, or resemble those told elsewhere, are curiously coloured by Celtic scenery and pervaded by Celtic imagination. In listening to them, one is specially impressed by a bare, desolate, woodless country; and this impression is not produced by any formal statement of fact; it arises partly from the paucity of actors in the stories and partly from the desert spaces over which the actors travel and partly from the number of carrion crows and ravens and malign hill-foxes which they encounter in their journeyings. The 'hoody' as the crow is called, hops and flits and croaks through all the stories. His black wing is seen everywhere. And it is the infrequent appearance of these beasts and birds, never familiar, never domesticated, always outside the dwelling and of evil omen when they fly or steal across the path, which gives to the stories much of their weird and direful character.

The Celt has not yet subdued nature. He cannot be sportive for the fear that is in his heart. In his legends there is no merry Puck, no Ariel, no Robin Goodfellow, no half-benevolent/half-malignant Brownie even. These creatures live in imaginations more emancipated from fear. The mists blind the Celt on his perilous mountainside, the sea is smitten white on his rocks, the wind bends and dwarfs his pine wood; and as Nature is cruel to him and his light and heat are gathered from the moor and his most plenteous food from the whirlpool and the foam, we need not be surprised that few are the gracious shapes that haunt his fancy.

Let us then to Skye this summer, to the misty, mystical, magic isle in the northern sea. But as any tale must have a beginning, so must my journey and it begins in the city wherein I live and work – the capital city of Scotland, Edinburgh.

Edinburgh

EVERY TRUE SCOTSMAN believes Edinburgh to be the most picturesque city in the world; and truly, standing on the Calton Hill
at early morning, when the smoke of fires newly-kindled hangs
in azure swathes and veils about the Old Town – which from
that point resembles a huge lizard, the Castle its head, church-
spires spikes upon its scaly back, creeping up from its lair beneath
the Crags to look out on the enthusiasm of the North Briton.
The finest view from the interior is obtained from the corner of
St Andrew Street, looking west. Straight before you the Mound
crosses the valley, bearing the white Academy buildings; beyond,
the Castle lifts, from greasy slopes and billows of summer foliage, its
weather-stained towers and fortification, the Half-Moon battery
giving the folds of its standard to the wind. Living in Edinburgh
there abides, above all things, a sense of its beauty. Hill, crag, castle,
rock, blue stretch of sea, the picturesque ridge of the old Town,
the squares and terraces of the New – these things seen once are
not to be forgotten. The quick life of today sounding around the
relics of antiquity and overshadowed by the august traditions of
a kingdom makes residence in Edinburgh more impressive than
residence in any other British city.

I have just come in – surely it never looked so fair before?
What a poem is that Princes Street! The puppets of the busy,
many-coloured hour move about on its pavement, while across
the ravine Time has piled up the Old Town, ridge on ridge, gray as
a rocky coast washed and worn by the foam of centuries peaked
and jagged by gable and roof; windowed from basement to cope;

the whole surmounted by St Giles's airy crown. The New is there looking at the Old. Two Times are brought face to face and are yet separated by a thousand years. Wonderful on winter nights, when the gully is filled with darkness and out of it rises, against the sombre blue and frosty stars, that mass and bulwark of gloom, pierced and quivering with innumerable lights. There is nothing in Europe to match that, I think. Could you but roll a river down the valley it would be sublime. Finer still, to place one's-self near the Burns Monument and look towards the Castle. It is more astonishing than an Easter dream. A city rises up before you painted by fire on night. High in air a bridge of lights leaps the chasm; a few emerald lamps, like glow-worms, are moving silently about in the railway station below; a solitary crimson one is at rest. That ridged and chimneyed bulk of blackness, with splendour bursting out at every pore, is the wonderful Old Town, where Scottish history mainly transacted itself; while, opposite, the modern Princes Street is blazing throughout its length. During the day the Castle looks down upon the city as if out of another world; stern with all its peacefulness, its garniture of trees, its slopes of grass. The rock is dingy enough in colour, but after a shower its lichens laugh out greenly in the returning sun, while the rainbow is brightening on the lowering sky beyond. How deep the shadow which the Castle throws at noon over the gardens at its feet where the children play! How grand when giant bulk and towery crown blacken against sunset! Fair, too, the New Town sloping to the sea. From George Street, which crowns the ridge, the eye is led down sweeping streets of stately architecture to the villas and woods that fill the lower ground and fringe the shore; to the bright azure belt of the Forth with its smoking steamer or its creeping sail; beyond, to the shores of Fife, soft blue and flecked with fleeting shadows in the keen clear light of spring, dark purple in the summer heat, tarnished gold in the autumn haze; and farther away still, just distinguishable on the paler sky, the crest of some distant peak, carrying the imagination into the illimitable world. Residence in Edinburgh is an education in itself. Its beauty refines one like being in love. It is perennial, like a play of Shakespeare's. Nothing can stale its infinite variety.

From a historical and picturesque point of view, the Old Town is the most interesting part of Edinburgh; and the great street running from Holyrood to the Castle – in various portions of its length called the Lawnmarket, the High Street and the Canongate – is the most interesting part of the Old Town. In that street the houses preserve their ancient appearance; they climb up heavenward, storey upon storey, with outside stairs and wooden panellings, all strangely peaked and gabled. With the exception of the inhabitants, who exist amidst squalor and filth, and evil smells undeniably modern, everything in this long street breathes of the antique world. If you penetrate the narrow wynds that run at right angles from it, you see traces of ancient gardens. Occasionally the original names are retained and they touch the visitor pathetically, like the scent of long-withered flowers. Old armorial bearings may yet be traced above the doorways. Two centuries ago fair eyes looked down from yonder window, now in possession of a drunken Irishwoman. If we but knew it, every crazy tenement has its tragic story; every crumbling wall could its tale unfold. The Canongate is Scottish history fossilised. What ghosts of kings and queens walk there! What strifes of steel-clad nobles! What wretches borne along, in the sight of peopled windows, to the grim embrace of the 'maiden'! What hurrying of burgesses to man the city walls at the approach of the Southron! What lamentations over disastrous battle days! James rode up this street on his way to Flodden. Montrose was dragged up hither on a hurdle and smote, with disdainful glance, his foes gathered together on a balcony. Jenny Geddes flung her stool at the priest in the church yonder. John Knox came up here to his house after his interview with Mary at Holyrood – grim and stern and unmelted by the tears of a queen. In later days the Pretender rode down the Canongate, his eyes dazzled by the glitter of his father's crown, while bagpipes skirled around and Jacobite ladies, with

white knots in their bosoms, looked down from lofty windows,
admiring the beauty of the 'Young Ascanius' and his long yellow
hair. Down here of an evening rode Dr Johnson and Boswell and
turned in to the White Horse. David Hume had his dwelling in
this street and trod its pavements, much meditating the wars of the
Roses and the Parliament and the fates of English sovereigns. One
day a burly ploughman from Ayrshire, with swarthy features and
wonderful black eyes, came down here and turned into yonder
churchyard to stand, with cloudy lids and forehead reverently
bared, beside the grave of poor Fergusson. Down the street, too,
often limped a little boy, Walter Scott by name, destined in after
years to write its *Chronicles*. The visitor starts a ghost at every step.
Nobles, grave senators, jovial lawyers, had once their abodes here.
In the old, low-roofed rooms, half-way to the stars, philosophers
talked, wits coruscated and gallant young fellows, sowing wild oats
in the middle of last century, wore rapiers and lace ruffles and
drank claret out of silver stoups. In every room a minuet has been
walked, while chairmen and linkmen clustered on the pavement
beneath. But the Canongate has fallen from its high estate. Quite
another race of people are its present inhabitants. The vices to
be seen are not genteel. Whisky has supplanted claret. Nobility
has fled and squalor taken possession. Wild, half-naked children
swarm around every doorstep. Ruffians lounge about the mouths
of the wynds. Female faces, worthy of the *Inferno*, look down from
broken windows. Riots are frequent; and drunken mothers reel
past scolding white atomies of children that nestle wailing in their
bosoms – little wretches to whom Death were the greatest bene-
factor. The Canongate is avoided by respectable people and yet
it has many visitors. The tourist is anxious to make acquaintance
with it. Gentlemen of obtuse olfactory nerve and of an antiquar-
ian turn of mind, go down its closes and climb its spiral stairs.
Deep down these wynds the artist pitches his stool and spends
the day sketching some picturesque gable or door way. The fever-
van comes frequently here to convey some poor sufferer to the
hospital. Hither comes the detective in plain clothes on the scent

of a burglar. And when evening falls and the lamps are lit, there is a sudden hubbub and crowd of people and presently from its midst emerge a couple of policemen and a barrow with poor, half-clad, tipsy woman from the sister island crouching up to it, her hair hanging loose about her face, her hands quivering with impotent rage and her tongue wild with curses. Attended by small boys, who bait her with taunts and nicknames and who appreciate the comic element which so strangely underlies the horrible sight, she is conveyed to the police cell and will be brought before the magistrate tomorrow – for the twentieth time perhaps – as a 'drunk and disorderly,' and dealt with accordingly. This is the kind of life the Canongate presents today – a contrast with the time when the tall buildings enclosed the high birth and beauty of a kingdom when the street beneath rang to the horse-hoofs of a king.

The New Town is divided from the Old by a gorge or valley, now occupied by a railway station; and the means of communication are the Mound, Waverley Bridge and the North Bridge. With the exception of the Canongate, the more filthy and tumble-down portions of the city are well kept out of sight. You stand on the South Bridge and, looking down, instead of a stream you see the Cowgate the dirtiest, narrowest, most densely peopled of Edinburgh streets. Admired once by a French ambassador at the court of one of the Jameses and yet with certain traces of departed splendour, the Cowgate has fallen into the sere and yellow leaf of furniture brokers, secondhand jewellers' and vendors of deleterious alcohol. These second-hand jewellers' shops, the trinkets seen by bleared gaslight, are the most melancholy sights I know. Watches hang there that once ticked comfortable in the fobs of prosperous men, rings that were once placed by happy bride-grooms on the fingers of happy brides, jewels in which lives the sacredness of deathbeds. What tragedies, what disruptions of households, what fell pressure of poverty brought them here! Looking in through the foul windows, the trinkets remind me of shipwrecked gold embedded in the ooze of ocean – gold that speaks of unknown, yet certain, storm and disaster, of the yielding of planks, of the cry of drowning men. Who has the heart to buy them, I wonder? The Cowgate is the Irish portion of the city. Edinburgh leaps over it with bridges; its inhabitants are morally and geographically the lower orders. They keep to their own quarters and seldom come up to the light of day. Many an Edinburgh man has never set foot in the street; the condition of the inhabitants is as little known to respectable Edinburgh as are the habits of moles, earthworms and the mining population. The people of the Cowgate seldom visit the upper streets. You may walk about the New Town for a twelve month before one of these Cowgate pariahs comes between the wind and your gentility. Should you wish to see that strange people 'at home', you must visit them. The Cowgate will not come to you: you must go to the Cowgate. The Cowgate holds high drunken carnivals every Saturday night; and to walk along it then, from the West Port, through the noble open space of the Grassmarket – where the Covenanters and Captain Porteous suffered – on to Holyrood, is one of the world's sights and one that does not particularly raise your estimate of human nature. For nights after, your dreams will pass from brawl to brawl, shoals of hideous faces will oppress you, sodden countenances of brutal men, women with loud voices and frantic gesticulations, children who have never known innocence. It is amazing of what ugliness the human face is capable. The devil marks his children as a shepherd marks his sheep – that he may know them and claim them again. Many a face flits past here bearing the sign-manual of the fiend.

But Edinburgh keeps all these evil things out of sight and smiles, with Castle, tower, church-spire and pyramid rising into sunlight out of garden spaces and belts of foliage. The Cowgate has no power to mar her beauty. There may be a canker at the heart of the peach – there is neither pit nor stain on its dusty velvet. And Edinburgh is at this moment in the full blaze of her beauty. The public gardens are in blossom. The trees that clothe the base of the Castle rock are clad in green: the 'ridgy back' of the Old

A Summer in Skye

Town jags the clear azure. Princes Street is warm and sunny – 'tis a very flowerbed of parasols, twinkling, rainbow-coloured. Shop windows are enchantment, the flag streams from the Half-Moon Battery, church spires sparkle sun-gilt, gay equipages dash past, the military band is heard from afar. The tourist is already here in wonderful tweed costume. Every week the wanderers increase – they stand on Arthur's Seat, they speculate on the birthplace of Mons Meg, they admire Roslin, eat haggis, attempt whisky-punch and crowd to Dr Guthrie's church on Sundays – and in a short time the city will be theirs. By August the inhabitants have fled.

Stirling and the North

EDINBURGH AND STIRLING are spinster sisters, who were both in their youth beloved by Scottish kings; but Stirling is the more wrinkled in feature, the more old-fashioned in attire and not nearly so well-to-do in the world. She smacks more of the antique time and wears the ornaments given her by royal lovers – sadly broken and worn now and not calculated to yield much if brought to the hammer – more ostentatiously in the public eye than does Edinburgh. On the whole, perhaps, her stock of these red sand-stone gewgaws is the more numerous.

In many respects there is a striking likeness between the two cities. Between them they, in a manner, monopolise Scottish history; kings dwelt in both and both have castles towering to heaven from the crests of up-piled rocks; both towns are hilly, rising terrace above terrace.

Many battles were fought in the seeing of Stirling's castle towers. Stirling Bridge, Carron, Bannockburn, Sauchieburn, Sheriffmuir, Falkirk – these battlefields lie in the immediate vicinity. From the field of Bannockburn you obtain the finest view of Stirling. The Ochils are around you; yonder sleeps the Abbey Craig where, on a summer day, Wight Wallace sat; you behold the houses climbing up, picturesque, smoke-feathered; and the wonderful rock, in which the grace of the lily and the strength of the hills are mingled and on which the castle sits as proudly as ever did rose on its stem.

The country around Stirling is interesting from its natural beauty no less than from its historical associations. Eastward from the castle ramparts stretches a great plain, bounded on either side by mountains and before you, the vast fertility dies into distance, flat as the ocean when winds are asleep. It is through this plain that the Forth has drawn her glittering coils – a silvery entanglement of loops and links – a watery labyrinth, which every summer the whole world flocks to see. Turn round, look in the opposite direction and the aspect of the country has entirely changed. It undulates like a rolling sea; heights swell up into the blackness of pines and then sink away into valleys of fertile green. At your feet the Bridge of Allan sleeps in azure smoke – the most fashionable of all the Scottish spas, wherein, by hundreds of invalids, the last new novel is being diligently perused. Beyond are the classic woods of Keir; and ten miles farther, what see you? A multitude of blue mountains climbing the heavens! The heart leaps up to greet them – the ramparts of a land of romance, from the mouths of whose glens broke of old the foray of the freebooter; and with a chief in front, with banner and pibroch in the wind, the terror of the Highland war. Stirling, like a huge brooch, clasps Highlands and Lowlands together.

It is from Stirling that I start on my summer journey and the greater portion of it I purpose to perform on foot. There is railway now to Callander, whereby time is saved and enjoyment destroyed – but the railway I shall in nowise patronise, meaning to abide by the old coach road. In a short time you are beyond the Bridge of Allan, beyond the woods of Keir and holding straight on to Dunblane. Reaching it, you pause for a little on the old bridge to look at the artificial waterfall and the ruined cathedral on the rising ground across the steam and the walks which Bishop Leighton paced. There is really not much to detain you in the little gray city and, pressing on, you will reach Doune, basking on the hill-side.

Possibly the reader may never have heard of Doune, yet it has its lions. What are these? Look at the great bulk of the ruined castle! These towers, rising from miles of summer foliage into fair sunlight, a great Duke of Albany beheld for a moment, with a shock of long-past happiness and home, as he laid down his head on the block at Stirling. Rage and shame filled the last heave of the heart, the axe flashed, and . . .

As you go down the steep town road, there is an old-fashioned garden and a well close to the wall. Look into it steadily – you observe a shadow on the sandy bottom and the twinkle of a fin. 'Tis a trout – a blind one, which has dwelt, the people will tell you, in its watery cage for ten years back. It is considered a most respectable inhabitant and the urchin daring to angle for it would hardly escape whipping.

You may leave Doune now. A Duke of Albany lost his head in the view of its castle, a blind trout lives in its well and visitors feel more interested in the trout than in the duke. The country in the immediate vicinity of Doune is somewhat bare and unpromising, but as you advance it improves and, a few miles on, the road skirts the Teith, the sweetest voiced of all the Scottish streams. The Roman centurion heard that pebbly murmur on his march even as you hear it now. The river, like all beautiful things, is coquettish and, just when you come to love her music, she sweeps away into the darkness of the woods and leaves you companionless on the dusty road. Never mind, you will meet her again at Callander and there, for a whole summer day, you can lean on the bridge and listen to her singing.

Callander is one of the prettiest of Highland villages. It was sunset as I approached it first, years ago. Beautiful the long crooked street of white-washed houses dressed in rosy colours. Prettily-dressed children were walking or running about; the empty coach was standing at the door of the hotel and the smoking horses were being led up and down; and right in front stood King Ben Ledi, clothing in imperial purple, the spokes of splendour from the sinking sun raying far away into heaven from behind his mighty shoulders.

Callander sits like a watcher at the opening of the glens and is a rendezvous of tourists. To the right is the Pass of Leny – well worthy of a visit. You ascend a steep path, birch trees on right and left; the stream comes brawling down, sleeping for a moment in black pools beloved by anglers and then hasting on in foam and fury to meet her sister in the Vale of Menteith below. When you have climbed the pass, you enter on a green treeless waste and soon approach Loch Lubnaig, with the great shadow of a hill blackening across it. The loch is perhaps cheerful enough when the sun is shining on it, but the sun in that melancholy region is but seldom seen. Beside the road is an old churchyard, for which no one seems to care – the tombstones being submerged in a sea of rank grass. The loch of the rueful countenance will not be visited on the present occasion.

My course lies round the left flank of Ben Ledi, straight on for the Trossachs and Loch Katrine. Leaving Callander you cross the waters of the Leny – changed now from the fury that, with raised voice and streaming tresses, leaped from rock to rock in the glen above – and walk into the country made immortal by *The Lady of the Lake*. Every step you take is in the footsteps of Apollo: speech at once becomes song. There is Coilantogle Ford; Loch Venachar, yonder, is glittering away in windy sunshine to the bounding hills. Passing the lake you come on a spot where the hillside drops suddenly down on the road. On this hillside Vich Alpine's warriors started out of the ferns at the whistle of their chief; and if you travelled on the coach, the driver would repeat half the poem with curious variations and point out the identical rock against which Fitz-James leaned – rock on which a dozen eye-glasses are at once levelled in wonder and admiration.

The loveliest sight on the route to the Trossachs is about to present itself. At a turn of the road Loch Achray is before you. Beyond expression beautiful is that smiling lake, mirroring the hills, whether bare and green or plumaged with woods from base to crest. Fair azure gem in a setting of mountains! The traveller – even if a bagman – cannot but pause to drink in its fairy beauty; cannot but remember it when far away amid other scenes and associations. At every step the scenery grows wilder. Loch Achray disappears. High in upper air tower the summits of Ben Aan and

40

Ben Venue. You pass through the gorge of the Trossachs, whose rocky walls, born in earthquake and fiery deluge, the fanciful summer has been dressing these thousand years, clothing their feet with drooping ferns and rods of foxglove bells, blackening their breasts with pines, feathering their pinnacles with airy birches that dance in the breeze like plumage on a warrior's helm. The wind here becomes a musician. Echo sits babbling beneath the rock. The gorge, too, is but the prelude to a finer charm; for before you are aware, doubling her beauty with surprise, there breaks on the right the silver sheet of Loch Katrine, with a dozen woody islands, sleeping peacefully on their shadows.

On the loch, the steamer *Rob Roy* awaits you and away you pant and fume towards a wharf and an inn, with an unpronounceable name, at the farther end. The lake does not increase in beauty as you proceed. All its charms are congregated at the mouth of the Trossachs and the upper reaches are bare, desolate and uninteresting. You soon reach the wharf and, after your natural rage at the toll of two pence exacted from you on landing has subsided and you have had a smack of something at the inn, you start on the wild mountain road towards Inversneyd. The aspect of the country has now changed. The hills around are bare and sterile, brown streams gurgle down their fissures, the long yellow ribbon of roads runs away before you, dipping out of sight sometimes and reappearing afar. You pass a turf hut and your nostrils are invaded by a waft of peat reek which sets you coughing and brings the tears into your eyes; and the juvenile natives eye you askance and wear the airiest form of the national attire. In truth, there is not a finer bit of Highland road to be found anywhere than that which runs between the inn – which might be immortal if the name of it could be pronounced – and the hotel at Inversneyd.

When you have travelled some three miles the scenery improves, the hills rise into nobler forms with misty wreaths about them and as you pursue your journey a torrent becomes your companion. Presently, a ruin rises on the hillside, the nettles growing on its melancholy walls. It is the old fort of Inversneyd, built in King

41

William's time to awe the turbulent clans. Nothing can be more desolate than its aspect. Sunshine seems to mock it; it is native and endued into its element when wrapt in mist or pelted by the wintry rain. Passing the old stone-and-lime mendicant on the hillside – by the way, tradition mumbles something about General Wolfe having been stationed there at the beginning of his military career – you descend rapidly on Loch Lomond and Inversneyd. The road by this time has become another Pass of Leny: on either side the hills approach, the torrent roars down in a chain of cataracts and, in a spirit of bravado, takes its proudest leap at the last.

Quite close to the fall is the hotel; and on the frail timber bridge that overhangs the cataract, you can see groups of picturesque-hunters, the ladies gracefully timid, the gentlemen gallant and reassuring. Inversneyd is beautiful and it possesses an added charm in being the scene of one of Wordsworth's poems; and he who has stood on the crazy bridge and watched the flash and thunder of the stream beneath him and gazed on the lake surrounded by mountains, will ever after retain the picture in remembrance, although to him there should not have been vouchsafed the vision of the *Highland Girl*.

Scott is here. If *The Lady of the Lake* rings in your ears at the Trossachs, then *The Legend of Montrose* haunts you at Inveraray. Every footstep of ground is hallowed by that noble romance. It is the best guidebook to the place.

No tourist should leave Inveraray before he ascends Duniquoich – no very difficult task either, for a path winds round and round it. When you emerge from the woods beside the watch-tower on the summit, Inveraray, far beneath, has dwindled to a toy – not a sound as in the streets; unheard the steamer roaring at the wharf and urging dilatory passengers to haste by the clashes of an angry bell. Along the shore nets stretched from pole to pole wave in the drying wind. The great boatless blue loch stretches away flat as a ballroom floor; and the eye wearies in its flight over endless miles of brown moor and mountain. Turn your back on the town and gaze towards the north! It is still 'a far cry to Loch Awe' and a wilderness of mountain peaks tower up between you and that noblest of Scottish lakes! – of all colours too – green with pasture, brown with moorland, touched with coming purple of the heather, black with a thunder cloud of pines. What a region to watch the sun go down upon! But for that you cannot wait; for today you lunch at Cladich, dine at Dalmally and sleep in the neighbourhood of Kilchurn – in the immediate presence of Ben Cruachan.

A noble vision of mountains is to be obtained from the road above Cladich. Dalmally is a very paradise of a Highland inn – quiet, sequestered, begirt with the majesty and the silence of mountains – a place where a world-weary man may soothe back into healthful motion jarred pulse and brain; a delicious nest for a happy pair to waste the honeymoon in. Dalmally stands on the shores of Loch Awe and in the immediate vicinity of Kilchurn Castle and Ben Cruachan.

The castle is picturesque enough to please the eye of the landscape painter and large enough to impress the visitor with a sense of baronial grandeur. And it is ancient enough and fortunate enough too – for to that age does not always attain – to have legends growing upon its walls like the golden lichens or the darksome ivies. The vast shell of a building looks strangely impressive standing there, mirrored in summer waters, with the great mountain looking down on it. It was built, it is said, by a lady in the Crusade times, when her Lord was battling with the infidel. The most prosaic man gazing on a ruin becomes a poet for the time being. You incontinently sit down and think how, in the old pile, life went on for generations – how children were born and grew up there – how brides were brought home there, the bridal blushes yet on their cheeks – how old men died there and had by filial fingers their eyes closed, as blinds are drawn down on the windows of an empty house and the withered hands crossed decently upon the breasts that will heave no more with any passions. The yule figures and the feast

43

fires that blazed on the old hearths have gone out now. The arrow of the foeman seeks no longer the window slit. Today and tonight, to winter and summer, Kilchurn stands empty as a skull; yet with no harshness about it; possessed rather of a composed and decent beauty – reminding you of a good man's grave, with the number of his ripe years and the catalogue of his virtues chiselled on the stone above him: telling of work faithfully done and of the rest that follows, for which all the weary pine.

Ben Cruachan, if not the monarch of Scottish mountains is, at all events, one of the princes of the blood. He is privileged to wear a snow wreath in presence of the sun at his midsummer levee and, like a prince he wears it on the rough breast of him. Ben Cruachan is seen from afar: is difficult to climb and slopes slowly down to the sea level, his base being twenty miles in girth, it is said.

From Ben Cruachan and Kilchurn, Loch Awe, bedropt with wooded islands, stretches Obanwards, presenting in its course every variety of scenery. Now the loch spreads like a sea, now it shrinks to a rapid river – now the banks are wooded like the Trossachs, now they are bare as the 'Screes' at Wastwater; and consider as you walk along what freaks light and shade are playing every moment – how shadows, hundred-armed, creep along the mountainside – how the wet rock sparkles like a diamond and then goes out – how the sunbeam slides along a belt of pines – and how, a slave to the sun, the lake quivers in light around her islands when he is unobscured and wears his sable colours when a cloud is on his face. On your way to Oban there are many places worth seeing: Loch Etive, with its immemorial pines, beloved by Professor Wilson; Benawe, Taynult, Connel Ferry, with its sea view and saltwater cataract; and Dunstaffnage Castle, once a royal residence and from which the stone was taken which is placed beneath the coronation chair at Westminster. And so, if the whole journey from Inveraray is performed on foot, Lune will light the traveller into Oban.

A steamer picks you up at Inversneyd and slides down Loch

Lomond with you to Tarbet, a village sleeping in the very presence of the mighty Ben, whose forehead is almost always covered with cloudy handkerchief. Although the loch is finer higher up, where it narrows towards Glen Falloch – more magnificent lower down, where it widens, many-isled, towards Balloch – it is by no means to be despised at Tarbet. Each bay and promontory wears its charm; and if the scenery does not astonish, it satisfies. Tarbet can boast, too, of an excellent inn, in which, if the traveller be wise he will – for one night at least – luxuriously take his ease.

Up betimes next morning, you are on the beautiful road which runs between Tarbet and Arrochar and begin, through broken, white upstreaming mists, to make acquaintance with the 'Cobbler' and some other peaks of that rolling country to which Celtic facetiousness had given the name of 'The Duke of Argyll's Bowling Green.' Escaping from the birches that line the road and descending on Arrochar and Loch Long, you can leisurely inspect the proportions of the mountain Crispin, a gruesome carle and inhospitable to strangers. The Cobbler's Wife sits a little way off – an ancient dame, to the full as withered in appearance as her husband and as difficult of access. They dwell in tolerable amity the twain, but when they do quarrel it is something tremendous!

You leave the little village of Arrochar, trudge round the head of Loch Long and, proceeding downward along the opposite shore and skirting the base of the Cobbler, strike for the opening of Glencroe, on your road to Inveraray. Glencroe is to the other Highland glens what Tennyson is to contemporary British poets. If Glencoe did not exist, Glencroe would be famous. It is several miles long, lonely, sterile and desolate. A stream rages down the hollow, fed by tributary burns that dash from the receding mountain tops. The hillsides are rough with boulders, as a sea-rock is rough with limpets. Showers cross the path a dozen times during the finest day. As you go along, the glen is dappled with cloud-shadows; you hear the bleating of unseen sheep and the chances are that, in travelling along its whole extent, opportunity will not be granted you of bidding 'good-morrow' to a single soul. If you are a murderer, you could shout out your secret here and no one be a bit the wiser.

At the head of the glen the road becomes exceedingly steep; and as you pant up the incline, you hail the appearance of a stone seat bearing the welcome motto, 'Rest and be thankful.' You rest, and *are* thankful. This seat was erected by General Wade while engaged in his great work of Highland road-making; and so long as it exists the General will be remembered. At this point the rough breast of a hill rises in front, dividing the road; the path to the left runs away down into the barren and solitary Hell's Glen, in haste to reach Loch Goil; the other to the right leads through bare Glen Ardkinglass, to St Catherine's and the shore of Loch Fyne, at which point you arrive after a lonely walk of two hours.

The only thing likely to interest the stranger at the little hostelry of St Catherine's is John Campbell, the proprietor of the same and driver of the coach from the inn to the steamboat wharf at Loch Goil. John has a presentable person and a sagacious countenance, his gray eyes are the homes of humour and shrewdness; and when seated on the box, he flicks his horses and manages the ribbons to admiration. He is a good storyteller and he knows it. He has not started on his journey a hundred yards when, from something or another, he finds you occasion for a story, which is sure to produce a roar of laughter from those alongside of, and behind, him. Encouraged by success, John absolutely coruscates, anecdote follows anecdote like flashes of sheet-lightning on a summer night; and by the time he is halfway, he is implored to desist by some sufferer whose midriff he has convulsed. John is naturally a humorist; and as every summer and autumn the Highlands are overrun with tourists he, from St Catherine's to Loch Goil, surveys mankind with extensive view. Everyone who tarries at St Catherine's should get himself driven across to Loch Goil by John Campbell and should take pains to procure a seat on the box beside him. When he returns to the south, he can relate over again the stories he hears and make himself the hero of them. The thing has been done before and will be again.

A small washtub of a steamer carries you across Loch Fyne to Inveraray in an hour. Arriving, you find the capital of the West Highlands a rather pretty place, with excellent inns, several churches, a fine bay, a ducal residence, a striking conical hill – Duniquoich the barbarous name of it – wooded to the chin and with an ancient watchtower perched on its bald crown. The chief seat of the Argylls cannot boast much of architectural beauty, being a square building with pepper-box-looking towers stuck on fine corners. The grounds are charming, containing fine timber, winding walks, stately avenues, gardens and, through all, spanned by several bridges, the Airy bubbles sweetly to the sea.

Oban

OBAN, WHICH, DURING the winter, is a town of deserted hotels, begins to get busy by the end of June. Yachts skim about in the little bay; steamers, deep-sea and coasting, are continually arriving and departing; vehicles rattle about in the one broad and the many narrow streets; and the inns, boots, chambermaid and waiter are distracted with the clangour of innumerable bells. Out of doors, Oban is not a bad representation of Vanity Fair. Every variety *Black's Guide*. Beauty, in the light attire, perambulates the principal street and taciturn Valour in mufti accompanies her. Sportsmen in knickerbockers stand in their groups at the hotel doors; Frenchmen chatter and shrug their shoulders; stolid Germans smoke curiously curved meerschaum pipes; and individuals who have not a drop of Highland blood in their veins flutter about in the garb of Gael, 'a hundredweight of cairngorms throwing a prismatic glory around their persons.' All kinds of people and all kinds of sounds are there. From the next street the tones of the bagpipe come on the ear; tipsy porters abuse each other in Gaelic. Round the corner the mail comes rattling from Fort William, the passengers clustering on its roof; from the pier the bell of the departing steamer urges passengers to make haste; and passengers who have lost their luggage rush about, shout, gesticulate and not unfrequently come into fierce personal collision with one of the tipsy porters.

A more hurried, nervous, frenzied place than Oban, during the summer and autumn months, it is difficult to conceive. People seldom stay there above the night. The tourist no more thinks of spending a week in Oban than he thinks of spending a week in a railway station. When he arrives his first question is after a bedroom; his second, as to the hour at which the steamer from the south is expected.

And the steamer, be it said, does not always arrive at a reasonable hour. She may be detained some time at Greenock; in dirty weather she may be 'on' the Mull of Kintyre all night, buffeted by the big Atlantic there; so that he must be a bold man, or a man gifted with the second sight, who ventures anything but a vague guess as to the hour of her arrival at Oban. And the weather *is* dirty; the panes are blurred with raindrops; outside one beholds an uncomfortable sodden world, a spongy sky above and, midway, a gull sliding sideways through the murky atmosphere. The streets are as empty now as they will be some months hence. Beauty is in her room, crying over *Enoch Arden* and Valour, taciturn as ever, is in the smoking saloon. The Oxford reading party – which, under the circumstances, has not the slightest interest in Plato – attempts, with no great success, to kill the time playing at pitch-and-toss. The gentleman in the highland dress remain indoors – birds with fine feathers do not wish to have them draggled – and the philabeg with an umbrella would be a combination quite too ridiculous. The tipsy porter is for the time silent; but from the next street the bagpipe grows in volume and torture. How the sound of it pains the nervous ear or a man half-maddened by a non-arriving steamer and a rainy day at Oban! Heavily the hours creep on; and at last the *Clansman* does steam in with wet decks – thoroughly washed by Atlantic brine last night – and her hundred and fifty passengers, two-thirds of whom are seasick.

I do not, however, proceed with the *Clansman*. I am waited for at Inverness; and so, when the weather has cleared, on a lovely morning, I am chasing the flying dazzle out of the sun up the lovely Linnhe Loch; past hills that come out on one and recede; past shores that continually shift and change; and am at length set down at Fort William in the shadow of Ben Nevis.

When a man goes to Caprera he, as a matter of course, brings a letter of introduction to Long John. This gentleman, the distiller of the place, was the tallest man I ever beheld out of an exhibition – whence his familiar *sobriquet* – and must, in his youth, have been of incomparable physique.

I presented my letter and was received with the hospitality and courteous grace so characteristics of the old Gael. He is gone now, the happy-hearted Hercules – gone like one of his own drams! His son distils in his stead – but he must feel that he is treading in the footsteps of a greater man. The machinery is the same, the malt is of quality as fine, but he will never produce whisky like him who is no more.

I saw Inverlochy Castle and thought of the craven Argyll, the gallant Montrose, the slaughtered Campbells. I walked up Glen Nevis; and then, one summer morning, I drove over to Bannavie, stepped on board a steamer and was soon in the middle of Loch Lochy.

And what a day and what a sail that was! What a cloudless sky above! What lights and shadows as we went! On Fort Augustus we descended by a staircase of locks and while there I spent half an hour in the museum of Roualeyn Gordon-Cumming. We then entered Loch Ness – stopped for a space to visit the Fall of Foyers which, from scarcity of water, looked 'seedy' as a moulting peacock; saw further on and on the opposite shore, a promontory run out into the lake like an arm and the vast ruin of Castle Urquhart at the end of it like a clenched fist – menacing all and sundry.

Then we went to Inverness, where I found my friend Fellowes who, for some time back, had been amusing himself in that pleasant Highland town reading law. We drove out to Culloden and stood on the moor at sunset. Here the butcher Cumberland trod out romance. Here one felt a Jacobite and a Roman Catholic. The air seemed scented by the fumes of altar incense, by the burning of pastilles. The White Rose was torn and scattered, but its leaves had not yet lost their odours.

'I should rather have died.' I said, 'like that wild chief who, when his clan would not follow him, burst into tears at the ingratitude of his children and charged alone on the English bayonets, than like any other man of whom I have read in history.'

'He wore the sole pair of brogues in the possession of his tribe,' said my companion. 'I should rather have died like Salkeld at the blowing in of the Dehli gate.'

Skye at Last

WHILE TARRYING AT Inverness, a note which we had been expecting for some little time reached Fellowes and myself from M'Ian junior, to the effect that a boat would be at our service at the head of Loch Eishart on the arrival at Broadford of the Skye mail; and that six sturdy boatmen would therefrom convey us to our destination. This information was satisfactory and we made our arrangements accordingly. The coach from Inverness to Dingwall – at which place we were to catch the mail – was advertised to start at four o'clock in the morning and to reach its bourne two hours afterwards; so, to prevent all possibility of missing it, we resolved not to go to bed. At that preposterous hour we were in the street with our luggage and in a short time the coach – which seemed itself not more than half awake – came lumbering up. For a while there was considerable noise; bags and parcels of various kinds were tumbled out of the coach office, mysterious doors were opened in the body of the vehicle into which these were shot. The coach stowed away its parcels in itself, just as in itself the crab stows away its food and *impedimenta*. We clambered up into the front beside the driver, who was enveloped in a drab great-coat of many capes; the guard was behind. 'All right,' and then, with a cheery chirrup, a crack of the whip, a snort and toss from the gallant roadsters, we were off.

There in nothing so delightful as travelling on a stagecoach, when you start in good condition and at a reasonable hour. For myself, I never tire of the varied road flashing past and could dream through a country in that way from one week's end to the other. On the other hand, there is nothing more horrible than starting at four a.m., half awake, breakfastless, the chill of the morning playing on your face as the dewy machine spins along. Your eyes close in spite of every effort, your blood thick with sleep, your brain stuffed with dreams; you wake and sleep and wake again; and no promise of the day ahead can rouse you into interest or blunt the keen edge of your misery.

I recollect nothing of this portion of our journey save its disagreeableness; and alit at Dingwall, cold, wretched and stiff, with cataract of needles and pins pouring down my right leg and making locomotion anything but a pleasure. However, the first stage was over and, on that, we congratulated ourselves. Alas! we did not know the sea of troubles into which we were about to plunge.

We entered the inn, performed our ablutions and sat down to breakfast with appetite. Towards the close of the meal my companion suggested that, to prevent accidents, it might be judicious to secure seats in the mail without delay. Accordingly I went in quest of the landlord and, after some difficulty, discovered him in a small office littered with bags and parcels, turning over the pages of a ledger. He did not lift his eyes when I entered. I intimated my wish to procure two places torward Broadford. He turned a page, lingered on it with his eye as if loath to leave it and then inquired my business. I repeated my message. He shook his head.

'You are too late; you can't get on today.'

'What! can't two places be had?'

'Not for love of money, sir. Last week Lord Deerstalker engaged the mail for his servants. Every place is took,'

'The deuce! do you mean to say we can't get on?'

The man, whose eyes had returned to the page, which he held all the while in one hand, nodded assent.

'Come now, this sort of thing won't do. My friend and I are anxious to reach Broadford tonight. Do you mean to say that we must either return or wait here till the next mail comes up, some three days hence?'

'You can post if you like: I'll provide you with a machine and horses.'

'You'll provide us with a machine and horses,' said I, while something shot through my soul like a bolt of ice.

I returned to Fellowes, who replied to my recital of the interview with a long whistle. When the mail was gone, we formed ourselves into a council of war. After considering our situation from every side, we agreed to post, unless the landlord should prove more than ordinarily rapacious. I went to the little office and informed him of our resolution. We chaffered a good deal, but at last a bargain was struck. I will not mention what current coin of realm was disbursed on the occasion; the charge was as moderate as in the circumstances could have been expected. I need only say that the journey was long and to consist of six stages, a fresh horse at every stage.

In due time a dog-cart was brought to the door, in which was harnessed a tall raw-boned white horse, who seemed to be entering in the sullen depths of his consciousness a protest against our proceedings. We got in and the animal was set in motion. There never was such a slow brute. He evidently disliked his work: perhaps he snuffed the rainy tempest imminent. Who knows! At all events, before he was done with us he took ample revenge for every kick and objurgation which we bestowed on him. Half an hour after starting, a huge raincloud was black above us; suddenly we noticed one portion crumble into a livid streak which slanted down to earth and in a minute or two it burst upon us as if it had a personal injury to avenge. Umbrellas and oil-skins – if we had had them – would have been useless. In less than a quarter of an hour we were saturated like a bale of cotton which has reposed for a quarter of a century at the bottom of the Atlantic; and all the while, against the fell lines of rain, heavy as bullets, straight as cavalry lances, jogged the white horse, heedless of cry and blow, with now and again but a livelier prick and motion of the ear, as if to him the whole thing was perfectly delightful. The first stage was a long one; and all the way from Strathpeffer to Garve, from Garve to Milltown, the rain rushed down on blackened wood, hissed in marshy tarn, boiled on iron crag. At last the inn was descried afar; a speck of dirty white in a world of rainy green. Hope revived us. Another horse could be procured there.

On our arrival, however, we were informed that certain travellers had, two hours before, possessed themselves of the only animal of which the establishment could boast. At this intelligence hope fell down stone dead as if shot through the heart. There was nothing for it but to give our steed a bag of oats and then to hie on. While the white was comfortable munching oats, we noticed from the inn door that the wet yellow road made a long circuit and it occurred to us that if we struck across country for the mile or so at once, we could reach the point where the road disappeared in the distance quite as soon as our raw-boned friend. In any case, waiting was weary work and we were as wet now as we could possibly be. Instructing our driver to wait for us should we not be up in time – of which we averred there was not the slightest possibility – we started. We had firm enough footing at first; but after a while our journey was the counterpart of the fiend's passage through chaos, as described by Milton. Always stick to beaten tracks; short cuts, whether the world of matter, or in the world of ethics, are bad things. In a little time we lost our way, as was to have been expected. The wind and rain beat right in our faces, we had swollen streams to cross, we tumbled into morasses, we tripped over knotted roots of heather. When, after a severe march of a couple of hours, we gained the crest of a small eminence and looked out on the wet, black desolation, Fellowes took out a half-crown from his waistcoat pocket and expressed his intention there and then to 'go in' for a Highland property. From the crest of this eminence too, we beheld the yellow road beneath and the dog cart waiting; and when we got down to it, found the driver so indignant that we thought it prudent to

propitiate him with our spirit flask. A caulker turneth away wrath
– in the Highlands at least.

Getting in again the white went at a better pace, the rain slack-
ened somewhat and our spirits rose in proportion. Our hilarity,
however, was premature. A hill rose before us, up which the yellow
road twisted and wriggled itself. This hill the white would nowise
take. The whip was of no avail; he stood stock-still. Fellowes
applied his stick to his ribs – the white put his fore legs steadily out
before him and refused to move. I jumped out, seized the bridle
and attempted to drag him forward; the white tossed his head
high in the air, showing at the same time a set of vicious teeth
and actually backed. What was to be done? Just at this moment
too, a party of drovers, mounted on red uncombed ponies, with
hair tangling over their eyes, came up and had the ill-feeling to
tee-hee audibly at our discomfiture. This was another drop of acid
squeezed into the bitter cup. Suddenly, at a well-directed whack,
the white made a desperate plunge and took the hill. Midway he
paused and attempted his old game, but down came a hurricane of
blows and he started off – ''Twere long to tell and sad to trace' the
annoyance that raw-boned quadruped wrought us. But it came to
an end at last. And at my parting I waved the animal, sullen and
unbeloved, my last farewell; and wished that no green paddock
should receive him in his old age, but that his ill-natured flesh
should be devoured by the hounds; that leather should be made
of his be-cudgelled hide and hoped that, considering its tough-
ness, of it should the boots and shoes of a poor man's children be
manufactured.

Late in the afternoon we reached Jean-Town, on the shores of
Loch Carron. 'Tis a tarry, scaly village, with a most ancient and
fish-like smell. The inhabitants have suffered a sea-change. The
men stride about in leather fishing-boots, the women sit at open
doors at work with bait baskets. Two or three boats are moored at
the stone-heaped pier. Brown, idle nets, stretched on high poles
along the beach, flap in the winds. We had tea at the primeval inn
and on intimating to the landlord that we wished to proceed to

Broadford, he went off to emerge with a boat and crew. In a short time an old sea-dog, red with the keen breeze and the redolent of fishy brine, entered the apartment with the information that everything was ready. We embarked at once, a sail was hoisted and on the vacillating puff of evening we dropped gently down on the loch. There was something in the dead silence of the scene and the easy motion of the boat that affected me. Weary with travel, worn out with the want of sleep yet, at the same time, far from drowsy, with every faculty and sense rather in a condition of wide and intense wakefulness, everything around became invested with a singular and frightful feeling. *Why*, I know not, for I have had no second experience of the kind; but on this occasion, to my overstrained vision, every object became instinct with a hideous and multitudinous life. The clouds congealed into faces and human forms. Figures started out upon me from mountain-sides. The rugged surfaces, seamed with torrent lines, grew into monstrous figures and arms with clutching fingers. The sweet and gracious shows of nature became, under the magic of lassitude, a phantasmagoria hateful and abominable. Fatigue changed the world for me – but the sublimity of one illusion will be memorable. For a barrier of mountains standing high above the glimmering lower world, distinct and purple against a 'daffodil sky', seemed the profile of a gigantic man stretched on a bier and the features in their sad imperial beauty, seemed those of the first Napoleon. Wonderful that mountain-monument, as we floated seaward into the distance – the figure sculptured by earthquake and fiery deluges sleeping up there, high above the din and strife of earth, robed in solemn purple, its background the yellow of the evening sky!

About ten we passed the rocky portals of the loch on the last sigh of evening and stood for the open sea. The wind came only in intermitting puffs and the boatmen took to the oars. The transparent autumn night fell upon us; the mainland was gathering in gloom behind us and before us rocky islands glimmered on the level deep. To the chorus of a Gaelic song of remarkable length and monotony the crew plied their oars and every plash awoke the lightening of the main. The sea was filled with elfin fire. I hung over the stern and watched our brilliant wake seething up into a kind of pale emerald and rushing away into the darkness. The coast on our left had lost form and outline, withdrawing itself into an undistinguishable mass of gloom, when suddenly the lights of a village broke clear upon it like a bank of glow-worms. I enquired its name and was answered, 'Plockton'.

In half an hour the scattered lights became massed into one; soon that died out in the distance. Eleven o'clock! Like one man the rowers pull. The air is chill on the ocean's face and we wrap ourselves more closely in our cloaks. There is something uncomfortable in the utter silence and loneliness of the hour – in the phosphorescent sea, with its ghostly splendours. The boatmen, too, have ceased singing. Would that I were taking mine ease with M'Ian!

Suddenly a strange sighing sound is heard behind. One of the crew springs up, hauls down the sail and the next moment the squall is upon us. The boatmen hang on their oars and we hear the rushing rain. Whew! how it hisses down on us, crushing everything in its passion. The long dim stretch of coast, the dark islands, are in a moment shut out; the world shrinks into a circumference of twenty yards; and within that space the sea is churned into a pale illumination – a light of misty gold. In a moment we are wet to the skin. The boatmen have shipped their oars, drawn their jacket collars over their ears and there we lie at midnight, shelterless to the thick hiss of the rain. But it has spent itself at last and a few stars are again twinkling in the blue. It is plain our fellows are somewhat tired of the voyage. They cannot depend upon a wind; it will either be a puff, dying as soon as born, or a squall roaring down on the sea, through the long funnels of the glens; and to pull all the way is a dreary affair. The matter is laid before us – the voices of the crew are loud for our return. They will put us ashore at Plockton – they will take us across in the morning. A cloud has again blotted the stars; we consent.

Our course is altered, the oars are pulled with redoubled vigour; soon the long dim line of coast rises before us, but the lights have burned out now and the Plocktonites are asleep. On we go; the boat shoots into a 'midnight cove' and we leap out upon masses of slippery sea-weed. The craft is safely moored. Two of the men seize our luggage and we go stumbling over rocks until the road is reached. A short walk brings us to the inn, or rather public-house, which is, however, closed for the night. After some knocking we were admitted, wet as Newfoundlands from the lake. Wearied almost to death, I reached my bedroom and was about to divest myself of my soaking garments when, after a low tap at the door, the owner of the boat entered.

He stated his readiness to take us across in the morning; he would knock us up shortly after dawn; but as he and his companions had no friends in the place they would, of course, have to pay for their beds and their breakfasts before they sailed; 'an' she was shure the shentlemens waana expect her to pay the same.' With a heavy heart I satisfied the cormorant. He insisted on being paid his full hire before he left Jean-Town, too! Before turning in, I looked what o'clock. One in the morning! In three hours M'Ian will be waiting in his galley at the head of Einshart's Loch. Unfortunates that we are!

At least, thought I when I awoke, there is satisfaction in accomplishing something quite peculiar. There are many men in the world who have performed extraordinary actions; but Fellowes and myself may boast, without fear of contradiction, that we were the only travellers who ever arrived at Plockton.

But, heavens! the boatmen should have been here ere this. Alarmed, I sprang out of bed, clothed in haste, burst into Fellowes' room, turned him out, and then proceeded downstairs. No information could be procured, nobody has seen our crew. That morning they had not called at the house. After a while a fisherman sauntered in and, in consideration of certain stimulants to be supplied by us, admitted that our fellows were acquaintances of his own; that they had started at daybreak and would now be far on their way to Jean-Town. The scoundrels, so overpaid too! Well, well, there's another world.

With some difficulty we gathered from our friend that a ferry from the mainland to Skye existed at some inconceivable distance across the hills and that a boat perhaps might be had there. But how was the ferry to be reached? No conveyance could be had at the inn. We instantly despatched scouts to every point on the compass to hunt for a wheeled vehicle. At height of noon our messengers returned with the information that neither gig, cart nor wheelbarrow could be had on any terms. What *was* to be done? I was smitten by a horrible sense of helplessness; it seemed as if I were doomed to abide for ever in that dreary place, girdled by these gray rocks scooped and honeycombed by the washing of the bitter seas – cut off from friends, profession and delights of social intercourse, as if spirited away to fairyland. I felt myself growing a fisherman, like the men about me; Gaelic seemed forming on my tongue. Fellowes, meanwhile, with that admirable practical philosophy of his, had lit a cigar and was chatting away with the landlady about the population of the village, the occupants of the inhabitants, their ecclesiastical history.

I awoke from my gloomy dream as she replied to a question of his – 'The last minister was put awa for drinkin'; but we've got a new ane, Mr Cammil, an' verra weel liket he is.'

The words were a ray of light and suggested a possible deliverance. I slapped him on the shoulder, crying, 'I have it! There was a fellow student of mine in Glasgow, a Mr Donald Campbell and it runs in my mind that he was preferred to a parish in the Highlands somewhere; what if this should prove to be the identical man? Let us call upon him.'

The chances were not very much in our favour; but our circumstances were desperate and the thing was worth trying. The landlady sent her son with us to point the way. We knocked, were admitted and shown to the tiny drawing-room. While waiting, I observed a couple of photograph cases on the table. These I opened. One contained the portrait of a gentleman in a white neckcloth, evidently a clergyman; the other that of a lady, in all likelihood his spouse. Alas! the gentleman bore no resemblance to *my* Mr Campbell: the lady I did not know. I laid the cases down in disappointment and began to frame an apology for our singular intrusion, then the door opened – and my old friend entered. He greeted us cordially and I wrung his hand with fervour. I told him our adventure with the Jean-Town boatmen and our consequent helplessness; at which he laughed and offered his cart to convey ourselves and luggage to Kyleakin ferry, which turned out to be only six miles off. Genial talk about college scenes and old associates brought on the hour of luncheon; that concluded, the cart was at the door. In it our things were placed; farewells were uttered and we departed.

It was a wild, picturesque road along which we moved; some-times comparatively smooth, but more frequently rough and stony, as the dry torrent's bed. Black dreary wastes spread around. Here and there we passed a colony of turf huts, out of which wild ragged children, tawny as Indians, came trooping to stare upon as we passed. But the journey was attractive enough; for before us rose a permanent vision of mighty hills, with their burdens of cloudy rack; and every now and then, from an eminence, we could mark, against the land, the blue of the sea flowing in, bright with sunlight. We were once more on our way; the minister's mare went merrily; the breeze came keen and fresh against us; and in less than a couple of hours we reached Kyleakin.

The ferry is a narrow passage between the mainland and Skye; the current is powerful there, difficult to pull against on gusty days; and the ferrymen are loath to make the attempt unless well remunerated. When we arrived, we found four passengers waiting to cross; and as their appearance gave prospect of an insufficient supply of coin, they were left sitting on the bleak windy rocks until some others should come up. It was as easy to pull across for ten shillings as it was for two!

One was a girl, who had been in service in the south, had taken ill there and was on her way home to some wretched turf hut on the hillside, in all liklihood to die; the second a little cheery Irish-woman, with a basketful of paper ornaments, with the gaudy colours and ingenious devices of which she hoped to tickle the aesthetic sensibilities and open the purses of the Gael. The third and fourth were men, apparently laborious ones; but the younger informed me he was a schoolmaster and it came out incidentally in conversation that his schoolhouse was a turf cabin, his writing-table a trunk, on which his pupils wrote by turns. Imagination sees his young kilted friends kneeling on the clay floor, laboriously forming pot-hooks there and squinting horribly the while.

The ferrymen began to bestir themselves when we came up; and in a short time the boat was ready and the party embarked. The craft was crank and leaked abominably, but there was no help; our bags were deposited in the bottom. The schoolmaster worked an oar in lieu of payment. The little Irishwoman, with her precious basket, sat high in the bow, the labourer and the sick girl behind us at the stern. With a strong pull of the oars we shot into the seething water. In a moment the Irishwoman is brought out in keen relief against a cloud of spray; but, nothing daunted, she laughed out merrily and seems to consider a ducking the funniest thing in the world. In another, I receive a slap in the face from a gush of blue water and emerged, half-blinded and soaked from top to toe. Ugh, this sea-waltz is getting far from pleasant. The leak is increasing fast and our carpet-bags are well-nigh afloat in the working bilge. We are all drenched now. The girl is sick and Fellowes is assisting her from his brandy-flask. The little Irishwoman, erst so cheery and gay, with spirits that turned every circumstance into a quip and crank, has sunk in a heap at the bow; her basket is exposed and the ornaments, shaped by patient fingers out of coloured papers, are shapeless now; the looped rosettes are ruined; her stock-in-trade, pulp — a misfortune great to her as defeat to an army, or a famine to a kingdom.

But we are more than halfway across and a little ahead the water is comparatively smooth. The boatmen pull with greater ease; the uncomfortable sensation at the pit of the stomach

is redressed; the white lips of the girl begin to redden somewhat; and the bunch forward stirs itself and exhibits signs of life.
Fellowes bought up the contents of her basket; and a contribution of a two-and-sixpence from myself made the widow's heart
to sing aloud for joy.

On landing, our luggage is conveyed in a cart to the inn and
waits our arrival there. Meanwhile we warm our chilled limbs
with a caulker of Glenlivet. 'Blessings be with it and eternal
praise.' How fine spirit melts into the wandering blood, like 'a
purer light in light!' How the soft benignant fire streams through
the labyrinthine veins, from brain to toe! The sea is checkmated;
the heart beats with fuller throb; and the impending rheumatism
flies afar. When we reached the inn, we seized our luggage, in the
hope of procuring dry garments. Alas! when I went upstairs, mine
might have been the carpetbag of a merman; it was wet to the
inmost core.

Soaked to the skin, it was our interest to proceed without
delay. We waited on the landlord, and desired a conveyance. The
landlord informed us that the only vehicle which he possessed was
a phaeton, at present on hire till the evening and advised us, now
that it was Saturday, to remain in this establishment till Monday,
when he could send us on comfortably. To wait till Monday,
however, would never do. We told the man our story, how for
two days we had been the sport of fortune, tossed hither and
thither; but he – feeling he had us in his power – would render
no assistance.

We wandered out towards the rocks to hold a consultation
and had almost resolved to leave our things where they were
and start out on foot, when a son of the innkeeper's joined us.
He – whether cognisant of his parent's statement, I cannot say
– admitted that there were a horse and gig in the stable; that he
knew Mr M'Ian's place and offered to drive us to a little fishing
village within three miles of it, where our things could be left and
a cart sent to bring them up in the evening. The charge was –
never mind what! But we closed with it at once.

We entered the inn while our friend went round to the stable to bring the machine to the door; met the landlord on the stairs, sent an indignant broadside into him, which he received with the utmost coolness. The imperturbable man! He swallowed our shot like a sandbank and was nothing the worse. The horse was now at the door, in a few moments our luggage was stowed away and we were off. Through seventeen miles of black moorland we drove almost without beholding a single dwelling. Sometimes, although rarely, we had a glimpse of the sea. The chief object that broke the desolation was a range of clumsy red hills, stretching away like a chain of gigantic dust heaps. Their aspect was singularly dreary and depressing.

About seven p.m. we reached the village, left our things, still soaked in seawater, in one of the huts, till Mr M'Ian could send for them and struck off on foot for the three miles which we were told yet remained. By this time the country had improved in appearance. The hills were swelling and green; up these the road wound, fringed with ferns, mixed with the purple bells of the foxglove. A stream, too, evidently escaped from some higher mountain tarn, came dashing along in a succession of tiny waterfalls. A quiet pastoral region, but so still, so deserted! Hardly a house, hardly a human being!

After a while we reached the lake, half covered with waterlilies and our footsteps startled a brood of wild ducks in its breast. How lonely it looked in its dark hollow there, familiar to the cry of the wild bird, the sultry summer cloud, the stars and meteors of night – strange to human faces and the sound of human voices. But what of our three miles? We have been walking for an hour and a half. Are we astray in the green wilderness? The idea is far from pleasant. Happily a youthful native came trotting along and we inquired our way. The boy looked at us and shook his head. We repeated the question, still the same shy puzzled look. A proffer of a shilling, however, quickened his apprehension and, returning with us a few paces, he pointed out a hillroad striking up through the moor. On asking the distance, he seemed put out for and then muttered, in difficult English, 'Four mile.' Nothing more could be procured in the way of information; so off went little Barelegs, richer than ever he had been in his life, at a long swinging trot, which seemed his natural pace and which, I suppose, he could sustain from sunrise to sunset. To this hillroad we now addressed ourselves.

It was sunset now. Up we went through the purple moor and in a short time sighted a crimson tarn, bordered with long black rushes and, as we approached, a duck burst from its face on 'squattering' wings, shaking the splendour into widening circles. Just then two girls came on the road with peats in their laps: anxious for information, we paused – they, shy as heath-hens, darted past and, when fifty-yards' distance, wheeled suddenly round and burst into shrieks of laughter, repeated and re-repeated. In no laughing mood we pursued our way.

The road now began to dip and we entered a glen plentifully covered with birchwood, a stream keeping us company from the tarn above. The sun was now down and objects at a distance began to grow uncertain in the evening mist. The horrible idea that we had lost our way and were doomed to encamp on the heather, grew upon us. On! on! We had walked six miles since our encounter with the false Barelegs. Suddenly we heard a dog bark; that was a sign of humanity and our spirits rose. Then we saw a troop of horses galloping along the bottom of the glen. Better and better.

All at once we heard the sound of voices and Fellowes declared he saw something moving on the road. The next moment M'Ian and a couple of shepherds started out of the gloom. At sight of them our hearts burned within us, like a newly-poked fire. Sincere was the greeting, immense the shaking of hands; and the story of our adventures kept us merry till we reached the house.

Of our doughty deeds at supper I will not sing, nor state how the toddy jugs were drained. Rather let me tell of those who sat with us at the board – the elder Mr M'Ian and Father M'Crimmon, then living in the house. Mr M'Ian senior was a man past eighty, but fresh and hale for his years. His figure was slight and wiry, his face a fresh pink, his hair like snow. Age, though it had bowed him somewhat, had not been able to steal the fire from his eye, nor the vigour from his limbs. He entered the army at an early age; carried colours in Ireland before the century came in; was with Moore at Corunna; followed Wellington through the Peninsular battles; was with the 42nd at Quatre Bras and hurt there when the brazen cuirassiers came charging through the tall rye-grass; and, finally, stood at Waterloo in a square that crumbled before the artillery and cavalry charges of Napoleon – crumbled, but never flinched!

M'Ian was an isleman of the old school; penetrated through every drop of blood with pride of birth and with a sense of honour which was like a second conscience. He had all the faults incidental to such a character. He was stubborn as the gnarled trunk of the oak, full of prejudices which our enlightenment laughs at, but which we need not despise, for well will it be for us with our knowledge and our science if we go to our graves with as stainless a name. He was quick of temper and contradiction brought fire from him like steel from flint. Short and fierce were his gusts of passion, but of these faults, however, this evening saw nothing.

The old gentleman was kind and hospitable; full of talk, but his talk seemed to us of old-world things. He talked of the French Revolution and the actors thereof as contemporaries; his heart was with his memory, in the older days when George III was king and not an old king neither.

Father M'Crimmon was a tall man, being in height considerably above six feet. He was thin, like his own island, where the soil is washed away by rain, leaving bare the rock. His face was mountainously bony, with great pits and hollows in it. His eyes were gray and had that depth of melancholy in them which is so often observed in men of his order. In heart he was simple as a child; in discourse slow, measured and stately. There was something in his appearance that suggested the silence and solitude of the wilderness; of hours lonely to the heart and bare spaces lonely to the eye.

Although of another and – as I think, else I should not profess it – a purer faith, I respected him at first and loved him almost when I came to know him. Was it wonderful that his aspect was sorrowful, that it wore a wistful look, as if he had lost something which could never be regained and that for evermore the sunshine was stolen from his smile? He was by his profession cut off from all the sweet ties of human nature, from all love of wife or child. His people were widely scattered: across the black moor, far up the hollow glens, blustering with winds or dimmed with rain-cloud. Thither the grim man followed them, officiating on rare festival occasions of marriage and christening; more frequently engaged dispensing alms, giving advice in disaster, waiting by the low pallets of the fever-stricken, listening to the confession of long-hoarded guilt, comforting the dark spirit as it passed to its audit.

Yet cold and cheerless as may be his life, he has his reward; for in his wanderings through the glens there is not an eye but brightens at his approach, not a mourner but feels he has a sharer in his sorrow; and when the tall, bony, seldom-smiling man is bourne at last to his grave, round many a fireside will tears fall and prayers be said for the good priest M'Crimmon.

All night sitting there, we talked of strange 'unhappy far-off things, and battles long ago,' blood-crusted clan quarrels, bitter wrongs and terrible revenges: of wraiths and bodings and pale death-lights burning on the rocks. The conversation was straight-forward and earnest, conducted with perfect faith in the subject matter; and I listened, I am not ashamed to confess, with a curious and not altogether unpleasant thrill of the blood.

A new world and order of things seemed to gather round us as we sat there, carried away from all that makes up the present and brought face to face with tradition; with the ongoings of men who lived in solitary places, whose ears were constantly filled with the *sough* of the wind, the clash of the wave on the rock;

whose eyes were open on the flinty cliff and the floating forms of mists and the dead silence of pale sky dipping down far off on the dead silence of black moor.

Perhaps it was the faith of the speakers that impressed me most. To them the stories were much a matter of course; the supernatural atmosphere had become so familiar to them that it had been emptied of all its wonder and the greatest part of its terror. Of this I am quite sure, that a ghostly story told in the pit of a theatre, or at Vauxhall, or walking through lighted London street, is quite a different thing from a ghost story told, as I heard it, in a lone Highland dwelling, cut off from every habitation by eight miles of gusty wind, the sea within a hundred feet of the walls, the tumble of the big wave and the rattle of the pebbles, as it washes away back again, distinctly heard where you sit and the talkers making the whole matter 'stuff o' the conscience.' Very different! You laugh in the theatre and call the narrator an ass; in the other case you listen silently, with a scalp creeping as if there were a separate life in it and the blood streaming coldly down my back.

At Mr M'Ian's

YOUNG M'IAN AWOKE me next morning. As I came down stairs
he told me, had it not been Sunday he would have roused me with
a performance on the bagpipes. Heaven forfend! I never felt so
sincere a Sabbatarian. He led me some little distance to a favourable point of rock and, lo! across a sea sleek as satin, rose a range
of hills, clear against the morning, jagged and notched like an old
sword-blade.

'Yonder,' said he, pointing, 'beyond the black mass in front,
just where the shower is falling, lies Lake Coruisk. I'll take you to
see it one of these days.'

The farm which Mr M'Ian rented was, in comparison with
many others in the island, of but moderate extent; and yet it
skirted the seashore for a considerable distance and comprised
within itself many a rough hill and many a green valley. The house
was old-fashioned, was harled all over with lime and contained
a roomy porch, over which ivies clustered, a dining-room, a
drawing-room, a lot of bedrooms and behind, and built out from
the house, an immense kitchen, with a flagged floor and a huge
fireplace.

A whole colony of turf huts, with films of blue smoke issuing from each, were scattered along the shore, lending a sort of
homely beauty to the wild picturesqueness. Beside the house,
with a ruined summer-seat at one end; was a large, carelessly-
kept garden, surrounded by a high stone wall. M'Ian kept the key
himself; and on the garden door were nailed ravens and other
feathered malefactors in different stages of decay.

Within a stone's throw from the porch, were one or two barns, a stable, a wool-house and other outhouses, in which several of the servants slept. M'Ian was careful of social degree and did not admit everyone to his dressing room. He held his interviews with the common people in the open air in front of the house. When a drover came for cattle he dined solitarily in the porch and the dishes were sent to him from M'Ian's table. The drover was a servant, consequently he could not sit at meat with my friend; he was more than a servant for the nonce, inasmuch as he was his master's representative and consequently he could not be sent to the kitchen – the porch was therefore a kind of convenient middle place; neither too high nor too humble, it was, in fact, a sort of social purgatory.

But Mr M'Ian did not judge a man by the coat he wore, nor by the amount of money in his purse – he valued a man for the sake of his grandfather rather than for the sake of himself.

The shepherds, the shepherds' dogs and the domestic servants, dined in the large kitchen. The kitchen was the most picturesque apartment in the house. There was a huge dresser near a small dusty window; in a dark corner stood a great cupboard in which crockery was stowed away. The walls and rafters were black with peat smoke. Dogs were continually sleeping on the floor with their heads resting on their outstretched paws; and from a frequent start and whine, I knew that in dream they were chasing a flock of sheep along the steep hillside, their masters shouting out orders to them from the valley beneath. The fleeces of sheep which had been found dead on the mountain were nailed on the walls to dry. Braxy hams were suspended from the roof; strings of fish were hanging above the fireplace. The door was almost continually open, for by the door light mainly entered. Amid a savoury stream of broth and potatoes, the shepherds and domestic servants drew in long backless forms to the table and dined, innocent of knife and fork, the dogs snapping and snarling among their legs; and when the meal was over the dogs licked the platters.

When Peter, the meek-faced violinist came, the kitchen was cleared after nightfall; the forms were taken away, candles stuck into battered tin sconces, the dogs unceremoniously kicked out and a somewhat ample ballroom was the result. Then in came the girls, with black shoes and white stockings, newly-washed faces and nicely smoothed hair; and with them came the shepherds and menservants, more carefully attired than usual. Peter took his seat near the fire; M'Ian gave the signal by clapping his hands; up went the inspiriting notes of the fiddle and away went the dancers, man and maid facing each other, the girl's feet twinkling beneath her petticoat, not like two mice, but rather like a dozen; her kilted partner pounding the flag-floor unmercifully; then man and maid changed step and followed each other through loops and chains; then they faced each other again, the man whooping, the girl's hair coming down with her exertions; then suddenly the fiddle changed time and with a cry the dancers rushed at each other, each pair getting linked arm in arm and away the whole floor dashed into the whirlwind of the reel of Hoolichan. It was dancing with a will – lyrical, impassioned; the strength of a dozen fiddlers dwelt in Peter's elbow; M'Ian clapped his hands and shouted and the stranger was forced to mount the dresser to get out of the way of whirling kilt and tempestuous petticoat.

Chief amongst the dancers on these occasions were John Kelly, Lachlan Roy and Angus-with-the-dogs. John Kelly was M'Ian's principal shepherd – a swarthy fellow, of Irish descent, I fancy and of infinite wind, endurance and capacity of drinking whisky. He was a solitary creature, irascible in the extreme; he crossed and re-crossed the farm I should think some dozen times every day and was never seen at church or market without his dog. With his dog only was John Kelly intimate and on perfectly confidential terms. I have often wondered what were his thoughts as he wandered through the glens at early morning and saw the fiery mists upstreaming from the shoulders of

Blaavin; or when he sat on a sunny knoll at noon smoking a black broken pipe and watching his dog bringing a flock of sheep down the opposite hillside. Whatever they were, John kept them strictly to himself.

In the absorption of whisky he was without a peer in my experience, although I have in my time encountered some rather distinguished practitioners in that art. If you gave John a glass of spirits, there was a flash and it was gone. For a wager I once beheld him drink a bottle of whisky in ten minutes. He drank it in cupfuls, saying never a word. When it was finished, he wrapt himself in his plaid, went out with his dog and slept all night on the hillside. I suppose a natural instinct told him that the night air would decompose the alcohol for him. When he came in the next morning his swarthy face was a shade paler than its wont; but he seemed to suffer no uneasiness and he tackled to his breakfast like a man.

Lachlan Roy was a little cheery, agile, red squirrel of a man and, like the squirrel, he had a lot of nuts stored away in secret hole against the winter time. A more industrious little creature I have never met. He lived near the old castle of Dunscaich, where he rented a couple of crofts or so; there he fed his score or two sheep and his half-dozen of black cattle; and from thence he drove them to Broadford market twice to thrice in the year, where they were sure to fetch good prices. He knew the points of a sheep or a stirk as well as any man in the island. He was about forty-five, had had a wife and children, but they had all died years before; and although a widower, Lachlan was as jolly, as merry-eyed and merry-hearted as any young bachelor shepherd in the country.

He was a kindly soul too, full of pity and was constantly performing charitable offices for his neighbours in distress. A poor woman in his neighbourhood had lost her suckling child and Lachlan came up to M'Ian's house with tears in his eyes, seeking some simple cordials and a bottle of wine.

'Ay, it's a sad thing, Mr M'Ian,' he went on, 'when death takes a child from the breast. A full breast and an empty knee, Mr M'Ian, makes a desolate house. Poor Mirren has a terrible rush of milk and cold is the lip today that could relieve her. And she's alone too, Mr M'Ian, for her husband is at Stornoway after the herring.'

Of course he got the cordials and the wine and, of course in a short space of time as was possible, the poor mother, seated on an upturned creel and rocking herself to and fro over her clasped hands, got them also, with what a supplementary aid Lachlan's own stores could afford. Lachlan was universally respected; and when he appeared every door opened cheerfully.

At all dance gatherings at M'Ian's he was certain to be present; and old as he was comparatively, the prettiest girl was glad to have him for a partner. He had a merry wit and when he joked, blushings and titterings overspread in a moment all the young women's faces. On such occasions I have seen John Kelly sitting in a corner gloomily biting his nails, jealousy eating his heart. But Lachlan cared nothing for John's mutinous countenance – he meant no harm and he feared no man.

Lachlan Roy, being interpreted means red Lachlan; and this cognomen not only drew its appropriateness from the colour of his hair and beard; it had, as I afterwards learned, a yet deeper significance. Lachlan, if the truth must be told, had nearly as fierce a thirst for strong waters as John Kelly himself and that thirst, on fair days, after he had sold his cattle at Broadford, he was wont plentifully to slake. His face, under the influence of liquor, became red as the harvest moon; and as of this physiological peculiarity in himself he had the most perfect knowledge, he was under the impression that if he drew rein on the side of high alcoholic inflammation of countenance, he was safe and on the whole rather creditably virtuous than otherwise. And so, perhaps, he would have been, had he been able to judge for himself, or had he been placed amongst boon companions who were ignorant of his weakness, or who did not wish to deceive him.

Somewhat suspicious, when a fresh jorum was placed on the table, he would call out – 'Donald, is my face red yet?'

Donald, who was perfectly aware of the ruddy illumination, would hypocritically reply, 'Hoots, Lachlan dear, what are ye speaking about? Your face is just its own natural colour. What should it be red for?'

'Duncan, you scoundrel,' he would cry fiercely at a later period, bringing his clenched fist down on the table and making the glasses dance – 'Duncan, you scoundrel, look me in the face!'

Thus adjured, Duncan would turn his uncertain optics on his flaming friend.

'Is my face red yet, Duncan?'

Duncan, too far gone for speech, would shake his head in the gravest manner, plainly implying that the face in question was *not* red and that there was not the least likelihood that it would ever become red.

And so, from trust in the veracity of his fellows, Lachlan was, at Broadford, brought to bitter grief twice or thrice in the year.

Angus-with-the-dogs was continually passing over the country like the shadow of a cloud. If he had a home at all, it was situated at Ardvasar, near Armadale; but there Angus was found but seldom. He was always wandering about with his gun over his shoulder, his terriers, Spoineag and Fruich, at his heels and the kitchen of every tacksman was open to him. The tacksmen paid Angus so much per annum and Angus spent his time in killing their vermin. He was a dead shot; he knew the hole of the fox and the cairn in which an otter would be found. If you wanted a brace of young falcons, Angus would procure them for you; if ravens were breeding on one of your cliffs, you had to wait till the young ones were half-fledged, send for Angus and, before the evening, the entire brood, father and mother included, would be nailed on your barn door. He knew the seldom-visited loch up amongst the hills which was haunted by the swan; the cliff of the Cuchullins on which the eagles dwelt; the place where, by moonlight, you could get a shot at the shy heron. He knew all the races of dogs. In the warm, blind pup he saw, at a glance, the future terrier or staghound. He could cure the distemper, could crop ears and dock tails. He could cunningly plait all kinds of fishing tackle; could carve quaichs and work you curiously-patterned dagger-hilts out of the black oak. If you wished a tobacco pouch made out of the skin of an otter or seal, you had simply to apply to Angus. From his variety of accomplishments he was an immense favourite.

The old farmers liked him because he was the sworn foe of polecats, foxes and ravens; the sons of farmers valued him because he was an authority on rifles and fowling-pieces and knew the warm shelving rocks on which bullet-headed seals slept and cairns on the seashore in which otters lived; and because if any special breed of dog was wanted he was sure to meet the demand.

He was a little, thick-set fellow, of great physical strength and of most obliging nature and he was called Angus-with-the-dogs, because without Spoineag and Fruich at his heels, he was never to be seen. The pipe was always in his mouth – to him tobacco smoke was as much a matter of course as peat reek is to a turf hut.

One day, after Fellowes had gone to the Landlord's, where I was to join him in a week or ten days, young M'Ian and myself waited for Angus-with-the-dogs on one of the rising grounds at a little distance from the house. Angus in his peregrinations had marked a cairn in which he thought an otter would be found and it was resolved that this cairn should be visited on a specified day about noon, in the hope that some little sport might be provided for the Sassenach.

About eleven a.m. therefore, on a specified day, we lay on the heather smoking. It was warm and sunny; M'Ian had thrown beside him on the heather his gun and shot-belt and lay back luxuriously on his fragrant couch, meerschaum in mouth, his

Glengarry bonnet tilted forward over his eyes, his left leg stretched out, his right drawn up and his brown hands clasped round the knee. Of my own position, which was comfortable enough, I was not at the moment specially aware; my attention being absorbed by the scenery around, which was wild and strange. We lay on purple heather and behind were the sloping birch woods – birch woods always remind me somehow of woods in their teens – which ran up to the bases of white cliffs traversed only by the shepherd and the shadows of hawks and clouds. The plateau on which we lay ran toward the sea and suddenly broke down to it in little ravines and gorges, beautifully grassed and mossed and plumed with bunches of ferns. Occasionally a rivulet came laughing and dancing down from rocky shelf to shelf.

Of course, from the spot where we lay, this breaking down of the hillface was invisible, but it was in my mind's eye all the same, for I had sailed along the coast and admired it a couple of days before. Right in front flowed Loch Eishart, with its islands and white seabirds. Down in the right-hand corner, reduced in size by distance, the house sat on its knoll, like a white shell; and beside it were barns and outhouses, the smoking turf huts on the shore, the clumps of birch wood, the thread of a road which ran down toward the stream from the house, crossed it by a bridge a little beyond the turf huts and the boatshed and then came right up towards us till it was lost in the woods.

Right across the loch were the round red hills that rise above Broadford; and the entire range of the Cuchillins – the outline wild, splintered, jagged, as if drawn by a hand shaken by terror or frenzy. A glittering mesh of sunlight stretched across the loch, blinding, palpitating, ever-dying, ever-renewed. The bee came booming past, the white seagull swept above, silent as a thought or dream. Gazing out on all this, somehow lost in it, I was suddenly startled by a sharp whistle and then I noticed that a figure was crossing the bridge below. M'Ian got up. 'That's Angus,' he said, 'let us go down and meet him.' And so, after knocking the ashes

76

out of his pipe and filling it anew, picking up his gun and slinging his shot-belt across his shoulder, he led the way.

At the bridge we found Angus seated, with his gun across his knee and Spoineag and Fruich coursing about and beating the bushes, from which a rabbit would occasionally bounce and scurry off. Angus looked more alert and intelligent than I had ever before seen him – probably because he had a business on hand. We started at once along the shore at the foot of the cliffs above which we had been lying half an hour before. Our way lay across large boulders which had rolled down from heights above and progression, at least to one unaccustomed to such rough work, was by no means easy. Angus and M'Ian stepped on lightly enough, the dogs kept up a continual barking and yelping and were continually disappearing in rents and crannies in the cliffs and emerging more ardent than ever. At a likely place Angus would stop for a moment, speak a word or two to the dogs and then they rushed barking at every orifice, entered with a struggle and ranged through all passages of the hollow cairn. As yet the otter had not been found at home.

At last when we came in view of a spur of the higher ground which, breaking down on the shore, terminated in a sort of pyramid of loose stones, Angus dashed across the broken boulders at a run, followed by his dogs. When they got up, Spoineag and Fruich, barking as they had never barked before, crept in at all kinds of holes and impossible fissures and were no sooner out than they were again in. Angus cheered and encouraged them and pointed out to M'Ian traces of the otter's presence. I sat down on a stone and watched the behaviour of the terriers. If ever there was an insane dog, it was Fruich that day; she jumped and barked and got into the cairn by holes through which no other dog could go and came out by holes through which no other dog could come. Spoineag, on the other hand, was comparatively composed; he would occasionally sit down and, taking a critical view of the cairn, run barking to a new point and to that point Fruich would rush like a fury and disappear.

Spoineag was a commander-in-chief, Fruich was a gallant general of the division. Fruich had disappeared for a time and, from the muffled barking, we concluded she was working her way to the centre of the citadel, when all at once Spoineag, as if moved by sudden inspiration, rushed to the top of the cairn began tearing up the turf with teeth and feet. Spoineag's eagerness now was as intense as ever Fruich's had been. Angus, who had implicit faith in Spoineag's genius, climbed up to assist and tore away at the turf with his hands. In a minute or so Spoineag had effected an entrance from the top and began to work his way downwards. Angus stood up against the sky with his gun in readiness. We could hear the dogs barking inside and evidently approaching a common centre, when all at once a fell tumult arose. The otter was reached at last and was using teeth and claws.

Angus made a signal to M'Ian, who immediately brought his gun to his shoulder. The combat still raged within and seemed to be coming nearer. Once Fruich came out howling with a bleeding foot, but a cry from Angus on the height sent her in again. All at once the din of the barking ceased and I saw a black lurching object flit past the stones towards the sea. Crack went M'Ian's gun from the boulder, crack went Angus's gun from the height and the black object turned half round suddenly and then lay still.

It was the otter; and the next moment Spoineag and Fruich were out upon it, the fire of the battle in their eyes and their teeth fixed in its bloody throat. They dragged the carcass backwards and forwards and seemed unable to sate their rage upon it. What ancient animosity existed between the families of otters and terriers? What wrong had been done never to be redressed?

Angus came forward at last, sent Spoineag and Fruich howling right and left with his foot, seized the otter by the tail and then, over the rough boulders, we began our homeward march. Our progress past the turf-huts nestling on the shore at the foot of the cliffs was a triumphal one. Old men, women and brown, half-naked children, came out to gaze upon us. When we got home the otter was laid on the grass in front of the house, where the elder M'Ian came out to inspect it and was polite enough to express his approval and to declare that it was not much inferior in bulk and strength to the otters he had hunted and killed at the close of the last century.

After dinner young M'Ian skinned his trophy and nailed and stretched the hide on the garden gate amid the dilapidated kites and ravens. In the evening, Angus, with his gun across his shoulder and Spoineag and Fruich at his heels, started for that mysterious home of his which was supposed to be at Ardvasar, somewhere in the neighbourhood of Armadale Castle.

A visit to Loch Coruisk had for some little time been medi-tated; and in the evening of the day on which the otter was slain the boat was dragged from its shed down towards the sea, launched and brought round to the rude pier, where it was moored for the night. We went to bed early, for we were to rise with the sun.

We got up, breakfasted and went down to the pier where two or three sturdy fellows were putting oars and row-locks to rights, tumbling in huge stones for ballast and carefully stowing away a couple of guns and a basket of provisions. In about an hour we were fairly afloat; the broad-backed fellows bent to their oars and soon the house began to dwindle in the distance, the irregular winding shores to gather into compact masses and the white cliffs, which we knew to be a couple of miles inland, to come strangely forward and to overhang the house and the surrounding strips of pasturage and clumps of birchwood.

On a fine morning there is not in the whole world a prettier sheet of water than Loch Eishart. Every thing about it is wild, beautiful and lonely. You drink a strange and unfamiliar air. You seem to be sailing out of the nineteenth century away back into the ninth. You are delighted and there is no remembered delight with which you can compare the feeling. Over the Loch the Cuchullins rise crested with tumult of golden mists; the shores are green behind; and away out, towards the horizon, the Island of Rum – ten miles long at the least – shoots up from the flat sea like a pointed flame.

It is a granite mass, you know, firm as the foundations of the world; but as you gaze the magic of morning light makes it a glorious apparition you might almost suppose to exist on sufferance and that breath would blow it away.

Between Rum, fifteen miles out yonder and the shores drawing together and darkening behind, the sea is smooth and flushed with more varied hues than ever lived on the changing opal – dim azures, tender pinks, sleek emeralds. It is one sheet of mother-of-pearl. The hills are silent. The voice of man has not yet awoke on their heathery slopes. But the sea, literally clad with birds, is vociferous. They make plenty of noise at their work, these fellows. Darkly the cormorant shoots across our tracks. The air is filled with a confused medley of sweet, melancholy and querulous notes. As we proceed, a quick head ducks: a troop of birds sinks suddenly to reappear far behind, or perhaps strips off the surface of the water, taking wing with a shrill cry of complaint. Occasionally too, a porpoise, or 'fish that hugest swims the ocean stream,' heaves itself slowly out of the element, its wet sides flashing for a moment in the sunlight and then heeling lazily over, sinks with never a ripple.

As we approached the Strathaird coast, M'Ian sat high in the bow smoking and covering with his gun every now and again some bird which came wheeling near, while the boatmen joked and sang snatches of many-chorused songs. As the coast behind became gradually indistinct, the coast in front grew bolder and bolder. I let my hand over the side of the boat and played listlessly with the water. I was lapped in a dream of other days. My heart was chanting ancient verses and sagas. The northern sea wind that filled the sails of the Vikings and lifted their locks of tarnished gold, was playing in my hair. And when the keel grated on the pebbles at Kilmaree I was brought back to my proper century and self – for by that sign I knew that my voyage was over for the present and that the way to Coruisk was across the steep hill in front.

The boat was moored to a rude pier of stones, very similar to the one from which we started a couple of hours before, the guns were taken out, so also was the basket of provisions and then the party, in long-drawn straggling procession, began to ascend the hill. The ascent was steep and laborious. At times I waded through heather as high as my knee; at other times I found myself in a bog, jumping perforce from solid turf to turf, Progress was necessarily slow; and the sun coming out strongly made my brows ache with intolerable heat. The hilltop was reached at last and I beheld a magnificent sight. Beneath, a blue loch flows in, on the margin of which stands the solitary farmhouse of Camasunary. Out on the smooth sea sleep the islands of Rum and Canna – Rum towered and mountainous, Canna flat and fertile. On the opposite side of the loch and beyond the solitary farmhouse, a great hill breaks down into ocean with shelf and precipice. On the right Blaavin towers up into the mists of the morning and at his base opens the desolate Glen Sligachan, to which Glencoe is Arcady. On the left, the eye travels along the whole south-west side of the island to the Sound of Sleat, to the hills of Knoydart, to the long point of Ardnamurchan, dim on the horizon.

In the presence of all this we sink down in heather or on boulder and wipe our heated foreheads; in the presence of all this M'Ian hands round the flask, which is received with the liveliest gratitude. In a quarter of an hour we begin the descent and in another quarter of an hour we are in the valley and approaching the solitary farmhouse.

While about three hundred yards from the door a man issued there from and came towards us. It would have been difficult to divine from dress and appearance what order of man this was. He was evidently not a farmer, he was as evidently not a sportsman. His countenance was grave, his eye was bright, but I could make little out of either; about him there was altogether a listless and weary look. He seemed to me to have held too constant communion with the ridges of Blaavin and the desolations of Glen Sligachan.

He was not a native of these parts for he spoke with an English accent. He addressed us frankly, discussed the weather, told us the family was from home and would be absent for some weeks yet; that he had seen us coming down the hill and that, weary of rocks and sheep and seabirds, he had come out to meet us. He then expressed a wish that we would oblige him with tobacco; that is, if we were in position to spare any; stating that tobacco he generally procured from Broadford in rolls of a pound weight at a time; that he had finished his last roll some ten days ago and that till this period, from some unaccountable accident, the roll which was more than a week due had never arrived. He feared it had got lost on the way – he feared that the bearer had been tempted to smoke a pipe of it and been so charmed with its exquisite flavour that he had been unable to stir from the spot until he had smoked the entire roll out. He rather thought the bearer would be about the end of the roll now and that, conscious of his atrocious conduct, he would never appear before him, but would fly the country – go to America, or the Long Island, or some other place where he could hold his guilt a secret. He found the paper in which the last roll had been wrapt, had smoked *that* and, by a strong effort of the imagination, had contrived to extract from it considerable enjoyment.

And so we made a contribution of Bird's-eye to the tobaccoless man, for which he returned us politest thanks and then strolled carelessly toward Glen Sligachan – probably to look out for the messenger who had been so long on the way.

'Who is our friend?' I asked my companion. 'He seems to talk in a rambling and fanciful manner.'

'I have seen him before,' said M'Ian; 'but I suspect he is one of those poor fellows who, from extravagance, or devotion to opium or strong waters, have made a mull of life and who are sent here to end it in a quiet way. We have lots of them everywhere.'

'But,' said I, 'this seems the very worst place you could send such a man to – it's like sending a man into the wilderness with his remorse. It is only in the world, amid its noise, its ambitions, its responsibilities, that men pick themselves up. Seabirds and misty mountains and rain and silence are the worst companions for such a man.'

'But then, you observe, seabirds and misty mountains and rain and silence hold their tongues and take no notice of peccadilloes. Whatever may be their faults, they are not scandalmongers. The doings in Skye do not cause blushes in London. The man dies here as silently as a crow; it is only a black-bordered letter, addressed in a strange hand, that tells the news; and the black-bordered epistle can be thrown into the fire – if the poor mother does not clutch at it and put it away – and no-one be a bit the wiser. It is sometimes to the advantage of his friends that a man should go into the other world by the loneliest and most sequestered path.'

So talking, we passed the farmhouse which, with the exception of a red-headed damsel who thrust her head out of a barn to stare, seemed utterly deserted and bent our steps towards the shore of the loch. Rough grass bordered a crescent of yellow sand and on the rough grass a boat lay on its side, its pitchy seams blistering in the early sunshine. Of this boat we immediately took possession, dragged it down to the sea margin, got in our guns and provisions, tumbled in stones for ballast, procured oars and pushed off. We had to go round the great hill which, from the other side of the valley, we had seen breaking down into the sea; and as we sailed and looked up, sheep were feeding on the green shelves and every now and again a white smoke of seabirds burst out clangorously from the black precipices.

Slowly rounding the rocky buttress, which on stormy days the Atlantic fillips with its spray, another headland, darker still and drearier, drew slowly out to sea and in a quarter of an hour we had passed from the main ocean into Loch Scavaig and every pull of the oars revealed another ridge of the Cuchullins. Between these mountain ramparts we sailed, silent as a boatfull of souls being conveyed to some Norse Hades. The Cuchullins were entirely visible now; and the sight midway up Loch Scavaig is more impressive even than when you stand on the ruined shore of Loch Coruisk itself – for the reason perhaps, that sailing midway, the mountain forms have a startling unexpectedness, while by the time you have pulled the whole way up you have had time to master them to some extent and familiarity has begun to the dull impression.

In half an hour or so we disembarked on a rude platform of rock and stepped out on the very spot on which, according to Sir Walter, the Bruce landed. Picking our steps carefully over huge boulder and slippery stone, we came upon the most savage scene of desolation in Britain. Conceive a large lake filled with dark green water, girt with torn and shattered precipices; the bases of which are strewn with ruin since an earthquake passed that way and whose summits jag the sky with grisly splinter and peak. There is no motion here save the white vapour steaming from the abyss, The utter silence weighed like a burden upon me; I felt like an intruder in the place. The hills seem to possess some secret; to brood over some unutterable idea which I can never know. I could not feel comfortable at Loch Coruisk and the discomfort arose in a great degree from the feeling that I was outside everything – that the thunder-splitten peaks have a life with which I could not intermeddle. The dumb monsters saddened and perplexed. Standing there I was impressed with the idea that the mountains are silent because they are listening so intently. And the mountains *are* listening, else why do they echo out voices in such a wonderful way?

M'Ian fired his gun and it reverberated into a whole battle of Waterloo. We kept the hills busy with shouts and the firing of guns and then M'Ian led us to a convenient place for lunching. As we trudge along something lifts itself from the rock – 'tis an eagle. See how grandly the noble creature soars away. What sweep of wings! What a lord of the air! And when I cast up my eyes I could see his brother hanging like a speck beneath the sun.

Under M'Ian's guidance we reached the lunching-place, unpacked our basket, devoured our bread and cold mutton, drank our bottled beer and then lighted our pipes and smoked – in strangest presence. Thereafter we bundled up our things, shouldered out guns and marched in the track of ancient earthquake towards our boat. Embarked once again and sailing between the rocky portals of Loch Scavaig, I said, 'I would not spend a day in that solitude for the world. I should go mad before evening.'

'Nonsense,' said M'Ian. 'Sportsmen erect tents at Coruisk and stay there by the week – capital trout too, are to be had in the loch. The photographer, with his camera and chemicals, is almost always here and the hills sit readily for his portraits. It's as well you have seen Coruisk before its glory had departed. Your friend, the Landlord, talks of mooring a floating hotel at the head of Loch Scavaig full of sleeping apartments, the best of meats and drinks and a brass band to perform the newest operatic tunes on summer evenings. At the clangour of the brass band the last eagle will take his flight for Harris.'

'The tourist comes and poetry flies before him as the red man flies before the white. His tweeds will make the secret top of Sinai commonplace some day.'

In due time we reached Camasunary and drew the boat up on the rough grass beyond the yellow sand. The house deserted as we passed. Our friend of the morning we saw seated on a rock, smoking and gazing up Glen Sligachan, still looking out for the appearance of his messenger from Broadford. At our shout he turned his head and waved his hand. We then climbed the hill and descended on Kilamaree. It was evening now and as we pulled homewards across the rosy frith, I sat in the bow and watched the monstrous bulk of Blaavin and the wild fringe of the Cuchullins, bronzed by sunset.

M'Ian steered and the rowers, as they bent to their work, sang melancholy Gaelic songs. It was eleven at night by the time we got across and the hills we had left were yet cutting, with dull purple, a pale yellow sky; for in summer in these northern latitudes there is no proper night, only a mysterious twilight of an hour and a sparkle of short-lived stars.

Broadford Fair

BROADFORD FAIR IS a great event in the island. The little town lies on the margin of a curving bay under the shadow of a somewhat celebrated hill. On the crest of the hill is a cairn of stones, the burying place of a Scandinavian woman, tradition informs me, whose wish it was to be laid high up there, that she might sleep right in the pathway of the Norway wind. In a green glen at its base stands the house of Corachatachin, breathing reminiscenses of Johnson and Boswell.

Broadford is a post town, containing a lime kiln, an inn and perhaps three dozen houses in all. It is a place of great importance. If Portree is the London of Skye, Broadford is its Manchester. The markets, held four times a year, take place on a patch of moorland, about a mile from the village. Not only are cattle sold and cash exchanged for the same, but there the Skye farmer meets his relations, from the brother of his blood to his cousin forty times removed. To these meetings he is drawn, not only by his love of coin, but by his love of kindred and – the *Broadford Mail* and the *Portree Advertiser* lying yet in the womb of time – by his love of gossip also.

The market is the Skyeman's exchange, his family gathering and his newspaper. From the deep sea of his solitude he comes up to breathe there and, refreshed, sinks again.

This fair at Broadford I resolved to see. The day before the market the younger M'Ian had driven some forty stirks from the hill and these, under the charge of John Kelly and his dog, started early in the afternoon that they might be present at rendezvous about eight o'clock on the following morning, at which hour business generally began. I saw the picturesque troop go past – wildly beautiful brutes of all colours – black, red, cream, dun and tan; all of a height too and so finely bred that, but for difference of colour, I could hardly distinguish the one from the other. What a lowing they made! how they tossed their slavering muzzles! how the breaths of each individual brute rose in a separate wreath! how John Kelly shouted and objurgated and how his dog scoured about! At last the bellowings of the animals grew fainter and fainter up the glen and finally on everything the wonted silence settled down.

Next morning before sunrise M'Ian and I followed in a dog-cart. We went along the glen down which Fellowes and I had come; and in the meadows over which, on that occasion, we observed a troop of horses galloping through the mist of evening, I noticed in the beamless light that preceded sunrise hay coops by the river side and an empty cart standing with its scarlet poles in the air. In a field nearer, a couple of male black-cocks with a loud *whirr-rr* were knocking their pugnacious heads together. Suddenly, above the hill in front, the sun showed his radiant face, the chill atmosphere was pierced and brightened by his fires, the dewy birch trees twinkled and there were golden flickerings on the pools of the mountain stream along whose margin our road ascended. We passed the lake near which the peat-girls had laughed at us; I took note of the very spot on which we had given Barelegs a shilling and related the whole story of our evening walk to my companion as we tooled along.

A mile or so after we had passed the little fishing village with which I had formerly made acquaintance, we entered on a very dismal district of country. It was precisely to the eye what the croak of the raven is to the ear. It was an utter desolation in which nature seemed deteriorated and at her worst. Winter could not possibly sadden the region; no spring could quicken it into flowers. The hills wore but for ornament the white streak of the torrent; the rocky soil clothed itself in heather to which the purple never came. Even man, the miracle worker, who transforms everything he touches, was defeated there. Labour was resultless, like a song without an echo.

A turf hut with smoke issuing from the roof and a patch of green round about, which reminded me of the smile of an ailing child and which would probably ripen, so far as it was capable of ripening, by November, was all that man could wrest from nature.

Gradually, however, as we proceeded, the aspect of the country changed, it began to exhibit traces of cultivation; and before long, the red hill with the Norwegian woman's cairn atop, rose before us, suggesting Broadford and the close of the journey. In a little while the road was filled with cattle, driven forward with oath and shout. Every now and then a dog-cart came skirring along and infinite was the confusion and dire the clangour of tongues, when it plunged into a herd of sheep or skittish 'three-year-olds'.

At the entrance to the fair, the horses were taken out of the vehicles and left, with a leathern thong fastened round their forelegs, to limp about in search of breakfast. On either side of the road stood hordes of cattle, the wildest-looking creatures, with fells of hair hanging over their eyes and tossing horns of preposterous dimensions. On knolls, a little apart, women with white caps and wrapped in scarlet tartan plaids, sat beside a staked cow or pony, or perhaps a dozen sheep, patiently awaiting the advance of customers.

Troops of horses neighed from stakes. Sheep were there, too, in restless throngs and masses, continually changing their shapes, scattering hither and thither like quicksilver, insane dogs and men flying along their edges. What a hubbub of sound! what lowing and neighing! what bleating and barking! Down in the hollow ground tents had been knocked up since dawn; there potatoes were being cooked for drovers who had been travelling all night; there also liquor could be had. To these places, I observed, contracting parties invariably repaired to solemnise a bargain.

At last we reached the centre of the fair and there stood John Kelly and his animals, a number of drovers moving around them and examining their points. By these men my friend was immediately surrounded and much chaffering and bargaining ensued; visits to one of the aforesaid tents being made at intervals. It was a strange sight, that rude primeval traffic. John Kelly kept a sharp eye on his beasts. Lachlan Roy passed by and low was his salute and broad the smile on his good-natured countenance.

I wandered about aimlessly for a time and began to weary of the noise and tumult. M'Ian had told me that he would not be able to return before noonday at earliest and that all the while he would be engaged in bargain-making on his own account, or on account of others and that during those hours I must amuse myself as best I could. As the novelty of the scene wore off, I began to fear that amusement would not be possible. Suddenly lifting my eyes out of the noise and confusion, there were the solitary mountain tops and the clear mirror of Broadford Bay, the opposite coast sleeping green in it with all its woods; and lo! the steamer from the south sliding in with her red funnel and breaking the reflection with a track of foam and disturbing the far-off morning silence with the thunders of her paddles. That sight solved my difficulty for me in a moment. I thought of Dr. Johnson and Boswell. 'I shall go,' I said, 'and look at the ruins of the House of Corachatachin, that lies in the green glen beneath the red hill, on top of which the Norse woman is buried.' And so saying I went.

To me, I confess, of all Hebridean associations, Dr. Johnson's visit is the pleasantest. How the doctor ever got there is a matter for perpetual wonder. He liked books, good cheer, club life, the roar of Fleet Street, good talk, witty companions. For fine scenery, Johnson did not care one rush. When Boswell in the fulness of his delight pointed out 'an immense mountain,' the doctor sincerely sneered, 'an immense protuberance'.

Johnson loved his ease; and a visit to the Western island was, in his day, a serious matter – about as serious as a visit to Kamtschatka would be in ours. In his wandering he was exposed to rain and wind, indifferent cookery, tempestuous seas and the conversation of persons who were neither witty nor learned. I protest, when I think of the burly doctor travelling in these regions, voluntarily resigning for a while all London delights, I admire him as a very hero.

Boswell commemorates certain outbreaks of petulance and spleen; but on the whole, the great man seems to have been pleased with his adventure. Johnson found in his wanderings beautiful and high-bred women, well-mannered and cultivated men – and it is more than probably that, if he were returning to the islands today, he would not find those admirable human qualities in greater abundance.

What puzzles me most is the courage with which the philosopher encountered the sea. I have, in a considerable steamer more than once, shivered at the heavy surge breaking on Ardnamurchan; and yet the doctor passed the place in an open boat on his way to Mull, 'lying down below in philosophical tranquillity, with a greyhound at his back to keep him warm,' while poor Bozzy remained in the rain above, clinging for dear life to a rope which a sailor gave him to hold, quieting his insurgent stomach as best he could with pious considerations and sadly disturbed when a bigger wave than usual came shouldering onward, making the boat reel.

Boswell's journal of the tour is delicious reading; full of amusing egotism; unconsciously comic when he speaks for himself and at the same time valuable, memorable, wonderfully vivid and dramatic in presentment when the 'Majestic Teacher of Moral and Religious Wisdom' appears. What a singular capacity the man had to exhibit his hero as he lived and at the same time to write himself complacently down as an ass! And yet the absurdity of Boswell has all the effect of the nicest art. Johnson floats, a vast galleon, in the sea of Boswell's vanity; and in contrast with the levity of the element in which it lives, its bulk and height appear all the more impressive.

In Skye one is every now and again coming on the track of the distinguished travellers. They had been at Broadford – and that morning I resolved I should go to Broadford also.

Picking my steps carefully through the fair – avoiding a flock of sheep on the one side and a column of big-horned black cattle on the other, with some difficulty getting out of the way of an infuriated bull that came charging up the road, scattering everything right and left, a dozen blown drovers panting at its heels – I soon got quit of the turmoil and in half an hour passed the lime-kiln, the dozen houses, the ten shops, the inn, the church, which constitute Broadford and was pacing along the green glen which ran in the direction of the red hills.

At last I came to a confused pile of stones, near which grew a solitary tree whose back the burden of the blast had bent and which, although not a breath of wind was stirring, could no more regain an upright position that can a round-shouldered labourer on a holiday. That confused pile of stones was all that remained of the old house of Corachatachin. I wandered around it more reverently than if it had been the cairn of a chief. It is haunted by no ghost. So far as my knowledge extends, no combat ever took place on the spot. But there Boswell, after Dr. Johnson had retired to rest, in company with some young Highland bloods – ah me! their very grandchildren must be dead or gray by this! – brewed and quaffed five gigantic bowls of punch, with what wild talk we fancy; and the friend of the 'Majestic Teacher of Moral and Religious Wisdom' went to bed at five in the morning and awoke with the headache of the reprobate. At noon the doctor burst in with the exclamation, 'What, drunk yet?'

'His tone of voice was not that of severe upbraiding,' writes the penitent Bozzy, 'so I was relieved a little.'

Did they fancy, these young men, as they sat that night and drank, that a hundred years after people would write of their doings? That the odour of their punchbowls would outlive themselves? No man knows what part of his life will be remembered, what forgotten. Picking my steps around the ruin, I thought curiously of the flushed faces which death has cooled for so long.

When I got back to the fair about noon, it was evident that a considerable stroke of business had been done. Hordes of bellowing cattle were being driven towards Broadford and drovers were rushing about in a wonderful manner, armed with tar-pot and stick and smearing their peculiar mark on the shaggy hides of their purchases. Rough-looking customers enough these fellows, yet they want not means. Some of them came here this morning with £500 in their pocketbooks and have spent every paper of it and this day three months they will return with as large a sum. As I advanced, the booths ranged along the side of the road – empty when I passed them several hours before – were plentifully furnished with confections, ribbons and cheap jewellery and around these, fair-headed and scarlet-plaided girls swarmed thickly as bees round summer flowers.

The fair was running its full career of bargain-making and consequent dram-drinking, rude flirtation and meeting of friend with friend; when up the middle of the road, hustling the passengers, terrifying the cattle, came three misguided young gentlemen – medical students I opined, engaged in botanical researches in these regions. But too plainly they had been dwellers in tents. One of them, gifted with a comic genius – his companions were desperately solemn – at one point of the road threw back the collar of his coat, after the fashion of Sambo when he brings down the applauses of the threepenny gallery and executed a shuffle in front of a bewildered cow. Crummie backed and shied, bent on retreat. He, agile as a cork, bobbed up and down in her front, turn whither she would, with shouts and hideous grimaces, his companions standing by the while like mutes at a funeral. The feat accomplished, the trio staggered on, amid the scornful laughter and derision of the Gael.

In a little while I encountered M'Ian, who had finished his business and was anxious to be gone. 'We must harness the horse ourselves,' he said, 'for that rascal, John Kelly, has gone off somewhere. He has been in and out of tents ever since the cattle were sold and I trust he won't come to grief. He has a standing quarrel with the Kyle men and may get a broken head.'

Elbowing our way through the crowd, we reached the dog-cart, got the horse harnessed and were just about to start, when Lachlan Roy came flying up. 'Maister Alic, Maister Alic, is my face red yet?' cried he, as he laid his hand on the vehicle.

'Red enough, Lachlan; you had better come with us, you may lose your money if you don't.'

'Aw, Maister Alic dear, don't say my face is red – it's no red, Maister Alic – it's no *vera* red,' pled the poor fellow.

'Will you come with us or will you not?' said M'Ian, as he gathered up the reins in his hand and seized the whip. At this moment three or four drovers issued from a tent in the neighbourhood and Lachlan heard his name shouted.

'I maun go back for my bonnet,' It wouldna do to ride with gentlemen without a bonnet,' and he withdrew his hand. The drovers shouted again and that second shout drew Lachlan towards it as the flame draws the moth.

'His face will be red enough before evening,' said M'Ian, as we drove away.

After we had driven about a quarter of an hour and got entirely free of the fair, M'Ian, shading his eyes from the sun with a curved palm, suddenly exclaimed, 'There's a red dog sitting by the roadside a little forward. It looks like John Kelly's.' When we got up, the dog wagged its tail and whined, but retained its recumbent position.

'Come out,' said M'Ian. 'The dog is acting as a sentinel and I daresay we shall find its master about.' We got out accordingly and soon found John stretched on the heather, snoring stentoriously, his necktie unloosened, his bonnet gone, the sun shining full on the rocky countenance of him.

'He's as drunk as the Baltic,' said M'Ian; 'but we must get him out of this. Get up, John.' But John made no response. We pinched, pulled and thumped, but John was immovable. I proposed that some water should be poured on his face and did procure some from a wet ditch near, with which his countenance was splashed copiously – not to its special adornment. The muddy water only produced a grunt of dissatisfaction.

'We must take him on his fighting side,' said M'Ian and then he knelt down and shouted in John's ear, 'Here's a man from Kyle says he's a better man than you.' John grunted inarticulate defiance. 'He says he'll fight you any day you like.'

'Tell him to strike me then,' said John, struggling with his stupor.

'He says he'll kick you.' Under the insult John visibly writhed.

'Kick him,' whispered M'Ian, 'as hard as you can. It's our only chance.'

I kicked and John was erect as a dart, striking blindly out and when he became aware against whom he was making such hostile demonstrations his hands dropped and he stood as if he had seen a ghost.

'Catch him,' said M'Ian, 'his rage has sobered him, he'll be drunk next moment; get him into the dog-cart at once.' So the lucid moment was taken advantage of, he was hoisted into the back seat of the vehicle, his bonnet was procured – he had fallen asleep on it – and placed on the wild head of him; we took our places and away we started, with the red dog trotting behind. John rolled off once or twice, but there was no great harm done and we easily got him in again. As we drove down the glen toward the house we set him down and advised him to dip his wildly-tangled head in the stream before he went home.

More of Mr M'Ian

THE HOUSE OF my friend Mr M'Ian is set down on the shore of one of the great lochs that intersect the island; and as it was built in smuggling times, its windows look straight down the loch towards the open sea. Consequently at night, when lighted up, it served all the purposes of a lighthouse: and the candle in the porch window, I am told, has often been anxiously watched by the rough crew engaged in running a cargo of claret or brandy from Bordeaux.

Right opposite, on the other side of the loch, is the great rugged fringe of the Cuchullin hills; and lying on the dry summer grass you can see it, under the influence of light and shade, change almost as the expression of a human face changes.

Behind the house the ground is rough and broken, every hollow filled, every knoll plumaged with birches and between the leafy islands, during the day, rabbits scud continually and in the evening they sit in the glades and wash their innocent faces.

A mile or two back from the house a glen opens into soft green meadows, through which a stream flows; and on these meadows Mr M'Ian, when the weather permits, cuts and secures his hay. The stream is quiet enough usually, but after a heavy day's rain, or when a waterspout has burst up among the hills, it comes down with a vengeance, carrying everything before it. On such occasions its roar may be heard a mile away. About a pistol-shot from the house the river is crossed by a plank bridge and in fine weather it is a great pleasure to sit down there and look about me. The stream flows sluggishly over the rocks, in the deep places of a purple or port-wine colour and lo! behind me, through the arch, slips a sunbeam and just beneath the eye there gleams a sudden chasm of brilliant amber.

The sea is at ebb and the shore is covered with stones and dark masses of sea-weed; and the rocks a hundred yards off – in their hollows they hold pools of clear seawater in which I have found curious and delicately-coloured ocean blooms – are covered with orange lichens, which contrast charmingly with the masses of tawny dulse and the stone-littered shore on the one side and the keen blue of the sea on the other. Beyond the blue of the sea the great hills rise, with a radiant vapour flowing over their crests. Immediately to the left a spur of high ground runs out to the sea edge – the flat top smooth and green as a billiard table, the sheep feeding on it white as billiard balls – and at the foot of this spur of rock a number of huts are collected. They are half lost in an azure veil of smoke, I can smell the peculiar odour of peat-reek, I can see the nets lying out on the grass to dry, I can hear the voices of children.

Immediately above and behind the huts and the spur of high ground, the hill falls back, the whole breast of it shaggy with birchwood; and just at the top there is a clearing and a streak of white stony road, leading into some other region as solitary and beautiful as the one in which I am at present.

And while I sit on the bridge in a state of half-sleepy content-ment – a bee muzzling in a bell-shaped flower within reach of my stick, the seagulls dancing silent quadrilles overhead, the white lightning flash of a rabbit from copse to copse twenty yards off – I hear a sharp whistle, then a shout and, looking round, there is M'Ian himself standing on a height, his figure clear against the sky: and immediately the men tinkering the boat on the shore drop work and stand and stare and out of the smoke that wraps the cottages rushes bonnetless, Lachlan Dhu, or Donald Roy, scattering a brood of poultry in his haste and marvelling much what has moved his master to such unwonted exertion.

My friend's white house is a solitary one, no other dwelling of the same kind being within eight miles of it. In winter, wind and rain beat it with a special spite; and the thunder of the sea creeps into my sleeping ears and my dreams are of breakers and reefs and ships going to pieces and the cries of drowning men. In summer, it basks as contentedly on its green knoll; green grass, with the daisy wagging its head in the soft wind, runs up to the very door of the porch. But although solitary enough – so solitary, that if he is asked to dine with his nearest neighbour he must mount and ride – there are many more huts about than those we have seen nestling on the shore beneath the smooth green plateau on which the sheep are feeding.

If I walk along to the west – and a rough path it is, for my course is over broken boulders – I come on a little bay with an eagle's nest of a castle – Dunscaich – perched on a cliff and there you will find a schoolhouse and a half-dozen huts, the blue smoke steaming out of the crannies in the walls and roofs. Dark pyramids of peat are standing about, sheep and cows are feeding on the bits of pasture, gulls are weaving their eternal dances above and during the day the schoolroom is murmuring like a bee-hive – only a much less pleasant task than the making of honey is going on within.

Behind the house to the east, hidden by the broken ground and the masses of birchwood, is another collection of huts; and in one of these lives the most interesting man in the place. He is an old pensioner, who has seen service in different quarters of the world; and frequently I have carried him a string of pigtail and shared his glass of usquebaugh and heard him, as he sat on a stone in the sunshine, tell tales of barrack life in Jamaica; of woody wilderness-esses filled with gorgeous undergrowth, of parasites that climbed like fluttering tongues of fire and of the noisy towns of monkeys and parrots in the upper branches. I have heard him also severely critical on the different varieties of rum.

Of every fiery compound he had a catholic appreciation, but rum was his special favourite.

So that, although Mr M'Ian's house was in a sense solitary, yet it was not altogether bereaved of the sight and sense of human habitations. On the farm there were existing perhaps, women and children included, some sixty souls; and to these the relation of the master was peculiar and perhaps without a parallel in the island.

When, nearly half a century ago, Mr M'Ian left the army and became tacksman, he found cotters on his farm and thought their presence as much a matter of course as that limpets should be found upon his rocks. They had their huts, for which they paid no rent; they had their patches of corn and potato ground, for which they paid no rent. There they had always been and there, so far as Mr M'Ian was concerned, they would remain. He had his own code of generous old-fashioned ethics, to which he steadily adhered; and the man who was hard on the poor, who would dream of driving them from the places in which they were born, seemed to him to break the entire round of Commandments. Consequently the huts still smoked on the hem of the shore and among the clumps of birchwood. The children who played on the green when he first became tacksman grew up in process of time and married; and on these occasions he not only sent them something on which to make merry withal, but he gave them – what they valued more – his personal presence, and he made it a point of honour, when the ceremony was over, to dance the first reel with the bride.

When old men or children were sick, cordials and medicines were sent from the house; when old man or child died, Mr M'Ian never failed to attend the funeral. He was a Justice of the Peace; and when disputes arose amongst his own cotters, or amongst the cotters of others – when, for instance, Katy M'Lure accused Effie M'Kean of stealing potatoes; when Red Donald raged against Black Peter on some matter relating to the sale of a dozen lambs; when Mary, in her anger at the loss of her sweetheart, accused Betty (to whom said sweetheart had transferred his allegiance) of the most flagrant breaches of morality – the contending parties were sure to come before my friend; and many a rude court of justice I have seen him hold at the door of his porch.

Arguments were heard *pro* and *con*, witnesses were examined, evidence was duly sifted and weighed, judgement was made and the case dismissed; and I believe these decisions gave in the long run as much satisfaction as those delivered in Westminster or the Edinburgh Parliament-House.

Occasionally too, a single girl or shepherd, with whose character liberties were being taken, would be found standing at the porch door anxious to make oath that they were innocent of the guilt or the impropriety laid to their charge. Mr M'Ian would come out and hear the story, make the party assert his or her innocence in his presence, on such and such a day, so and so had sworn that certain charges were unfounded, false and malicious. Armed with this certificate, the aspersed girl or shepherd would depart in triumph. He or she had passed through the ordeal by oath and nothing could touch them farther.

Mr M'Ian paid rent for the entire farm; but to him the cotters paid no rent, either for their huts or for their patches of corn and potato ground. But the cotters were by no means merely pensioners – taking and giving nothing in return. The most active of the girls were maids of various degree in Mr M'Ian's house; the cleverest and strongest of the lads acted as shepherds and cow-men; and these of course received wages. The grown men amongst the cotters were generally at work in the south, or engaged in fishing expeditions, during the summer; so that the permanent residents on the farm were chiefly composed of old men, women and children.

When required, Mr M'Ian demands the services of these people just as he would the services of his household servants and they comply quite as readily. If the crows are to be kept out of the corn, or the cows out of the turnip field, an urchin is remorselessly reft away from his games and companions. If a boat is out of repair, old Dugald is deputed to the job and when his task is completed, he is rewarded with ten minutes chat and a glass of spirits up at the house. When fine weather comes, every man, woman and child is ordered to the hayfield and Mr M'Ian potters amongst them the whole day and takes care that no-one shirks his duty. When his corn or barley is ripe the cotters cut it and when the harvest operations are completed, he gives the entire cotter population a dance and harvest-home.

But between Mr M'Ian and his cotters no money passes; by a tacit understanding he is to give them house, corn ground, potato ground and they are to remunerate him with labour.

Mr M'Ian, it will be seen, is a conservative and hates change; and the social system by which he is surrounded wears an ancient and patriarchal aspect to a modern eye. It is a remnant of the system of clanship. The relation of cotter and tacksman, which I have described, is a bit of antiquity quite as interesting as the old castle on the crag – nay, *more* interesting, because we value the old castle mainly in virtue of its representing an ancient form of life and here is yet lingering a fragment of the ancient form of life itself. If an ancient tool or weapon is dug up in a moor, it is carefully placed in a museum: here, as it were, is the ancient tool or weapon in actual use.

No doubt Mr M'Ian's system has grave defects: it perpetuates comparative wretchedness on the part of the cotters, it paralyses personal exertion, it begets an ignoble contentment; but on the other hand it sweetens sordid conditions, so far as they can be sweetened, by kindliness and good services. If Mr M'Ian's system is bad, he makes the best of it and draws as much comfort and satisfaction out of it, both for himself and for others, as is perhaps possible.

He would carry with him a sense of strangeness in a city and among men of the present generation; but here he creates no surprise – he is a natural product of the region, like the red heather, or the bed of the dried torrent. He is a master of legendary lore. He knows the history of every considerable family in the island: he circulates like a sap through every genealogical tree; he is an enthusiast in Gaelic poetry and is often fond of reciting compositions of native bards, his eyes lighted up and his tongue moving glibly over the rugged clots of consonants.

He has a servant cunning upon the pipes; and, dwelling there this summer, I heard Ronald wandering near the house, solacing himself with their music; now a plaintive love song, now a coronach for a chieftain borne to his grave, now a battle march, the notes of which, melancholy and monotonous at first, would soar into a higher strain and then hurry and madden as if beating time to the footsteps of the charging clan.

I am the fool of association; and the tree under which a king has rested, the stone on which a banner was planted on the morning of some victorious or disastrous day, the house in which some great man first saw the light, are to me the sacredest things.

This slight, gray, keen-eyed man gives me a thrill like an old coin with its half-obliterated effigy, a druid stone on a moor, a stain of blood on the floor of a palace. He stands before me a living figure and history groups itself behind by way of background. We are accustomed to lament the shortness of life; but it is wonderful how long it is notwithstanding. Often a single life, like a summer twilight, connects two historic days. Count back four lives and King Charles is kneeling on the scaffold at Whitehall. To hear M'Ian speak, I could not help thinking in this way. In a short run across the mainland with him one summer, we reached Culloden Moor. The old gentleman with a mournful air – for he is a great Jacobite – pointed out the burial grounds of the clans. Struck with his manner, I inquired how he came to know their red resting places. As if hurt, he drew himself up, laid his hand on my shoulder, saying, 'Those who put them in told me.'

Heavens, how a century and odd years collapsed and the bloody field – the battle-smoke not yet cleared away and where Cumberland's artillery told the clansmen sleeping in thickest swathes – unrolled itself from the horizon down to my very feet!

Dwellers in cities have occasionally seen a house that has the reputation of being haunted and heard a ghost story told. City people laugh when these stories are told, even though the blood should run chill the while. But Skye is steeped in a ghostly atmosphere; men walk about here gifted with the second sight. There has been something weird and uncanny about the island for some centuries; it is haunted by legends; as full of noises as Prospero's Island. One such legend, concerning Ossian and his poems, struck me as a good deal.

Near Mr M'Ian's place is a ruined castle, a mere hollow shell of a building, Dunscaich by name, built in Fingalian days by the chieftain Cuchullin and so called by him in honour of his wife. The ruins stands on a rocky headland bearded by gray-green lichens. It is quite desolate and but seldom visited. The only sounds heard there are the whistle of the salt breeze, the bleat of a strayed sheep, the cry of wheeling seabirds.

M'Ian and myself sat one summer day on the ruined stair. Loch Eishart lay calm and bright beneath, the blue expanse broken only by a creeping sail. Across the loch rose the great red hill, in the shadow of which Boswell got drunk, on the top of which is perched the Scandinavian woman's cairn; and out of the bare heaven, down on the crests of the Cuchullins, flowed a great white vapour which gathered in the sunlight in mighty fleece on fleece. The old gentleman was the narrator and the legend goes as follows.

The castle was built by Cuchullin and his Fingalians in a single night. The chieftain had many retainers, was a great hunter and terrible in war. With his own arm he broke batallions; and every night at feast the minstrel Ossian sang his exploits. Ossian, on one occasion, wandering among the hills, was attracted by strains of music which seemed to issue from a round green knoll on which the sun shone pleasantly. He sat down to listen and was lulled asleep by the melody. He had no sooner fallen asleep than the knoll opened and he beheld the underworld of the fairies. That afternoon and night he spent in revelry and in the morning he was allowed to return. Again the music sounded and the senses of the minstrel were steeped in forgetfulness; and on the sunny knoll he awoke, a gray-haired man, for into one short afternoon and evening had been crowded a hundred of our human years.

In his absence the world had been entirely changed, the Fingalians were extinct and the dwarfish race whom we now call men were possessors of the country. Longing for companionship and weary of singing his songs to the earless rocks and sea waves, Ossian married the daughter of a shepherd and in process of time a little girl was born to him. Years passed on, his wife died and his daughter, woman grown now, married a pious man – for the people were Christianised by this time – called, from his love of psalmody, Peter of the Psalms.

Ossian, blind with age and bearded like the cliff yonder, went to reside with his daughter and her husband. Peter was engaged all day in hunting and when he came home at evening and the lamp was lighted, Ossian, sitting in a warm corner, was wont to recite the wonderful songs of his youth and to celebrate the mighty battles and hunting feats of the big-boned Fingalians – and in these songs Cuchullin stood with his terrible spear upraised and his beautiful wife sat amid her maids plying the distaff.

To these songs Peter of the Psalms gave attentive ear and, being something of a penman, carefully inscribed them in a book. One day Peter had been more than usually successful in the chase and brought home on his shoulders the carcass of a huge stag. Of this stag a leg was dressed for supper and, when it was picked bare, Peter triumphantly inquired of Ossian, 'In the Fingalian days you sing about, killed you ever a stag so large as this one?' Ossian balanced the bone in his hand, then sniffing intense disdain, replied, 'This bone, big as you think it, could be dropped into the hollow of a Fingalian blackbird's leg.' Peter of the Psalms, enraged at what he considered an unconscionable *crammer* on the part of his father-in-law, started up, swearing that he would not peril his soul by preserving any more of his lying songs and flung the volume in the fire: but his wife darted forward and snatched it up, half-charred from the embers.

At this conduct on the part of Peter, Ossian groaned in spirit and wished to die, that he might be saved from the envies and stupidities of the little people whose minds were as stunted as

their bodies. When he went to bed he implored his ancient gods
– for he was a sad heathen and considered psalm-singing no better
than the howling of a dog – to resuscitate, if but for one hour, the
hounds, the stags and the blackbirds of his youth, that he might
confound and astonish the unbelieving Peter. His prayers done,
he fell on slumber and just before dawn a weight upon his breast
awoke him. He put forth his hands and stroked a shaggy hide.

Ossian's prayers were answered, for there, upon his breast, in
the dark of the morning, was couched his favourite hound. He
spoke to it, called it by name and the faithful creature whimpered
and licked his hands and face. Swiftly he got up and called his
little grandson and they went out with the hound. When they
came to the top of a little eminence, Ossian said to the child,
'Put your fingers in your ears, little one, else I will make you deaf
for life.' The little boy put his fingers in his ears and then Ossian
whistled so loud that the whole sky rang as if it had been the roof
of a cave. He then asked the child if he saw anything.

'Oh, such large deer!' said the child. 'But a small herd by the
trampling of it,' said Ossian; 'we will let that herd pass.' Presently
the child called out, 'Oh, *such* large deer!' Ossian bent his ear to
the ground to catch the sound of their coming and then, as if
satisfied, he let slip the hound, who speedily overtook and tore
down seven of the fattest. When the animals were skinned and
dressed. Ossian groped his way toward a large lake, in the centre
of which grew a wonderful bunch of rushes. He waded into the
lake, tore up the rushes and brought to light the great Fingalian
kettle, which had lain there for more than a century. Returning
to his quarry, a fire kindled, the kettle containing the seven
carcasses was placed thereupon; and soon a most savoury smell
flew abroad on all the winds. When the animals were stewed
after the approved fashion of his ancestors, Ossian sat down to his
repast. At last, when the kettle was emptied, he lay down on the
grass perfectly satisfied and silent as the ocean when the tide is full.

Recovering himself, he gathered all the bones together – set
fire to them and the smoke which ascended made the roof of

the firmament as black as the roof of the turf hut at home. 'Little one,' then said Ossian, 'go up to the knoll and tell me if you see anything.' 'A great bird is flying hither,' said the child; and immediately the great Fingalian blackbird alighted at the feet of Ossian, who at once caught and throttled it. The fowl was carried home and was in the evening dressed for supper. After it was devoured, Ossian called for the stag's thigh-bone which had been the original cause of quarrel and, before the face of the astonished and convicted Peter of the Psalms, dropped it into the hollow of the blackbird's leg.

Ossian died on the night of his triumph and the only record of his songs is the volume which Peter in his rage threw into the fire and from which, when half consumed, it was rescued by his wife.

'But,' said I, when the old gentleman had finished his story, 'how came it that the big-boned Fingalians were extirpated during the hundred years that Ossian was asleep among the fairies?'

'Well,' said the old gentleman, 'a woman was the cause of that, just as a woman is the cause of most of the other misfortunes that happen in the world. I told you that this castle was built by Cuchullin and that he and his wife lived in it. Now tallest, bravest, strongest, handsomest of all Cuchullin's warriors was Diarmid and many a time his sword was red with the blood of the little people who came flocking over here from Ireland in their wicker and skin-covered boats.

'Now, when Diarmid took off his helmet at feast, there was a fairy mole right in the centre of his forehead, just above the eyes and between his curling locks; and on this beauty spot no woman could look without becoming enamoured of him. One night Cuchullin gave a feast in the castle; the great warrior was invited; and while he sat at meat with his helmet off, Cuchullin's wife saw the star-like mole in the centre of his forehead and at once fell in love with him. Cuchullin discovered his wife's passion and began secretly to compass the death of Diarmid. He could not slay him openly for fear of his tribe; so he consulted an ancient witch who lived over the hill yonder. Long they consulted and at last they matured their plans.

'Now, the Fingalians had a wonderful boar which browsed in Gasken – the green glen which you know leading down to my house – and on the back of this boar there was a poisoned bristle which, if it pierced the hand of any man, the man would certainly die. No-one knew the secret of the bristle save the witch and the witch told it to Cuchullin. One day, therefore, when the chief and his warriors were sitting on the rocks hereabout the conversation was cunningly led to the boar. Cuchullin wagered the magic whistle which was slung around his neck, that the brute was so many handbreadths from the snout to the tip of the tail. Diarmid wagered the shield that he was polishing – the shield which was his mirror in peace, by the aid of which he dressed his curling locks and with which he was wont to dazzle the eyes of his enemies on a battle day – that it was so many handbreadths less.

'The warriors heard the dispute and were divided in opinion; some agreeing with Cuchullin, others agreeing with Diarmid. At last it was arranged that Diarmid should go and measure the boar; so he and a number of the warriors went. In a short time they came back laughing and saying that Diarmid had won his wager, that the length of the boar was so many handbreadths, neither more or less. Cuchullin bit his white lips when he saw them coming; and then he remembered that he had asked them to measure the boar from the snout to the tail, being the way the pile lay; whereas, in order to carry out his design, he ought to have asked them to measure the boar *against* the pile.

'When, therefore, he was told that he had lost his wager, he flew into a great rage, maintained that they were all conspiring to deceive him, that the handbreadths he had wagered were the breadths of Diarmid's own hands and declared that he would not be satisfied until Diarmid would return and measure the boar from tip of the tail to the snout. Diarmid and the rest went away; and when he reached the boar he began measuring it from the tail onward, his friends standing by to see that he was measuring

properly and counting every handbreadth. He had measured halfway up the spine, when the poisoned bristle ran into his hand.
'Ah,' he said, and turned pale as if a spear had been driven into his
heart. To support himself, he caught two of his friends round the
neck and in their arms he died. Then the weeping warriors raised
the beautiful corpse on their shoulders and carried it to the castle
and laid it down near the drawbridge. Cuchullin then came out
and when he saw his best warrior dead he laughed as if a piece of
great good fortune had befallen him and directed that the corpse
should be carried into his wife's chamber.

'But Cuchullin had cause to repent soon after. The little
black-haired people came swarming over from Ireland in their
boats by hundreds and thousands, but Diarmid was not there to
oppose them with his spear and shield. Every week a battle was
fought and the little people began to prevail; and by the time that
Ossian made his escape from the fairies, every Fingalian, with the
exception of two, slept in their big graves – and at times the peat
digger comes upon their mighty bones when he is digging in the
morasses.'

'And the two exceptions?' asked I.

'Why, that's another story,' said M'Ian, 'and I getting tired of
legends. Well, if you will have it, the two last Fingalians made
their escape from Skye, carrying with them the magic whistle
which Cuchullin wore around his neck and took up their abode
in a cave in Ross-shire. Hundreds of years after, a man went into
that cave and in the half twilight of the place saw the whistle on
the floor and lifted it up. He saw it was of the strangest workman-
ship and, putting it to his lips, he blew it. He had never heard a
whistle sound so loudly and yet so sweetly. He blew it a second
time and then he heard a voice: 'Well done, little man; blow the
whistle a third time;' and turning to the place from which the
sound proceeded, he saw a great rock like a man leaning on his
elbow and looking up at him. 'Blow it the third time, little man
and relieve us from our bondage!' What, between the voice and
the strange human-looking rock, the man got so terrified that

he dropped the whistle on the floor of the cave, where it was smashed into a thousand pieces and ran out into the daylight. He told his story; and when the cave was again visited, neither he nor his companions could see any trace of the broken whistle on the floor, nor could they discover any rock which resembled a weary man leaning on his elbow and looking up.'

The Second Sight

THE QUIRANG IS one of the wonderful sights of Skye and if you once visit it you will believe ever afterwards the misty and spectral Ossian to be authentic. The Quirang is a nightmare of nature; 'tis a huge spire or cathedral of rock some thousand feet in height, with rocky spires or needles sticking out of it. It stands in a region as wild as itself; the country around is strange and abnormal, rising into rocky ridges here, like the spine of some huge animal, sinking into hollows there, with pools in the hollows – glimmering almost always through drifts of misty rain. On a clear day, with a bright sun above, the ascent of Quirang may be pleasant enough; but a clear day is seldom found, for on spectral precipices and sharp-pointed rocky needles, the weeping clouds of the Atlantic have made their chosen home.

I have climbed it in rain and wind, with every ledge and block slippery, every runnel a torrent, the wind taking liberties with my cap and making my plaid stream like a meteor to the troubled air, white tormented mists boiling up from black chasms and caldrons, rain making disastrous twilight of noon-day – horror shot through my pulse, my brain swam on the giddy pathway and the thought of my room in the vapoury underworld rushed across my soul like the fallen Adam's remembrance of his paradise.

Then I learned, as perhaps I never learned before, that nature is not always gracious; that not always does she outstretch herself and heavy-uddered cattle low; but that she has fierce hysterical moods in which she congeals into granite precipice and peak and draws around herself and her companions the winds that moan

110

and bluster, veils of livid rains. An English-man habitually knows her in her gracious, a Skyeman in her fiercer, moods.

No-one is independent of scenery and climate. A Saxon, nurtured in fat Kent or Sussex, amid flats of heavy wheat and acorn-dropping oaks, must of necessity be a different creature from the Celt who gathers his sustenance from the bleak sea-board and who is daily drenched by the sea-cloud from Cuchullin. The Skyeman will be, at best, of sharper spirit, because it has been more keenly whetted on difficulty; if not more intrepid, at least more consciously so; of sadder mood habitually, but *when* happy, happier, as the gloomier the cloud the more dazzling the rainbow; at his worst, either beaten down, subdued and nerveless, or gaunt, suspicious and crafty, like the belly-pinched wolf. The Celt is the more superstitious; the more poetical; with an anger swift and transient, like the flame that consumes the dried heather. He is the most melancholy of men; he has turned everything to superstitious uses and every object of nature, even the unreasoning dreams of sleep, are mirrors which flash back death upon him. He, least of all me, requires to be reminded that he is mortal. The howling of his dog will do him that service.

During the last few weeks I have had opportunity of witnessing something of life as it passes in the Skye wildernesses and have been struck with its self-containedness, not less than with its remoteness. A Skye family has everything within itself. The bare mountains yield mutton, which possesses a flavour and delicacy unknown in the south. The copses swarm with rabbits; and if a net is set overnight at the Black Island, there is abundance of fish to breakfast. The farmer grows his own corn, barley and potatoes, digs his own peats, makes his own candles; he tans leather, spins cloth shaggy as a terrier's pile and a hunch-backed artist in the place transforms the raw materials into boots or shepherd garments.

Twice every year a huge hamper arrives from Glasgow, stuffed with all the little luxuries of housekeeping – tea, sugar, coffee and the like. At more frequent intervals comes a ten-gallon flask from

Greenock, whose contents can cunningly draw the icy fangs of a north-easter, or take the chill out of the clammy mists.

And once a week the *Inverness Courier*, like a window suddenly opened on the roaring sea, brings a murmur of the outer world, its politics, its business, its crimes, its literature, its whole multitudinous and unsleeping life, making the stillness yet more still.

To the Islesman the dial face of the year is not artificially divided, as in cities, by parliamentary session and recess, college terms, vacations short and long, by the rising and sitting of courts of justice; nor yet, as in more fortunate soils, by imperceptible gradations of coloured light – the green flowery year deepening into the sunset of the October hollyhock; the slow reddening of burdened orchards; the slow yellowing of wheaten plains. Not by any of these.

To the Islesman the year rises into interest when the hills, yet wet with melted snows, are pathetic with newly-weaned lambs and it completes itself through the successive steps of weaning, fleecing, sorting, fattening, sale, final departure and cash in pocket. The shepherd life is more interesting than the agricultural, inasmuch as it deals with a higher order of being; for I suppose a couchant ewe, with her young one at her side, or a ram cropping the herbage, is a more pleasing object to the aesthetic sense that a field of mangel-wurzel, flourishing ever so gloriously.

The shepherd inhabits a mountain country, lives more completely in the open air and is acquainted with all the phenomena of storm and calm, the thunder smoke coiling in the wind, the hawk hanging stationary in the breathless blue. He knows the faces of hills, recognises the voices of the torrents as if they were children of his own, can unknit their intricate melody as he lies with his dog beside him on the warm slope at noon, separating tone from tone and giving this to rude crag, that to pebbly bottom. Every member of his flock wears to his eye its special individuality and he recognises the countenance of a 'wether' as he would the face of a human acquaintance. Sheep-farming is a picturesque occupation: and I think a multitude of sheep descending a hillside, now outspreading in bleating leisure, now huddling together in the haste of fear – the dogs, urged more by sagacity than by the shepherd's voice, flying along the edges, turning, guiding, changing the shape of the mass – one of the prettiest sights in the world.

The milking of the cows is worth going a considerable distance to see. The cows browse about on the hills all day and at sunset they are driven into a sort of green oasis, amid the surrounding birchwood. The rampart of rock above is dressed in evening colours, the grass is golden green; everything – animals, herds and milkmaids – is throwing long shadows. All about, the cows stand lowing in picturesque groups.

The milkmaid approaches one, caresses it for a moment, draws in her stool and, in an instant, the rich milk is hissing into the pail. All at once there arises a tremendous noise and, pushing through the clumps of birch wood down towards a shallow rivulet which skirts the oasis, breaks a troop of wild-looking calves, attended by a troop of wilder-looking urchins armed with sticks and the branches of trees. The cows low more than ever and turn their wistful eyes; the bellowing calves are halted on the further side of the rivulet and the urchins stand in the water to keep them back.

An ardent calf, however, breaks through the cordon of urchins, tumbles one into the streamlet, climbs the bank amid much Gaelic exclamation and ambles awkwardly toward his dam. Reaching her, he makes a wild push at the swollen udder, drinks, his tail shaking with delight; while she, turning her head round, licks his shaggy hide with fond maternal tongue. In about five minutes he is forced to desist and with a branch-bearing urchin on each side of him, is marched across the rivulet again. One by one the calves are allowed to cross, each makes the same wild push at the udder, each drinks, the tail ecstatically quiverring; and on each the dam fixes her great patient eyes and, turning, licks the hide, whether it be red, black, brindled, dun or cream-coloured.

When the calves have been across the rivulet and back again and the cows are being driven away to their accustomed pasturage, a milkmaid approaches with her pail and, holding it up, gives me to drink, as long ago Rebecca gave to drink the servant of Abraham. By this time the grass is no longer golden green; the red light has gone off the rocky ramparts and the summer twilight is growing in the hollows and in amongst the clumps of birch wood. Afar I hear the noise of retiring calves and urchins. The milkmaids start off in long procession with their pails and stools. A rabbit starts out from a bush at my feet and scurries away down the dim field. And when following, I descend the hillside toward the bridge I see the solemn purple of the Cuchullins cutting the yellow pallor of evening sky – perhaps with a feeling of deeper satisfaction I notice that a light is burning in the porch of Mr M'Ian's house.

'The fold,' as the milking of the cows is called, is pretty enough; but the most affecting incident of shepherd life is the weaning of the lambs – affecting, because it reveals passions in the fleecy flocks, which we tend to consider exclusive to ourselves.

From all the hills men and dogs drive the flocks down into a fold, or 'fank', as it is called here, consisting of several chambers or compartments. Into these compartments the sheep are huddled and then the separation takes place. The ewes are returned to the mountains, the lambs are driven away to some spot where the pasture is rich and where they are watched day and night. Midnight comes with dews and stars; the lambs are peacefully couched. Suddenly they are restless, ill at ease, goaded by some sore unknown want and seem disposed to scatter wildly in every direction; but the shepherds are wary, the dogs swift and sure and after a little while the perturbation is allayed and they are quiet again. I walk up now to the fank. The full moon is riding between the hills, filling the glens with lustres and floating mysterious glooms.

Listen! I hear it on every side of me, till it dies away in the silence of distance – the fleecy Rachel weeping for her children! The turf walls of the fank are in shadow, but something seems to be moving there. As I approach, it disappears with a quick short bleat and a hurry of tiny hooves. Wonderful mystery of instinct!

Affection all the more affecting that it is so wrapt in darkness, hardly knowing its own meaning. For nights and nights the creatures will be found haunting about those turfen walls seeking the young that have been taken away. Thoughts of these touching and delightful events took me down the path towards the house.

In the stories which are told round the island peat fires it is abundantly apparent that the Celt has not yet subdued nature. In these stories you can detect a curious subtle hostility between man and his environments; a fear of them, a want of absolute trust in them. In these stories and songs man is not at home in the world. Nature is too strong for him; she rebukes and crushes him. The elements, however calm and beautiful they may appear for the moment, are malign and deceitful at heart and merely bide their time.

And this curious relation between man and nature grows out of the climatic conditions and the forms of Hebridean life. In his usual avocations the Islesman rubs clothes with death as he would with an acquaintance. Gathering wildfowl, he hangs, like a spider on its thread, over a precipice on which the sea is beating a hundred feet beneath. In his crazy boat he adventures into whirlpool and foam. He is among the hills when the snow comes down making everything unfamiliar and stifling the strayed wanderer. This death is ever near him and that consciousness turns everything into omen.

The mist creeping along the hillside by moonlight is an apparition. In the roar of the waterfall, or the murmur of the swollen ford, he hears the water spirit calling out for the man for whom it has waited so long. He sees death candles burning on the sea, marking the place at which a boat will be upset by some sudden squall. He hears spectral hammers clinking in an outhouse and he knows that ghostly artificers are preparing a coffin there. Ghostly fingers tap at his window, ghostly feet are about his door; at midnight his furniture cries out as if it had seen a sight and could not restrain itself. Even his dreams are prophetic and point ghastly issues for himself or for others.

And just as there are poets who are more open to beauty than other men and whose duty and delight it is to set forth that beauty anew; so in the Hebrides there are seers who bear the same relation to the other world that the poet bears to beauty, who are cognisant of its secrets and who make those secrets known. The seer does not inherit his power. It comes upon him at haphazard, as genius or personal beauty might come. He is a lonely man among his fellows; apparitions cross his path at noonday; he never knows into what a ghastly something the commonest object may transform itself – the table he sits at may suddenly become the resting place of a coffin; and the man who laughs in his cups with him may, in the twinkling of an eye, wear a death shroud up to his throat. He hears river voices prophesying death and shadowy and silent funeral processions are continually defiling before him.

When the seer beholds a vision his companions know it; for the inner part of his eyelids turn so far upwards that, after the object disappears, he must draw them down with his fingers and sometimes employs others to draw them down, which he finds to be much the easier way.

From long experience of these visions and by noticing how closely or tardily fulfilment has trodden upon their heels, the seer can extract the meaning of the apparition that flashes upon him and predict the period of its accomplishment. Other people can make nothing of them, but *he* reads them.

These visions, it would appear, conform to rules, like everything else. If a vision be seen early in the morning, it will be accomplished in a few hours; if at noon, it will usually be accomplished that day; if in the evening, that night; if after candles are lighted, certainly that night. When a shroud is seen about a person it is a sure prognostication of death. And the period of death is estimated by the height of the shroud about the body. If it lies about the legs, death is not to be expected before the expiry of a year and perhaps it may be deferred a few months longer. If it is seen near the head, death will occur in a few days, perhaps in a few hours. To see houses and trees in a desert place is a sign that buildings will be erected there anon. To see a spark of fire falling on the arms or breast of a person is the sign that a dead child will shortly be in the arms of those persons. To see a seat empty at the time of sitting in it is a sign of that person's death being at hand.

The seers are said to be extremely temperate in habit; they are neither drunkards nor gluttons; they are not subject to convulsions nor hysterical fits; there are no madmen amongst them; nor has a seer ever been known to commit suicide.

The literature of the second sight is extremely curious. The writers have perfect faith in the examples they adduce; but their examples are far from satisfactory. They are seldom obtained at first hand, they almost always live on hearsay; and even if everything be true, the professed fulfilment seems nothing other than a rather singular coincidence. Still, these stories are devoutly believed in Skye and it is almost as perilous to doubt the existence of a Skyeman's ghost as it is to doubt the existence of a Skyeman's ancestor. In *Treaties on the Second Sight* compiled by Theophilus Insulanus, the following stories are related.

John Campbell, younger of Ardsliguish, in Ardnamurchan, in the year 1729, returning home with Duncan Campbell, his brother, as they drew near the house, observed a young girl whom they knew to be one of their domestics, crossing the plain and, having called her by name, she did not answer, but ran into the thicket. As the two brothers had been some days from home and willing to know what happened in their absence, the youngest, John, pursued after, but could not find her. Arriving home they acquainted their mother of the incident of the girl; upon which they were told she had departed this life that same day. Related by James Campbell in Girgudale, a young man of known modesty and candour, who had the story from the said John Campbell.

Mr Anderson lay in bed with his spouse towards the dawning of the 16th of April 1746, when he heard very audibly a voice at his bedhead inquiring if he was awake; who answered he was, but then took no further notice of it. A little time after, the voice repeated, with greater vehemence, if he was awake. And he answering, as formerly, that he was, there was some stop until the voice, louder, asked the same question yet again and he made the same answer, but asking what the voice had to say; upon which it replied, 'The prince is defeated, defeated, defeated!' For on that day, the Duke of Cumberland defeated Prince Charles at Culloden, which news was received within forty-eight hours.

Captain Macdonald of Castletown tells of a Knoydart man on board a vessel at anchor in the sound of Oronsay who went at night from the cabin onto the deck and, being missed by his company, some of them went to call him down; but not finding him, concluded that he had dropt from his ship's side. When day came on, they got a long line furnished with hooks which, having cast from the ship's side, some of the hooks got hold of his clothes, so that they got the corpse taken up. The owner of the long line who lived close by the shore, told Captain Macdonald that for a quarter of a year before that accident happened, he and his servants, on every calm night, heard lamentable cries at the shore where the corpse was landed; and that the long lines which pulled up the corpse, being hung on a pin in his house, all of them would hear an odd jingling of the hooks before and after going to bed, without any person, dog or cat touching them; and at other times, by firelight, see the long lines covered over with droplets such as are seen falling from oars at night.

The foregoing tales are examples of the general superstitions that prevail in the islands; those that follow relate to the second sight.

The Lady Coll informs of one M'Lean of Knock, an elderly reputable gentleman, living on their estate who, walking in the fields before sunset, saw a neighbouring person who had been sick for a long time, coming his way, accompanied by another man; and as they drew nearer, he asked them some questions and how far they intended to go. The first named the village they were making for and then pursued his journey with a more than ordinary pace. Next day, early in the morning, M'Lean was invited to his neighbour's internment, which surprised him much; he was then told that the neighbour had been confined to his bed for seven weeks and had departed this life a little before sunset, the preceding day.

Margaret Macleod, an honest woman advanced in years, knew, when a young woman, a dairymaid in the family of Grishornish who daily used to herd the calves in a park close to the house; there she observed at different times, a woman resembling herself in shape and attire, walking solitarily at no great distance from her; and being surprised at the apparition, to make further trial, she one day wore her gown back to front — and anon the phantom was dressed in the same manner, which made her uneasy, believing it portended some fatal consequence to herself. In a short time she was seized with a fever, which brought her to her end; but before her sickness and again on her deathbed, declared this second sight to several.

Neil Betton, an elder in the session of Diurinish, learned from the Reverend Mr Kenneth Betton of Trotternish, that a farmer in the village of Airadh, on the west side of the country, being towards evening to quit his work, observed a traveller coming towards him as he stood close by the highway; and as he knew the man, waited his coming up; but when he began to speak with him, the traveller broke off the road abruptly to the shore that was hard by; and as he reached the shore, he gave a loud cry and at the middle of the shore, gave another loud cry; and went on until he reached a river running through the shore, which he entered and gave a third loud cry, then disappeared. On the farmer's return home he told all that he had heard and seen: so the story spread until it reached the traveller's ears and he sought out the farmer and inquired of him narrowly about it; and he told what he had seen and heard. Less than a year later, the traveller, going with two others to cut wattling for creels in Coille-na-Skiddil, all three were drowned in the river where he had given the third cry.

Some inhabitants of Harris were sailing round the Isle of Skye, intending to go to the opposite mainland, when they were strangely surprised by an apparition of two men hanging down by the ropes which secured the mast, but could not think what it meant. They pursued the voyage; but the wind turned contrary and forced them into Broadford, where they found Sir Donald Macdonald conducting a sheriff's court and two criminals receiving sentence of death. The ropes and masts of that very boat were made use of to hang those criminals.

Such are some of the stories laboriously gathered together and set down in perfect good faith by Theophilus Insulanus. It will be seen that they are loosely reported, are always at second or third hand and that, if the original teller of the stories could be placed in the witness box, a strict cross-examination would make sad havoc with him and them. But although sufficiently ridiculous and foolish in themselves, they exemplify the strange ghostly atmosphere which pervades the western islands. Every one of the people amongst whom I now live believes in apparitions and the second sight. Mr M'Ian has seen a ghost himself, but he will not willingly speak about it. A woman gifted with the second sight dwells in one of the smoking turf huts on the shore.

At night, round a precipitous rock that overhangs the sea, about a hundred yards from the house, a light was often seen to glide and evil was apprehended. At last a boy, the son of one of the cotters, climbing about the rock, missed his footing, fell into the sea and was drowned and from that hour the light was never more visible. At a ford up amongst the hills, the people tell me doleful cries have been heard at intervals for years. The stream has waited long for its victim, but I am assured that it will get it at last. That a man will yet be drowned there is an article of faith amongst the cotters. But who? I suspect *I* am regarded as the likely person. Perhaps the withered crone down in the turf hut yonder knows the features of the doomed man.

This prevailing superstitious feeling takes curious possession of me somehow. I cannot live in a ghostly atmosphere without being more or less affected by it. Lying a-bed, I don't like to hear the furniture of my bedroom creak. At sunset I am suspicious of the prodigious shadow that stalks alongside of me across the gold-green fields. I become more than usually impressed by the multitudinous and unknown voices of the night. Gradually I get the idea that nature and I are alien; and it is in that feeling of alienation that superstition lives.

Father M'Crimmon and I had been out rabbit-shooting and, tired of the sport, we sat down to rest on a grassy knoll. The ghostly island stories had taken possession of my mind and as we sat down and smoked I inquired if the priest was a believer in ghosts generally and in the second sight in particular. The gaunt, solemn-voiced, melancholy-eyed man replied that he believed in the existence of ghosts just as he believed in the existence of America – he had never seen America, he had never seen a ghost, but the existence of both he considered was amply borne out by testimony.

'I know there is such a thing as the second sight,' he went on, 'because I have had cognisance of it myself. Six or seven years ago I was staying with my friend Mr M'Ian, as I am staying now and just as we were sipping a tumbler of punch after dinner we heard a great uproar outside. We went out and found all the farm servants standing on the grass and gazing seawards. On inquiry, we learned that two brothers, M'Millan by name, who lived down at Stonefield, beyond that point yonder, fishermen by trade and well versed in the management of a boat, had come up to the islands here to gather razorfish for bait. When they had secured plenty of bait, they steered for home, although a stiff breeze was blowing. They kept a full sail on and went straight on the wind. A small boy, Hector, who was employed in herding cows, was watching the boat trying to double the point. All at once he came running into the kitchen where the farm servants were at dinner. 'Men, men,' he cried, 'come out fast; M'Millan's boat is sinking – I saw her heel over.'

'Of course the hinds came rushing out bareheaded and it was the noise they made that disturbed my friend and myself at our punch. All this we gathered in less time than I have taken to tell you. We looked narrowly seaward, but no boat was to be seen. Mr M'Ian brought out his telescope and still the sea remained perfectly blue and bare. Neither M'Ian nor his servants could be brought to believe Hector's story – they thought it extremely unlikely that on a comparatively calm day any harm could befall such experienced sailors. It was universally agreed that the boat *had* rounded the point and Mr M'Ian rated the herdboy for raising a false alarm.

'Hector still persisting that he had seen the boat capsize and go down, got his ears soundly boxed for his obstinacy and was sent whimpering away to his cows and enjoined in future to mind his own business. Then the servants returned to their dinner in the kitchen and, going back with me to our punch which had become somewhat cold, Mr M'Ian resumed his story of the eagle that used to come down the glen in the early mornings and carry away his poultry and told how he shot it at last and found that it measured six feet from wingtip to wingtip.

'But although Hector got his ears boxed it turned out that he had in all probability spoken the truth. Towards the evening of the next day the M'Millan sisters came up to the house to inquire after the boat, which had never reached home. The poor girls were in a dreadful state when they were told that their brothers' boat had left the islands the previous afternoon and what Hector the cowherd averred he had seen. Still, there was room for hope; it was possible that Hector was mistaken, it was possible that the M'Millans might have gone somewhere, or been forced to take shelter somewhere – and so the two sisters, mustering up the best heart they could, went across the hill to Stonefield when the sun was setting and the sea a sheet of gold leaf and looking as if it could never be angry or have the heart to drown anything.

'Days passed and the boat never came home, nor did the brothers. It was on Friday that the M'Millans sailed away on the fresh breeze and on the Wednesday following the bay down there was a sorry sight. The missing sailors were brave, good-looking, merry-hearted and were liked along the whole coast; and on the

Wednesday I speak of no fewer than two hundred and fifty boats were sailing slowly up and down, crossing and re-crossing, trawling for the bodies. I remember the day perfectly. It was dull and sultry, with but little sunshine; the hills over there (Blaavin and the others) were standing dimly in a smoke of heat; and on the smooth pallid sea the mournful multitude of black boats were moving slowly up and down, across and back again.

'In each boat two men pulled and the third sat in the sterm with the trawling-irons. The day was perfectly still and I could hear through the heated air the solemn pulses of the oars. The bay was black with the slowly-crawling boats. A sorry sight,' said the good priest, filling his second pipe from a tobacco pouch made of otter's skin.

'I don't know how it was,' went on the Father, holding his newly-filled pipe between his forefinger and thumb; 'but looking on the black dots of boats and hearing the sound of their oars, I remembered that old Mirren, who lived in one of the turf huts yonder, had the second sight; and so I thought I would go down and see her. When I got to the hut, I met Mirren coming up from the shore with a basket full of whelks, which she had been gathering for dinner. I went into the hut along with her and sat down. "There's a sad business in the bay today," said I. "A sad business," said Mirren, as she laid down her basket. "Will they get the bodies?" Mirren shook her head. "The bodies are not there to get; they have floated out past Rum to the main ocean." "How do you know?" "Going out to the shore about a month ago I heard a scream and, looking up, saw the boat off the point, with two men in it, caught in a squall and going down. When the boat sank the men still remained in it – the one entangled in the fishing net, the other in the ropes of the sails. I saw them float out to the main sea between the two wines," – that's a literal translation,' said the Father, parenthetically.

'You have seen two liquors in a glass – the one floating on top of the other? Very well; there are two currents in the sea and when my people wish to describe anything sinking down and floating between these two currents, they use the image of two liquors in a wine glass. Oh, it's a fine language the Gaelic and admirably adapted for poetical purposes, but to return.

'Mirren told me that she saw the bodies float out to sea between the two wines and that the trawling boats might trawl forever in the bay before they would get what they wanted. When evening came, the boats returned home without having found the bodies of the drowned M'Millans. Well,' and here the Father lighted his pipe, 'six weeks after, a capsized boat was thrown on the shore in Uist, with two corpses inside; one entangled in the fishing net, the other in the ropes of the sails. It was the M'Millan's boat and it was the two brothers who were inside. Their faces were all eaten away by the dogfishes; but the people who had done business with them in Uist identified them by their clothes. This I know to be true,' said the Father emphatically and shutting the door on all argument or hint of scepticism.

'And now, if you are not tired, suppose we try our luck in the copses down there? 'Twas a famous place for rabbits when I was here last year.'

In a Skye Bothy

I AM QUITE alone here. England may have been invaded and London sacked, for aught I know. Several weeks since a newspaper, accidently blown to my solitude, informed me that the *Great Eastern*, with the second American telegraphic cable on board, had got under way and was about to proceed to sea. There is great joy, I perceive. Human nature stands astonished at itself – felicitates itself on its remarkable talent and will for months to come complacently purr over its achievement in magazines and reviews. A fine world that will attain to heaven – if in the power of steam. A very fine world; yet for all that, I have withdrawn from it for a time and would rather not hear of its remarkable exploits. In my present mood I do not value them the coil of vapour on the brow of Blaavin which, as I gaze, smoulders into nothing in the fire of sunrise.

Goethe informs us that in his youth he loved to shelter himself in the scripture narratives from the marching and countermarching of armies, the cannonading, fighting and retreating, that went on everywhere around him. He shut his eyes, as it were and a whole war-convulsed Europe wheeled away into silence and distance; and in its place, lo! the patriarchs with their tawny tents, their manservants and maidservants and countless flocks in perceptible procession whitening the Syrian plains.

In this, my green solitude, I appreciate the full sweetness of the passage. Everything here is silent as the Bible plains themselves. The noise of the world does not touch me. I live too far inland to hear the thunder of the reef. To this place no postman comes; no tax gatherer. This region never heard the sound of the churchgoing bell. The land is pagan as when the yellow-haired Norsemen landed a thousand years ago. I almost feel a pagan myself.

Not using a notched stick, I have lost all count of time and don't know Saturday from Sunday. Civilisation is like a soldier's stock, it makes you carry your head a good deal higher, makes the angels weep a little more at your fantastic tricks and half-suffocates you the while. I have thrown it away and breathe freely.

My bed is the heather, my mirror the stream from the hills, my comb and brush the sea breeze, my watch the sun, my theatre the sunset and my evening service – not without a rude natural religion in it – watching the pinnacles of the hills of Cuchullin sharpening in intense purple against the pallid orange of the sky, or listening to the melancholy voices of the seabirds and the tide; that over, I am asleep, till touched by the earliest splendour of the dawn. I am, not without reason, hugely enamoured of my vaga-bond existence.

My bothy is situated on the shores of one of the lochs that intersect Skye. The coast is bare and rocky, hollowed into fantastic chambers; and when the tide is making, every cavern murmurs like a seashell. The land, from frequent rain, green as emerald, rises into soft pastoral heights and about a mile inland soars suddenly up into peaks of bastard marble, white as the cloud under which the lark sings at noon and bathed in rosy light at sunset. In front are the Cuchullin hills and the monstrous peak of Blaavin; then the green strath runs narrowing out to sea and the Island of Rum, with a white cloud upon it, stretches like a gigantic shadow across the entrance of the loch and completes the scene.

Twice every twenty-four hours the Atlantic tide sets in upon the hollowed shores; twice is the sea withdrawn, leaving spaces of smooth sand on which mermaids, with golden combs, might sleek alluring tresses; and black rocks, heaped with brown dulse and tangle and lovely ocean blooms of purple and orange; and bare islets – marked at full of tide by a glimmer of pale green amid the universal sparkle – where most the seafowl love to congregate. To these islets, on favourable evenings, come the crows and sit in sable parliament; business despatched, they start into air as at a gun and stream away through the sunset to their roosting place in the Armadale woods.

The shore supplies for me the place of books and companions. Of course Blaavin and the Cuchullin hills are the chief attractions and I never weary watching them. In the morning they wear a great white caftan of mist; but that lifts away before noon and they stand with all their scars and passionate torrent lines bare to the blue heavens, with perhaps a solitary shoulder for a moment gleaming wet to the sunlight. After a while a vapour begins to steam up from the abysses, gathering itself into strange shapes, knotting and twisting itself like smoke; while above, the terrible crests are now lost, now revealed, in a stream of flying rack. In an hour a wall of rain, gray as granite, opaque as iron to the eye, stands up from the sea to heaven. The loch is roughening before the wind and the islets, black dots a second ago, are patches of roaring foam. I hear the fierce sound of its coming. Anon, the lashing tempest sweeps me and looking behind, up the long inland glen, I can see the birchwoods and over the sides of the hills, driven on the wind, the white smoke of the rain.

Though fierce as a charge of Highland bayonets these squalls are seldom of long duration and I bless them when I creep from my shelter, for out comes the sun and the birchwoods are twinkling and more intensely flash the levels of the sea and at a stroke the clouds are scattered from the wet brow of Blaavin and to the whole a new element has been added; the voice of the swollen stream as it rushes red over a hundred tiny cataracts and roars river-broad into the sea, making turbid the azure.

Then I have my amusements in this solitary place. The mountains are of course open and this morning at dawn, a roe swept past me like the wind, with its nose to the dewy ground – 'tracking,' they call it here. Above all, I can wander on the ebbed beach.

Hogg speaks of that 'undefined and mingled hum, Voice of the desert, never dumb.' But far from that the murmuring and insecty air of the moorland does the wet chirk-chirking of the living shore give one the idea of crowded and multitudinous life.

Did the reader ever hunt razorfish? – not sport like tiger-hunting, I admit; yet it has its pleasure and excitements and can kill a forenoon for an idle man agreeably. On the wet sands yonder the razorfish are spouting like the fountains at Versailles on a *fête* day. The shy fellow sinks on discharging his watery *feu de joie*. If I am quickly after him through the sand, I catch him and then comes the tug of war. Address and dexterity are required. If I pull vigorously, he slips out of his sheath a 'mother-naked' mollusc and escapes. If I do my spiriting gently, I drag him up to light, a long thin case, with a white fishy bulb protruding at one end like a root. Rinse him in seawater, toss him into my basket and plunge after another watery flash. These razorfish are excellent eating, the people say and when used as bait no fish that swims the ocean stream – cod, whiting, haddock, flat skate, broad-shouldered crimson bream, no, not the detested dogfish himself, this summer swarming in every loch and becursed by every fisherman – can keep himself off the hook and in an hour my boat is laden with glittering spoil.

Then, if I take my gun to the low islands – and I can go dry-shod at ebb of tide – I have my chance of seafowl. Gulls of all kinds are there, dookers and divers of every description, flocks of shy curlews and specimens of a hundred tribes to which my limited ornithological knowledge cannot furnish a name. The solan goose yonder falls from heaven into the water like a meteor-stone. See the solitary scart, with long narrow wing and outstretched neck, shooting towards some distant promontory. Anon, high above head, come wheeling a covey of lovely sea-swallows. I fire, one flutters down, never more to skim the horizon or to dip in the sea-sparkle. Lift it up; is it not beautiful? The wild, keen eye is closed, but see the delicate slate colour of the wings and the long tailfeathers white as the creaming foam. There is a stain of blood on the breast, hardly brighter than the scarlet of its beak and feet. Lay it down, for its companions are dashing round and round, uttering harsh cries of rage and sorrow; and had I the heart, I could shoot them one by one.

At ebb of tide wild-looking children, from turf cabins on the hillside, come down to hunt shellfish. Even now a troop is busy; how their shrill voices go the while! Old Effie I see is out today, quite a picturesque object, with her white cap and red shawl. With a tin can in one hand, an old reaping-hook in the other, she goes picking among the tangle. Let me see what sport she has had.

She turns round at my salutation – very old, old almost as the worn rocks around. She might have been the wife of Wordsworth's 'Leech-gatherer.' Her can is sprawling with brown crabs; and, opening her apron, she exhibits a large black and blue lobster – a fellow such as she alone can capture. A queer woman is Effie and an awesome. She is familiar with ghosts and apparitions. She can relate legends that have power over the superstitious blood and with little coaxing will sing those wild Gaelic songs of hers – of dead lights on the sea, of fishing boats going down in squalls, of unburied bodies tossing day and night upon the gray peaks of the waves and of the girls that pray God to lay them by the sides of their drowned lovers, although for them should never rise mass nor chant and although their flesh should be torn asunder by the wild fishes of the sea.

Rain is my enemy here; and at this writing I am suffering siege. For three days this rickety dwelling has stood assault of wind and rain. Yesterday a blast breached the door and the tenement fluttered for a moment like an umbrella caught in a gust. All seemed lost; but the door was got closed again, heavily barred across and the enemy foiled. An entrance, however, had been effected and that portion of the attacking column which I had imprisoned by my dexterous manoevre, maddened itself into whirlwind, rushed up the chimney, scattering my turf fire as it went and so escaped. Since that time the windy columns have retired to the gorges of the hills, where I can hear them howl at intervals; and the only thing I am exposed to is the musketry of the rain. How viciously the small shot peppers the walls! Here must I wait till the cloudy armament breaks up. My own mind is a dull companion in such circumstances.

Books are the only refuge on a rainy day; but in Skye bothies books are rare. To me, however, the gods have proved kind – for in my sore need I found on a shelf here two volumes of the old *Monthly Review* and I have sauntered through those dingy literary catacombs with considerable satisfaction. What a strange set of old fogies the writers are! To read them is like conversing with the antediluvians. Their opinions have fallen into disuse long ago and resemble today the rusty armour and gimcracks of an old curiosity shop.

Mr Henry Rogers has written a fine essay on the *Glory and Vanity of Literature* – in my thoughts, out of this dingy material before me I can frame a finer.

These essays and criticisms were thought brilliant, I suppose, when they appeared last century; and authors praised therein doubtless considered themselves rather handsome flies preserved in pure critical amber for the inspection and admiration of posterity. The volumes were published, I notice, from 1790 to 1792 and exhibit a period of wonderful literary activity. Not to speak of novels, histories, travels, farces, tragedies, upwards of two hundred poems, short and long, are brought to judgement; and several of these – with their names and the names of their authors I have, during the last two days, made acquaintance for the first time – are assured of immortality. Perhaps they deserved it; But they have gone down like the steamship *President* and left no trace.

On the whole, these Monthly Reviewers worked hard and with a proper spirit and deftness. They had a proud sense of the importance of their craft, they laid down the law with great gravity and, from critical benches, shook their awful wigs on offenders. How it all looks *now!*

'Let us indulge ourselves with another extract,' quoth one, 'and contemplate once more the tear of grief before we are called upon to witness the tear of rapture.' *Both* tears dried up long ago.

Hear this other, stern as Rhadamanthus. Behold Duty steeling itself against human weakness! 'It grieves us to wound a young man's feelings: but our judgement must not be biased by any plea whatsoever. Why will men apply for our opinion when they know that we cannot be silent and that we will not lie?'

Listen to this prophet in Israel and say if there be not a plaintive touch of pathos in him: 'Fine words do not make fine poems. Scarcely a month passes in which we are not obliged to issue this decree. But in these days of universal heresy our decrees are no more respected than the bulls of the Bishop of Rome.' Oh that men would hear, that they would incline their hearts to wisdom!

One peculiarity I have noticed – the advertisements sheets which accompanied the numbers are bound up with them and form an integral portion of the volumes. And just as the tobacco-less man whom we met at the entrance to Glen Sligachan smoked the paper in which his roll of pigtail had been wrapped, so when I had finished the criticisms I attacked the advertisements and found them much the more amusing reading. Might not the magazine-buyer of today follow the example of the unknown Islesman? Depend upon it, to the reader of the next century the advertising sheets will be more interesting than the poetry, or the essays, or the stories.

The two volumes were a godsend; but at last I began to weary of the old literary churchyard in which the poet and his critic sleep in the same oblivion. When I closed the books and placed them on their shelves, the rain peppered the walls as pertinaciously as when I took them down.

Next day it rained still. It was impossible to go out; the volumes of the *Monthly Review* were sucked oranges and could yield no further amusement or interest. What was to be done? I took refuge with the Muse. Certain notions had got into my brain – certain stories had taken possession of my memory – and these I resolved to versify and finally to dispose of. This I accomplished at last in seven poems, *Poems Written in a Skye Bothy* which the competent critic can see at a glance are the vilest plagiarisms – that as throughout I have called the sky *blue* and the grass *green*, I have stolen from every English poet from Chaucer downwards; he will observe also, from occasional uses of *all* and *and*, that they are the merest Tennysonian echoes. But they served their purpose – they killed for me the languor of the rainy days, which is more than they are likely to do for the critic.

These verses I had no sooner copied out in my best hand than, looking up, I found that the rain had ceased from sheer fatigue and that great white vapours were rising up from the damp valleys. Here was release at last – the beleaguering army had raised the siege; and better than all, I heard the sound of wheels on the boggy ground: and just when the staunched rainclouds were burning into a sullen red at sunset, I had the M'Ian's, father and son, in my bothy and pleasant human intercourse. They came to carry me off with them.

I am to stay with M'Ian tonight. A wedding has taken place up among the hills and the whole party have been asked to make a night of it. The mighty kitchen has been cleared for the occasion; torches are stuck up, ready to be lighted; and I already hear the first mutterings of the bagpipe's storm of sound. The old gentleman wears a look of brightness and hilarity and vows that he will lead off the first reel with the bride. Everything is prepared; and even now the bridal party are coming down the steep hillroad. I must go out to meet them. Tomorrow I return to my bothy to watch; for the weather has become fine now, the sunny mists congregating on the crests of Blaavin – Blaavin on which the level heaven seems to lean.

Riding through Skye

AFTER SPENDING ANOTHER ten days or thereabouts with Mr M'Ian and at my bothy, I intimated my intentions of paying a visit to my friend the Landlord – with whom Fellowes was then staying – who lived some forty miles off in the north-western portion of the Island. The old gentleman was opposed to rapid decisions and movements and asked me to remain with him yet another week. Now his speech was as old-fashioned as he was himself; ancient matters turned up on his tongue just as ancient matters turned up on his farm. There might be an old grave or an old implement on the one, so would be found an old proverb or an old scrap of Gaelic poem on the other.

When he found I was resolute he glanced at the weather-gleam and the troops of mists gathering on Cuchullin, muttering as he did so, ' "Make ready my galley," said the king, "I shall sail for Norway on Wednesday." "Will you?" said the wind, who flying about, had overheard what was said. "You had better ask my leave first." '

As M'Ian had predicted, I could only move from his house if the weather granted permission; and this permission the weather did not seem disposed to grant. For several days it rained as I had never seen it before; a waterspout too had burst up among the hills and the stream came down in mighty flood. There was a great hubbub at the house. Mr M'Ian's hay, which was built in large stacks in the valley meadows, was in danger and the fiery cross was sent through the cotters.

Up to the hayfields every available man was dispatched with carts and horses, to remove the stacks to some spot where the waters could not reach them; while at the bridge nearer the house women and boys were stationed with long poles and what rudely-extemporised implements Celtic ingenuity could suggest, to intercept and fish out piles and trusses which the thievish stream was carrying away with it seaward. These piles and trusses would at least serve for the bedding of cattle.

For three days the rainy tempest continued; at last, on the fourth, mist and rain rolled up like a vast curtain in heaven and then again were visible the clumps of birchwood and the bright sea and the smoking hills and, far away on the ocean floor, Rum and Canna, without a speck of cloud on them, sleeping in the coloured calmness of early afternoon. This uprising of the elemental curtain was, so far as the suddenness of the effect was concerned, like the uprising of the curtain of the pantomime on the transformation scene – all at once a dingy, sodden world had become a brilliant one and all the newly-revealed colour and brilliancy promised to be permanent.

Of this happy change in the weather I, of course, took immediate advantage. About five o'clock in the afternoon my dog-cart was brought to the door; and after a parting cup with Mr M'Ian – who pours a libation both to his arriving and his departing guest – I drove away on my journey to remote Portree and to the unimagined country that lay beyond Portree, but which I knew held Dunvegan, Duntulm, MacLeod's Tables and Quirang. I drove up the long glen with a pleasant exhilaration of spirit. I felt grateful to the sun, for he had released me from my rainy captivity.

The drive, too, was pretty; the stream came rolling down in foam, the smell of the wet birch trees was in the brilliant air, every mountain top was strangely and yet softly distinct; and looking back, there were the blue Cuchullins looking after me, as if bidding me farewell! At last I reached the top of the glen and emerged on a high plateau of moorland, in which were dark inky tarns with big white waterlillies on them; and skirting across the plateau I dipped down on the parliamentary road, which, like a broad white belt, surrounds Skye. Better road to drive on you will not find in the neighbourhood of London itself! and just as I was descending, I could not help pulling up.

The whole scene was of the extremest beauty – exquisitely calm, exquisitely coloured. On my left was a little lake with a white margin of waterlillies, a rocky eminence throwing a shadow halfway across it. Down below, on the seashore, was the farm of Knock, with white outhouses and pleasant patches of cultivation, the schoolhouse and the church, while on a low spit of land the old castle of the Macdonalds was mouldering. Still lower down and straight away stretched the sleek blue Sound of Sleat, with not a sail or streak of steamer smoke to break its vast expanse and with a whole congregation of clouds piled up on the horizon, soon to wear their evening colours. I let the sight slowly creep into my study of imagination, so that I might be able to reproduce it at pleasure; that done, I drove down to Isle Oronsay by pleasant sloping stages of descent, with green hills on right and left and, along the roadside, like a guard of honour, the purple stalks of the foxglove.

The evening sky was growing red above me when I drove into Isle Oronsay, which consists of perhaps fifteen houses in all. It sits on the margin of a pretty bay, in which the cry of the fisher is continually heard and into which the *Clansman* going to or coming from the south steams twice or thrice in the week. At a little distance is a lighthouse with a revolving light – an idle building during the day, but when night comes, awakening to full activity – sending now a ray to Ardnamurchan, now piercing with a fiery arrow the darkness to Glenelg.

In Isle Oronsay is a merchant's shop, in which every conceivable article may be obtained. At Isle Oronsay the post runner drops a bag, as he cries on to Armadale Castle. At Isle Oronsay I supped with my friend Mr Fraser. From him I heard that the little village had been, like M'Ian's house, fiercely scourged by rains. On the supper table was a dish of trouts.

'Where do you suppose I procured these?' he asked.

'In one of your burns, I suppose.'

'No such thing; I found them in my potato-field.'

'In your potato field! How came that about?'

'Why, you see the stream, swollen by three days' rain, broke over a potato field of mine on the hillside and carried the potatoes away and left these plashing in poll and runnel. The Skye streams have a slight touch of honesty in them!'

I smiled at the conceit and expounded to my host the law of compensation which pervades the universe, of which I maintained the trouts on the table were a shining example. Mr Fraser assented; but held that Nature was a poor valuator – that her knowledge of the doctrine of equivalents was slightly defective – that the trouts were well enough, but no reimbursement for the potatoes that were gone.

Next morning I resumed my journey. The road, so long as it skirted the seashore, was pretty enough; but the seashore it soon left and entered a waste of brown monotonous moorland. The country round about abounds in grouse and was the favourite shooting ground of the late Lord Macdonald. By the roadside his lordship had erected a stable and covered the roof with tin; and so at a distance it flashed as if the Koh-i-noor had been dropped by accident in that dismal region.

As I went along, the hills above Broadford began to rise; then I drove down the slope, on which the market was held – the tents all struck, but the stakes yet remaining in the ground – and after passing the six houses, the lime kiln, the church and the two merchants' shops, I pulled up at the inn door and sent the horse round to the stable to feed and rest an hour.

After leaving Broadford the traveller drives along the margin of the ribbon of salt water which flows between Skye and the island of Scalpa. Up this narrow sound the steamer never passes and it is only navigated by the lighter kinds of sailing craft. Scalpa is a hilly island of some three or four miles in length, by one and a half in breadth, is gray-green in colour and as treeless as the palm of my hand. It has been the birthplace of many soldiers.

After passing Scalpa the road ascends; and I noticed as I drove along that during the last hour or so the frequent streams have changed colour. In the southern portion of the island they come down as if the hills ran sherry – here they are pale as shallow sea-water. This difference in hue arises of course from a difference of bed. About Broadford they come down through the mossy moor-land, here they run over marble, Of marble the island is full; and it is not impossible that the sculptors of the twentieth century will patronise the quarries of Strath and Kyle rather than the quarries of Carrara. But wealth is needed to lay bare these mineral treas-ures. The fine qualities of Skye marble will never be obtained until they are laid open by a golden pickaxe.

Over past Scalpa, I approached Lord Macdonald's deer forest. I had turned the flank of the Cuchullins now and was taking them in rear and I skirted their bases very closely too. The road is full of wild ascents and descents and on my left, for a couple of miles or so, I was in continual presence of bouldered hillside sloping away upward to some invisible peak, overhanging wall of wet black precipice, far-off serrated ridge that cuts the sky like a saw. Occasionally these mountain forms open up and fall back and I saw the sterilest valleys running no man knows whither. Altogether the hills here have a strange weird look. Each is as closely seamed with lines as the face of a man of a hundred and these myriad reticulations are picked out with a pallid gray-green, as if through some mineral corrosion.

Passing along I was strangely impressed with the idea that some vast chemical experiment has been going on for some thousands of years; that the region is nature's laboratory and that down these wrinkled hill-fronts she had spilt her acids and undreamed-of combinations. I never think of verdure in connection with that network of gray-green, but only of rust, or of some metallic discolouration. I cannot help fancying that if a sheep fed on one of those hillsides it would to a certainty be poisoned. Altogether the sight is very grand, very impressive and very uncomfortable and it was with the liveliest satisfaction that, tearing down one of the long descents, I turned my back on the mountain monsters and beheld in front the green Island of Raasay, with its imposing modern mansion, basking in sunshine. It is like passing from the world of gnomes to the world of men.

I have driven across Lord Macdonald's deer forest in sunshine and in rain and am constrained to confess that, under the latter atmospherical condition, the scenery is the more imposing. Some months ago I drove in the mail-gig from Sligachan to Broadford. There was a high wind, the sun was bright and consequently a great *carry* and flight of sunny vapours. All at once, too, every half-hour or so, the turbulent brightness of wind and cloud was extinguished by fierce squalls of rain. I could see the coming rain-storm blown out on the wind toward me like a sheet of muslin cloth. On it came racing in its strength and darkness, the long straight watery lines pelting on road and rock, churning in marsh and pool. Over the unhappy mail-gig it rushed, bidding defiance to plaid or waterproof cape and wetting everyone to the skin.

The mail jogged on as best it could through the gloom and the fury and then the sunshine came again, making to glisten, almost too brightly for the eye, every rain pool on the road. In the sunny intervals there was a great race and hurry of towered vapour, as I said; and when a shining mass smote one of the hillsides, or shrouded for a while one of the more distant serrated crests, the concussion was so palpable to the eye that the ear felt defrauded and silence seemed unnatural. And when the vast mass passed onward to impinge on some other mountain barrier, it was singular to notice by what slow degrees, with what evident reluctance the laggard skirts combed off.

All these effects of rain and windy vapour I remember vividly and I suppose that the vividness was partly due to the lamentable condition of a fellow traveller. He was a meek-faced man of fifty. He was dressed in sables, his swallow-tailed coat was threadbare and withal seemed made for a smaller man. There was an uncomfortable space between the wrists of his coat and his black-thread gloves. He wore a hat and against the elements had neither protection of plaid or umbrella. No-one knew him, to no-one did he explain his business. To my notion he was bound for a funeral at some place beyond Portree. He was not a clergyman – he might have been a schoolmaster who had become green-moulded in some out-of-the-way locality.

Of course one or two of the rainy squalls settled the meek-faced man in the threadbare sables. Emerging from one of these he resembled a draggled rook and the rain was pouring from the brim of his pulpy hat as it might from the eaves of a cottage. A passenger handed him his spirit flask, the meek-faced man took a hearty pull and, returning it, said plaintively, 'I'm but poorly clad, sir, for this God-confound climate.' I think often of the utterance of the poor fellow: it was the only thing he said all the way; and when I think of it, I see again the rain blown out towards me on the wind like a waving sheet of muslin cloth and the rush, the concussion, the up-break and the slow reluctant trailing off from the hillside of the sunny cloud. The poor man's plaintive tone is the anchor which holds these things in my memory.

The forest is of course treeless. Nor are deer seen there frequently. Indeed, only once did I get a sight of antlers in that place. Carefully I crept up, sheltering myself behind a rocky haunch of the hill to where the herd were lying and then rushed out upon them with a halloo. In an instant they were on their feet and away went the beautiful creatures, doe and fawn, a stag with branchy head leading. They dashed across a torrent, crowned an eminence one by one and disappeared. Such a sight is witnessed but seldom; and the traveller passing through the brown desolation sees usually no sign of life. In Lord Macdonald's deer forest neither trees nor deer were visible.

When once quit of the forest, I came on a shooting-box, perched on the seashore; then I passed the little village of Sconser and, turning the sharp flank of a hill, drove along Loch Sligachan to Sligachan Inn, about a couple of miles distant. This Inn is a famous halting place for tourists. There are good fishing streams about, I am given to understand, and through Glen Sligachan you can find your way to Camasunary and take the boat from thence to Loch Coruisk as we did. It was down this glen that the messenger was to have brought the tobacco to our peculiar friend. If you go you may perhaps find his skeleton scientifically articulated by the carrion crow and the raven!

From the inn door the ridges of the Cuchullins are seen wildly invading the sky and in closer proximity there are other hills which cannot be called beautiful. Monstrous, abnormal, chaotic, they resemble the other hills on the earth's surface as Hindu deities resemble human beings. The mountain, whose sharp flank I turned after I passed Sconser, can from here be inspected leisurely and is, to my mind, supremely ugly. In summer it is red as copper, with great ragged patches of verdure upon it, which look for all the world as if the coppery mass had *rusted* green. On these green patches cattle feed from March to October.

I baited at Sligachan – dined on trout which a couple of hours before were darting hither and thither in the stream – and then drove leisurely along to Portree while the setting sun was dressing the wilderness in gold and rose. And all the way the Cuchullins followed me. The wild irregular outline, which no familiarity can stale, haunts me at Portree, as it does in nearly every quarter of Skye.

Portree folds two irregular ranges of white houses, the one range rising steeply above the other, around a noble bay, the entrance to which is guarded by rocky precipices. At a little distance the houses are white as shells and as in summer they are all set in the greenness of foliage the effect is strikingly pretty; and if the sense of prettiness departs to a considerable extent on a closer acquaintance, there is yet enough left to gratify me so long as I remain there and to make it a pleasant place to think about when I am gone. The lower range of houses consists mainly of warehouses and fish-stores; the upper, of the main hotel, the two banks, the courthouse and the shops. A pier runs out into the bay and here, when the state of tide permits, comes the steamer on its way to or from Stornoway and unlades.

Should the tide be low the steamer lies to in the bay and her cargo and passengers come to shore by means of boats. She usually arrives at night; and at low tide, the burning of coloured lights at the mast-heads, the flitting hither and thither of busy lanterns, the pier boats coming and going with illuminated wakes and ghostly fires on the oar-blades, the clatter of chains and the shock of the crank hoisting the cargo out of the hold, the general hubbub and storm of Gaelic shouts and imprecations make the arrival at once picturesque and impressive.

In the bay the yacht of the tourist is continually lying and at the hotel door his dog-cart is continually departing or arriving and on the evenings of market days, in the large public rooms, farmers and cattle dealers sit over tumblers of smoking punch and discuss noisily the prices and the qualities of stock.

Besides the hotel and the pier, the banks and the courthouse already mentioned, there are other objects of interest in the little island town – three churches, a post office, a poorhouse and a cloth manufactory. And it has more than meets the eye – one of the Jameses landed here on a visitation of the Isles, Prince Charles was here on his way to Raasay, Dr Johnson and Boswell were here; and somewhere on the green hill on which the pretty church stands, a murderer is buried – the precise spot of burial is unknown and so the entire hill gets the credit that of right belongs only to a single yard of it.

In Portree the tourist seldom abides long; he passes through it as a fortnight before he passed though Oban. It does not seem to the visitor a specially remarkable place, but everything is relative in this world. It is an event for the Islesman at Dunvegan or the Point of Sleat to go to Portree, just as it is an event for a Yorkshireman to go to London.

When I drove out of Portree I was in Macleod's country and I discovered that the character of the scenery had changed. Looking back, the Cuchullins are wild and pale on the horizon, but everything around is brown, softly-swelling and monotonous. The hills are round and low and except when an occasional boulder crops out on their sides like a wart, are smooth as a seal's back. They are gray-green in colour and may be grazed to the top. Expressing once to a shepherd my admiration of the Cuchullins, the man replied, while he swept with his arm the entire range, 'There's no feeding there for twenty wethers!' Here, however, there is sufficient feeding to compensate for any lack of beauty.

About three miles out of Portree I came upon a solitary-looking schoolhouse by the wayside and a few yards farther to a division of the roads. A fingerpost informed me that the road to the right led to Uig, that to the left to Dunvegan. As I am at present bound for Dunvegan, I skirr along to the left and after an hour's drive come in sight of Loch Snizort, with Skeabost sitting whitely on its margin. Far inland from the broad Minch, like one of those wavering swords which medieval painters place in the hands of archangels, has Snizort come wandering; and it is the curious mixture of brine and pastureland, of mariner life and shepherd life which gives its charm to this portion of the island.

The lochs are narrow and I fancy a strong-lunged man could shout across. The sea-gull skims above the feeding sheep, the shepherd can watch the sail of the sloop, laden with meal, creeping from point to point. Above all places which I have seen in Skye, Skeabost has a lowland look. There are almost no turf huts to be seen in the neighbourhood; the houses are built of stone and lime and are tidily whitewashed. The hills are low and smooth; on the lower slopes corn and wheat are grown; and from a little distance the greenness of cultivation looks like a palpable smile – a strange contrast to the monotonous district through which, for an hour or so, I have driven.

As I pass the inn and drive across the bridge, I notice that there is an island in the stony stream and that this island is covered with ruins, The Skyeman likes to bury his dead in islands and this one in the stream at Skeabost is a crowded cemetery. I forded the stream and wandered for an hour amongst the tombs and broken stones. There are traces of an ancient chapel on the island, but tradition does not even make a guess at its builder's name or the date of its erection. There are old slabs, lying sideways, with the figures of recumbent men with swords in their hands and inscriptions – indecipherable now – carved on them. There is the grave of a Skye clergyman who, if his epitaph is to be trusted, was a burning and a shining light in his day. I never saw a churchyard so mounded and so evidently overcrowded. Here laird, tacksman and cotter elbow each other in death. Here no-one will make way for a newcomer, or give the wall to his neighbour.

And standing in the little ruined island of silence and the dead, with the river perfectly audible on either side, I could not help thinking what a picturesque sight a Highland funeral would be, creeping across the moors with wailing pipe music, fording the river and his bearers making room for the dead man amongst the older dead as best they could. And this sight, I am told, may be seen any week in the year. To this island all the funerals of the countryside converge. Standing there, too, I could not help thinking that this space of silence, girt by river noises, would be an *eerie* place by moonlight. The broken chapel, the carved slabs lying sideways, as if the dead man beneath had grown restless and turned himself and the headstones jutting out of the mounded soil at every variety of angle, would appear in the ink of shadow and the silver of moonbeam. In such circumstances I would hear something more in the stream as it ran past than the mere breaking of water on stones.

After passing the river and the island of graves I drove down between hedges to Skeabost church, school, post office and manse and thereafter I climbed the steep hill towards Bernesdale and its colony of turf huts; and when I reached the top I had a noble view of the flat blue Minch and the Skye headlands, each precipitous, abrupt and reminding me somehow of a horse which has been suddenly reined back to its haunches. But the grand vision is not of long duration, for the road descends rapidly towards Taynlone

Inn. In my descent I beheld two barefooted and bareheaded girls
yoked to a harrow and dragging it up and down a small plot of
delved ground.

Sitting in the inn it began to remember me how frequently I
had heard in the south of the destitution of the Skye people and
the discomfort of the Skye hut. During my wanderings I had the
opportunity of visiting several of these dwellings and seeing how
matters were transacted within. Frankly speaking, the Highland
hut is not a model edifice. It is open to wind and almost always
pervious to rain. An old bottomless herring firkin stuck in the roof
usually serves for a chimney, but the blue peat-reek disdains that
aperture and steams wilfully through the door and the crannies
in the walls and roof. The interior is seldom well-lighted – what
light there is proceeding rather from the orange glow of the peat
fire, on which a large pot is simmering, than from the narrow pane
with its great bottlegreen bull's-eye. The rafters which support the
roof are black and glossy with soot, as can be seen by the sudden
flashes of firelight. The sleeping accommodation is limited and
the beds are composed of heather or ferns. The floor is the beaten
earth, the furniture scanty; there is hardly ever a chair – stools and
stones, worn smooth by the usage of several generations, have to
do instead.

One portion of the hut is not unfrequently a byre and the
breath of the cow is mixed with the odour of peat-reek and the
baa of the calf mingles with the wranglings and swift ejaculations
of the infant Highlanders. In such a hut as this there are sometimes three generations. The mother stands knitting outside,
the children are scrambling on the floor with the terrier and
the poultry and a ray of cloudy sunshine from the narrow pane
smites the silver hairs of the grandfather near the fire, who is
mending fishing nets against the return of his son-in-law from
the south.

Am I inclined to lift my hands in horror at witnessing such a
dwelling? Certainly not. I have only given one side of the picture.
The hut I speak of nestles beneath a rock, on the top of which

dances the ash tree and the birch. The emerald mosses on its roof are softer and richer than the velvets of kings. Twenty yards down that path is a well that needs no ice in the dog days. At a little distance, from rocky shelf to rocky shelf, trips a mountain burn, with abundance of trout in the brown pools. At the distance of a mile is the sea, which is not allowed to ebb and flow in vain; for in the smoke there is a row of fishes drying; and on the floor a curly-headed urchin of three years or thereby is pommeling the terrier with the scarlet claw of a lobster. Methought, too when I entered I saw beside the door a heap of oyster shells.

Within the hut there is good food, if a little scant at times; without there is air that will call colour back to the cheek of an invalid, pure water, play, exercise, work. That the people are healthy, can be seen from their strong frames, brown faces and the age to which many attain; that they are happy and light-hearted, the shouts of laughter that ring around the peat fire of an evening may be taken as sufficient evidence.

I protest I cannot become pathetic over the Highland hut. I have sat in these turfen dwellings, amid the surges of blue smoke received hospitable welcome and found amongst the inmates good sense, industry, family affection, contentment, piety, happiness. And when I have heard philanthropists, with more zeal than discretion, maintain that these dwellings are a disgrace to the country in which they are found, I have thought of districts of great cities which I have seen, of evil scents and sights and sounds: of windows stuffed with rags; of female faces that look out of a sadder Inferno than that of Dante's; of faces of men containing the debris of the entire decalogue, faces which hurt more than a blow would: of infants poisoned with gin, of children bred for the prison and the hulks.

Depend upon it there are worse odours than peat smoke, worse nextdoor neighbours than a cow or a brood of poultry; and although a couple of girls dragging a harrow be hardly in accordance with our modern notions, yet we need not forget that there are worse employments for girls than even that.

I do not stand up for the Highland hut; but in one of these smoky cabins I would a thousandfold rather spend my days than in the Cowgate of Edinburgh or in one of the streets that radiate from Seven Dials.

The Landlord's Walk

AFTER TRAVELLING THREE or four days from Mr M'Ian's house
in the south, I beheld on the other side of a long, blue, river-
like loch, the house of the Landlord. From the point at which
I now paused, a boat could have taken me across in half an
hour, but as the road wound round the top of the loch, I had
yet some eight or ten miles to drive before my journey was
accomplished. Meantime the loch was at ebb and the sun
was setting. On the hillside, on my left as I drove, stretched a
long street of huts covered with smoky wreaths and in front
of each a strip of cultivated ground ran down to the road
which skirted the shore. Potatoes grew in one strip, turnips in
a second, corn in a third and, as these crops were in different
stages of advancement, the entire hillside, from the street of
huts downward, resembled one of those counterpanes which
thrifty housewives manufacture by sewing together the patches
of different patterns.

Along the road running at the back of the huts a cart was passing; on the moory hill behind, a flock of sheep, driven by men
and dogs, was contracting and expanding itself like quicksilver.
The women were knitting at the hut doors, the men were at
work in the cultivated patches in front. On all this scene of cheerful and fortunate industry, on men and women, on turnips, oats
and potatoes, on cottages set in azure films of peat-reek, the rosy
light was striking – making a pretty spectacle enough. From the
whole hillside breathed peace, contentment, happiness and a
certain sober beauty of usefulness. Man and nature seemed in

perfect agreement and harmony – man willing to labour, nature to yield increase.

Down to the head of the loch the road sloped rapidly and at the very head a small village had established itself. It contained an inn, a schoolhouse, in which divine service was held on Sundays: a smithy, a merchant's shop – all traders are called *merchants* in Skye – and, by the side of a stream which came brawling down from rocky steep to steep, stood a corn mill, the big wheel lost in a watery mist of its own raising, the door and windows dusty with meal.

Behind the village lay a stretch of black moorland intersected by drains and trenches and from the black huts which seemed to have grown out of the moor and the spaces of sickly green here and there, I could see that the desolate and forbidding region had its colonists and that they were valiantly attemping to wring a sustenance out of it. Who were the squatters on the black moorland? I had no-one to inform me at the time; meanwhile the sunset fell on these remote dwellings, lending them what beauty and amelioration of colour it could, making a drain sparkle for a moment, turning a far-off pool into gold leaf and rendering, by contrast of universal warmth and glow, yet more beautiful the smoke which swathed the houses. Yet, after all, the impression made upon me was cheerless enough. Sunset goes but a little way in obviating human wretchedness, Misery is often picturesque, but the picturesqueness is in the eyes of others, not in her own. The black moorland and the banished huts abode in my mind during the remainder of my drive.

Between the Landlord and M'Ian there were many likenesses and divergences. Both were Skyemen by birth, both had the strongest love for their native island, both had the management of human beings, both had shrewd heads and hearts of the kindest texture. But at this point the likenesses ended and the divergences began. Mr M'Ian had never been out of the three kingdoms. The Landlord had spent the best part of his life in India, was more familiar with huts of ryots, topes of palms, tanks in which the

indigo plant was steeping, than with the houses of Skye cotters
and the process of sheep farming. He knew the streets of Benares
or Delhi better than he knew the streets of London; and, when he
first came home, Hindustani would occasionally jostle Gaelic on
his tongue. The Landlord, too, was rich, would have been considered a rich man even in the southern cities; he was owner of many
a mile of moorland and the tides of more than one far-winding
loch rose and rippled on shores that called him master.

In my friend the Landlord there was a sort of contrariety, a
sort of mixture or blending of opposite elements which was not
without its fascination. He was, in some respects, a resident in two
worlds. He liked motion; he had a magnificent scorn of distance:
to him the world seemed comparatively small; and he would start
from Skye to India with as much composure as other men would
take the night train to London. He paid taxes in India and he paid
taxes in Skye. His name was as powerful in the markets of Calcutta
as it was at the Muir of Ord. He read the *Hurkaru* and the *Inverness
Courier*. He had known the graceful salaam of the East, as he now
knew the touched bonnets of his shepherds. And in living with
him, in talking with him, one was now reminded of the green
western island on which sheep fed, anon of the tropical heats, of
pearl gold, of mosque and pinnacle glittering above belts of palm
trees. In his company you were in imagination travelling backwards and forwards. You made the overland route twenty times
a day. Now you heard the bagpipe, now the monotonous beat of
the tomtom and the keen clash of silver cymbals. In the West with
a half-glass of bitters in the morning, in the East with the curry
at dinner.

The Landlord, when he entered on the direction of his property, exploded every ancient form of usage, actually *ruled* his
tenants; would permit no factor, middleman or go-between; met
them face to face and had it out with them. The consequence
was that the poor people were at times sorely bewildered. They
received their orders and carried them out, with but little sense of
the ultimate purpose of the Landlord – just as the sailor, ignorant

of the principles of navigation, pulls ropes and reefs and sails and does not discover that he gains much thereby, the same sea crescent being around him day by day, but in due time a cloud rises on the horizon and he is in port at last.

Everything about a man is characteristic, more or less; and in the house of the Landlord I found that singular mixture of hemispheres which I had before noticed in his talk and in his way of looking at times. Greshornish House was plain enough externally, but its furniture was curious and far-brought. The interior of his porch was adorned with heads of stags and tusks of elephants. He had Highland relics and curiosities from sacked Eastern palaces; the tiny porcelain cup out of which Prince Charles drank tea at Kingsburgh and the signet ring which was stripped from the dead fingers of Tippoo Sahib; modern breech-loaders and revolvers in his gun room alongside matchlocks from China and Nepal; Lochaber axes, claymores and targets that might have seen service at Inverlochy and hideous krises, Afghan daggers, curiously-curved swords, scabbards thickly crusted with gems. On the drawing room table were ivory card cases wrought by the patient Hindu, as finely as we work our laces, Chinese puzzles that baffled all European comprehension and comical squab-faced deities in silver and bronze.

And then there were the pets, all kinds, with which he surrounded himself and lived on the most intimate terms. When he entered the breakfast room his terriers barked and frisked and jumped about him; his great black harehound, Maida, got up from the rug on which it had been basking and thrust its sharp nose into his hand; his canaries broke into emulous music, as if the sunshine had come into the room; the parrot in the porch clambered along the cage with horny claws, settled itself on its perch, bobbed its head up and down for a moment and was seized with whooping cough. When he went out the black harehound followed at his heel; the peacock, strutting on the gravel in the shelter of the larches, unfurled its starry fan; in the stable his horses turned round to smell his clothes and to have their foreheads stroked: melodious thunder broke from the dog kennel when he came: and at his approach his falcons did not withdraw; they listened to his voice and a gentler something tamed for a moment the fierce cairngorms of their eyes. When others came near they ruffled their plumage and uttered sharp cries of anger.

After breakfast it was his habit to carry the parrot out to a long iron garden seat in front of the house – where, if sunshine was to be had at all, we were certain to find it – and placing the cage beside him, smoke a cheroot. The parrot would clamber about the cage, suspended head downwards would take a crafty stock of me with an eye which had perhaps looked out on the world for a century or so and then, righting itself, insist that Polly should put on the kettle and that the boy should shut up the grog.

On one special morning, while the Landlord was smoking and the parrot whooping and whistling, several men, dressed in rough pilot cloth which had seen much service and known much darning, came along the walk and respectfully uncovered. Returning their salutation, the Landlord threw away the end of his cheroot and went forward to learn their message. The conversation was in Gaelic; slow and gradual at first, it quickened anon and broke into gusts of altercation; and on these occasions I noticed that the Landlord would turn impatiently on his heel, march a pace or two back to the house and then, wheeling round, return to the charge.

He argued in the unknown tongue, gesticulated, was evidently impressing something on his auditors which they were unwilling to receive, for at intervals they would look in one another's faces – a look implying, 'Did you ever hear the like?' – and give utterance to a murmured *chit, chit, chit* of dissent and humble protestation. At last the matter got itself amicably settled, the deputation – each man making a short sudden duck before putting on his bonnet – withdrew and the Landlord came back to the parrot which had now with one eye, now with the other, been watching the proceeding. He sat down with a slight air of annoyance.

'These fellows are wanting more meal,' he said, 'and one or two are pretty deep in my books already.'

'Do you, then, keep regular accounts with them?'

'Of course, I give nothing for nothing. I wish to do them as much good as I can. They are a good deal like my old ryots, only the ryot was more supple and obsequious.'

'Where do your friends come from?' I asked.

'From the village over there,' pointing across the narrow blue Loch. 'Pretty Polly! Polly!'

The parrot was climbing up and down the cage, taking hold of the wires with beak and claw as it did so.

'I wish to know something of your villagers. The cotters on the hillside seem comfortable enough, but I wonder about the black land and the lonely huts behind.'

'Oh,' said he, laughing, 'that is my penal settlement – I'll drive you over tomorrow.' He then got up, tossed a stone into the shrubbery, after which Maida dashed, thrust his hands into his breeches pocket for a moment and marched into the house.

Next morning we drove across to the village and pretty enough it looked as we alighted. The big water wheel of the mill whirred industrious music, flour flying about the door and windows. Two or three people were standing at the merchant's shop. At the smithy a horse was haltered and within were brilliant showers of sparks and the merry clink of hammers. The sunshine made pure amber the pools of the tumbling burn and in one of these a girl was rinsing linen, the light touching her hair into a richer colour.

Our arrival at the inn created some little stir. The dusty miller came out, the smith came to the door rubbing down his apron with a horny palm, the girl stood upright by the burnside shading her eyes with her hand, one of the men at the merchant's shop went to tell her the news, the labourers in the field round about stopped work to stare.

The machine was no sooner put to rights and the horses taken round to the stable than the mistress of the house complained that the roof was leaky and she and the Landlord went in to inspect the same. Left alone for a little, I could observe that, seeing my friend had arrived, the people were resolved to make some use of him and here and there I noticed them laying down their crooked spades and coming down towards the inn. One old woman, with a white handkerchief tied round her head, sat down on a stone opposite and when the Landlord appeared – the matter of the leaky roof having been arranged – she rose and dropped a courtesy.

She had a complaint to make, a benefit to ask, a wrong to be redressed. I could not, of course, understand a word of the conversation, but curiously sharp and querulous was her voice, with a slight suspicion of the whine of the mendicant in it and every now and then she would give a deep sigh and smooth down her apron with both her hands. I suspect the old lady gained her object, for when the Landlord cracked his joke at parting the most curious sunshine of merriment came into the withered features, lighting them up and changing them and giving one, for a flying second, some idea of what she must have been in her middle age, perhaps in her early youth, when she as well as other girls had a sweetheart.

In turn we visited the merchant's shop, the smithy and the mill; then we passed the schoolhouse which was one confused murmur, the sharp voice of the teacher striking through at intervals – and turning up a narrow road, came upon the black region and the banished huts.

The cultivated hillside was shining in sunlight, the cottages smoking, the people at work in their crofts – everything look-ing blithe and pleasant and under the bright sky and the happy weather the penal settlement did not look nearly so forbidding as it had done when, under the sunset, I had seen it a few evenings previously. The houses were rude, but they seemed sufficiently weathertight, Each was set down in a little oasis of cultivation, a little circle in which by labour the sour land had been coaxed into a smile of green; each small domain was enclosed by a low turfen wall and on the top of one of these a wild-goat-looking sheep was feeding, which, as we approached, jumped down with an alarmed bleat and then turned to gaze on the intruders. The land was sour and stony, the dwellings framed of the rudest materials and the people – for they all came forward to meet him and at each turfen wall the Landlord held a *levee* – especially the older people, gave me the idea somehow of worn-out tools. In some obscure way they reminded me of bent warped oars, battered spades and blunted pickaxes. On every figure was written hard, unremitting toil that had twisted their frames, seamed and puckered their leathern faces, made their hands horny, bleached their grizzled locks. My fancy had to run back along years and years of labour before it could arrive at the original boy or girl.

Still, they were cheerful-looking after a sort, content and loquacious withal. The man took off his bonnet, the woman dropped her courtesy, before pouring into the Landlord's ear how the wall of the house wanted mending, how a neighbour's sheep had come into the corn, had been *driven* into the corn out of foul spite and envy it was suspected, how new seed would be required for next year's sowing, how the six missing fleeces had been found in the hut of the old soldier across the river and all the other items which made up their world.

And the Landlord, his black hound couched at his feet, would sit down on a stone, or lean against the turf wall and listen to the whole of it and consult as to the best way to repair the decaying house and discover how defendant's sheep came into complainant's corn and give judgement and promise new seed to old Donald and walk over to the soldier's and pluck the heart out of the mystery of the missing fleeces.

And in going in and out amongst his people, his functions were manifold. He was not Landlord only – he was leech, lawyer, divine. He prescribed medicine, he set broken bones and tied up sprained ankles; he was umpire in a hundred petty quarrels and damped out wherever he went every flame of wrath. Nor, when it was needed, was he without ghostly counsel. On his land he would permit no unbaptized child; if Donald was drunk and brawling at a fair, he would, when the inevitable headache and nausea were gone, drop in and improve the occasion, to Donald's much discomfiture and his many blushes; and with the bed-ridden woman or the palsied man, who for years had sat in the corner of the hut as constantly as a statue sits within its niche, he held serious conversations and uttered words which come usually from the lips of a clergyman.

We then went through the cottages on the cultivated hill-side and there another series of *levees* were held. One cotter complained that his neighbour had taken advantage of him in this or the other matter: another man's good name had been aspersed by a scandalous tongue and ample apology must be made, else the sufferer would bring the asperser before the sheriff. Norman had borrowed for a day Neil's plough, had broken the shaft and when requested to make a reparation, had refused in terms too oppro-brious to be repeated. The man from Sleat who had a year or two ago come to reside in these parts and with whom the world had gone prosperously, was minded at next fair to buy another cow – would he therefore be allowed to rent the croft which lay alongside that which he already possessed?

To these cotters the Landlord gave attentive ear, standing beside the turf dike, leaning against the walls of their houses, sitting down inside in the peat smoke – the children gathered in the farthest corner regarding him with no awe. And so he came to know all the affairs of his people – who was in debt, who had money in the bank; and going daily amongst them he was contin-ually engaged in warning, expostulation, encouragement, rebuke. When he found that argument had no effect on the obstinate or the pig-headed, he suddenly changed his tactics and descended in a shower of *chaff*, which is to the Gael an unknown and terrible power, dissolving opposition as salt dissolves a snail.

The last cotter seen, the last *levee* held, we then climbed up to the crown of the hill to visit the traces of an old fortication, or *dun*, as the Skye people call it. These ruins – and they are thickly scat-tered over the island – are supposed to be of immense antiquity;

so old, that Ossian may have sung in each to a circle of Fingalian chiefs. When we reached the *dun* – a loose congregation of mighty stones, scattered in a circular form, with some rude remnants of an entrance and a covered way – we sat down and the Landlord lighted a cheroot.

Beneath lay the little village covered with smoke. Far away to the right, Skye stretched into ocean, pale headland after headland. In front, over a black wilderness of moor, rose the conical forms of Macleod's Tables and I thought of the 'restless bright Atlantic plain' beyond, the endless swell and shimmer of watery ridges, the clouds of seabirds, the sudden glistening upheaval of a whale and its disappearance, the smoky trail of a steamer on the horizon, the tackling of a white-sailed craft. On the left there was nothing but moory wilderness and hill, with something on a slope flashing in the sunshine like a diamond. A falcon palpitating in the intense blue above, the harehound cocked her ears and looked out alertly, the Landlord with his field-glass counted the sheep feeding on the hillside a couple of miles off. Suddenly he closed the glass and lay back on the heather, puffing a column of white smoke into the air.

'I suppose,' said I, 'your going in and out amongst your tenants today is very much the kind of thing you used to do in India?'

'Exactly. I know those fellows, every man of them – and they know me. We get on very well together. I know all their secrets, all their family histories, everything they wish and everything they fear. I think I have done them some good since I came amongst them.'

'But,' said I, 'I wish you to explain to me your system of penal servitude, as you call it. In what respect do the people on the cultivated hillside differ from the people in the black ground behind the village?'

'Willingly. But I must premise that the giving away of money in charity is, in nine cases out of ten, tantamount to throwing money into the fire. It does no good to the bestower: it does absolute harm to the receiver. You see I have taken the management of these people into my own hands. I have built a schoolhouse for them – on which we will look in and overhaul on our way down – I have built a shop, as you see, a smithy and a mill. I have done everything for them and I insist that, when a man becomes my tenant, he shall pay me rent. If I did not so insist I should be doing an injury to myself and to him.

'The people on the hillside pay me rent; not a man Jack of them is at this moment one farthing in arrears. The people down there in the black land behind the village, which I am anxious to reclaim, don't pay rent. They are broken men, broken sometimes by their own fault and laziness, sometimes by culpable imprudence, sometimes by stress of circumstances. When I settle a man there I build him a house, make him a present of a bit of land, give him tools, should he require them and set him to work. He has the entire control of all he can produce. He improves my land and can, if he is industrious, make a very comfortable living. I won't have a pauper on my place: the very sight of a pauper sickens me.'

'But why do you call the black lands your penal settlement?'

Here the Landlord laughed. 'Because, should any of the crofters on the hillside fall into arrears, I transport him at once. I punish him by sending him among the people who pay no rent. It's like taking the stripes off a sergeant's arm and degrading him to the ranks; and if there's any spirit in the man he tries to regain his old position. I wish my people to respect themselves and to hold poverty in horror.'

'And do many get back to the hillside again?'

'Oh, yes! and they are all the better for their temporary banishment. I don't wish residence there to be permanent in any case. When one of these fellows gets on, makes a little money, I have him up here at once among the rent-paying people. I draw the line at a cow.'

'How?'

'When a man by industry out of self-denial has saved money enough to buy a cow, I consider the black land is no longer the place for him. He is able to pay rent and he must pay it. I brought

an old fellow up here the other week and very unwilling he was
to come. He had bought himself a cow and so I marched him up
here at once. I wish to stir all these fellows up, to put into them a
little honest pride and self-respect.'

'And how do they take your system?'

'Oh, they grumbled a good deal at first and thought their lines
were hard; but discovering that my schemes have been for their
benefit, they are content enough now. In these black lands, you
observe, I not only rear corn and potatoes, I rear and train men,
which is the most valuable crop of all. But let us be going. I wish
you to see my scholars. I think I have got one or two smart lads
down here.'

In a short time we reached the schoolhouse, a plain, substan-
tial-looking building, standing midway between the inn and the
banished huts. As it was arranged that neither schoolmaster nor
scholar should have the slightest idea that they were to be visited
that day, we were enabled to see the school in its ordinary aspect.
When we entered the master came forward and shook hands with
the Landlord, the boys pulled their red forelocks, the girls dropped
their best courtesies. Sitting down on a form I noted the bare
walls, a large map hanging on one side, the stove with a heap of
peats near it, the ink-smeared bench and the row of girls' heads,
black, red, yellow and brown, surmounting it and the boys, barefooted and in tattered kilts, gathered near the window.

The girls regarded us with a shy, curious, gaze which was not
ungraceful; and in several of the freckled faces there were the
rudiments of beauty, or of comeliness at least. The eyes of all,
boys as well as girls, kept twinkling over our persons, taking silent
note of everything. I don't think I ever before was the subject of
so much curiosity. I was pricked all over by quick-glancing eyes
as pins.

We had come to examine the school and the ball opened by
a display of copybooks. Opening these, we found pages covered
with *Emulation is a generous passion* and *Emancipation does not
make man*, in very fair and legible handwriting. Expressing our

satisfaction, the schoolmaster bowed low and the prickling of thirty or forty curious eyes became yet more keen and rapid. The schoolmaster then called for those who wished to be examined in geography – very much as the colonel might seek volunteers for a forlorn hope – and in a trice six scholars, kilted, of various ages and sizes, were drawn up in a line in front of the large map. A ruler was placed in the hand of a little fellow at the end who, with his eyes fixed on the schoolmaster and his body bent forward eagerly, seemed as if waiting the signal to start off in a race.

'Number one, point out the river Tagus.'

Number one charged the Peninsula with his ruler as ardently as a great-grandfather in all probability charged the French at Quebec.

'Through what country does the Tagus flow?'

'Portugal.'

'What is the name of the capital city?'

'Lisbon'

Number one having accomplished his mission, the ruler was handed on to number two, who traced the course of the Danube and answered several questions thereanent with considerable intelligence. Numbers three and four acquitted themselves creditably, number four boggling a little about Constantinople, much to the vexation of the schoolmaster; number five was a little fellow who was asked to point out Portree and, as the Western Isles hung too high in the north for him to reach, he jumped at them, went into the North Sea the first time but, on his second attempt, he smote Skye with his ruler very neatly. After satisfactory number six, slates were produced and the six geographers – who were the cream of the school, I daresay – were prepared for the arithmetical action.

As I was examiner and had no desire to get into deep waters, the efforts of my kilted friends were, at my request, confined to the good old rule of simple addition. The schoolmaster called out ten or eleven ranks of figures and then cried, 'Add.' Six swishes of the slate pencil were heard and then began the arithmetical tug of war. Each face was hidden behind a slate and we could hear the quick tinkle of pencils. All at once there was a hurried swish and the redhead, who had boggled about Constantinople, flashed round his slate on me with the summation fairly worked out. Flash went another slate, then another, till the six were held out. All the answers corresponded and totting up the figures I found them correct.

Then books were procured and we listened to English reading. In a loud tone of voice, as if they were addressing someone on an opposite hillside and with barbarous intonation, the little fellows read off about a dozen sentences each. Now and again a big word brought a reader to grief, now and again a reader went through a word, but on the whole, they deserved the commendation which they received.

The Landlord expressed his satisfaction and mentioned that he had left at the inn two baskets of gooseberries for the scholars. The schoolmaster again bowed; and although the eyes of the scholars were as bright and curious as before, they had laid their heads together and were busily whispering now.

The schools in Skye bear the same relationship to the other educational establishments of the country that a turf hut bears to a stone-and-lime cottage. These schools are scattered thinly up and down the Island and the puplis are unable to attend steadily on account of the distances they have to travel and the minor agricultural occupations in which they are at intervals engaged. The schoolmaster is usually a man of no surpassing intelligence or acquirement: he is wretchedly remunerated and his educational aids and appliances, such as books, maps etc., are defective. But still, a turf hut is better than no shelter and a Skye school is better than no school at all.

The school, for instance, which we had just visited, was an authentic light in the darkness. There boys and girls were taught reading, writing and ciphering – plain and homely accomplishments it is true, but accomplishments that bear the keys of all doors that lead to wealth and knowledge. The boy or girl who can read, write and cast up accounts deftly, is not badly equipped for the battle of life; and although the school which the Landlord has established is plain and unostentatious in its forms and modes of instruction, it at least with tolerable success, teaches these. For the uses made of them by the pupils in after life, the pupils are themselves responsible.

Orbost and Dunvegan

PUNCTUALLY AT NINE next morning there was a grating of wheels on the gravel and Malcolm and his dog-cart were at the door. My good friend Fellowes, who had left Greshornish for a few days tramping the hills the day before I arrived from the south, had not yet returned and so I was to explore this region without awaiting him. After a little delay I took my place on the vehicle and we drove off. Malcolm was a thick-set, good-humoured, red-haired and whiskered little fellow, who could be silent for half a day if needed, but who could speak and speak to the point, too, when required. When driving and especially when the chestnut mare exhibited any diminution of speed, he kept up a running fire of ejaculations. 'Go on,' he would say, as he shook the reins, for the whip he mercifully spared, 'what are you thinking about?' 'Hoots! chit, chit, chit! I'm ashamed of you!' 'Now then. Hoots!' and these reproaches seemed to touch the mare's heart, for at every ejaculation she made a dash forward as if the whip had touched her.

On the way from Greshornish to Dunvegan, about a couple of miles from the latter place, a road branches off to the right and runs away downward through the heathery waste; and about forty yards onward we came to a bridge spanning a gully and into this gully three streams leap and become one and then the sole stream flows also to the right with shallow fall and brawling rapid, the companion of the descending road. The road up to the bridge is steep, but it is steeper beyond and at the bridge Malcolm jumped down and walked alongside with the reins in his hands.

In the slow progression my eye naturally followed the road and the stream; and beyond the flank of a hill sloping gradually down to the purple gloom of undulating moorland, I caught a glimpse of a bit of blue sea, some white broken cliffs that drop down to it; and, leaning on these cliffs, a great green sunny strath, with a white dot of a house upon it. The glimpse of sea and white cliffs and stretch of sunny greenness is pleasant; the hill, which we had yet to climb, kept the sun from me and all around were low heathery eminencies. I stared at the far-off sunlit greenness and, having satisfied myself therewith, began to examine the ground above and on either side of the bridge and found it possessed of much pastoral richness and variety. The main portion was covered with heather, but near me there were clumps of ferns and further back were soft banks and platforms of verdure on which kine might browse and ruminate and which only required the gilding of sunshine to make them beautiful.

'What bridge is this?' I asked of Malcolm, who was still trudging alongside with the reins in his hand.

'The Fairy Bridge.' And then I was told that the fairy sits at sunset on the green knolls and platforms of pasture chirming and singing songs to the cows; and that when a traveller crosses the bridge and toils up the hill, she is sure to accompany him.

As this was our own course, I asked, 'Is the fairy often seen now?'

'Not often. It's the old people who know about her. The shepherds sometimes hear her singing when they are coming down the hill; and years ago, a pedlar was found lying across the road up there, dead; and it was thought that the fairy had walked along with him. But, indeed, I never saw or heard her myself – only, that is what the old people say.' And so, in a modern dog-cart, I was slowly passing through one of the haunted places in Skye!

I fancy Malcolm must have seen that this kind of talk interested me. 'Did you ever hear, sir, about the Battle of the Spoiling of the Dikes down at Trompton Kirk, yonder?' and he pointed with his whip to the yellow-green strath which broke down in cliffs to the sea.

I answered that I never had and Malcolm's narrative flowed on at once.

'You see, sir, there was a feud between the Macdonalds of the Mainland and the Macleods of Trotternish; and one Sunday, when the Macleods were in church, the Macdonalds came at full of tide, unknown to anyone and fastened their boats to the arched rocks on the shore – for it's a strange coast down there, full of caves and natural bridges and arches. Well, after they had fastened their boats, they surrounded the church, secured the door and set it on fire. Everyone was burned that Sunday, except one woman, who squeezed herself through a window – it was so narrow that she left one of her breasts behind her – and escaped carrying the news. She raised the country with her crying and the sight of bloody clothes. The people – although it was Sunday – rose, men and women and came down to the burning church and there the battle began.

'The men of Macleod's country fought and the women picked up the blunted arrows, sharpened them on the stones and then gave them to the men. The Macdonalds were beaten at last and made for their boats. But by this time it was ebb of tide; and what did they see but the boats in which they had come and which they had fastened to the rocky arches, hanging in the air! Like an otter, when its retreat to the sea is cut off, the Macdonalds turned on the men of Macleod's country and fought till the last of them fell and in the sheughs of the sand their blood was running down red into the sea.

'At that time the tide came further in than it does now and the people had built a turf dike to keep it back from their crops. Then they took the bodies of the Macdonalds and laid them down side by side at the foot of the dike and tumbled it over on the top of them. That was the way they were buried. And after they had tumbled the dike they were vexed, for they minded then that the sea might come in and destroy their crops. That's the reason that the battle is called the Battle of the Spoiled Dikes.'

'The men of Macleod's country would regret the spoiling of the dikes, as Bruce the battleaxe with which, on the evening before Bannockburn and in the seeing of both armies, he cracked the skull of the English knight who came charging down upon him,' said I. But undiverted by my remark, Malcolm went on.

'Maybe, sir, you have seen the Sgurr of Eigg as you came past in the steamer?'?

'Yes and I know the story. The Macdonalds were cooped up in a cave and the Macleods ranged over the island and could find no trace of them. They then in high dudgeon returned to their boats, meaning to depart next morning. There was a heavy fall of snow during the night, was there not? and just when the Macleods were about to sail, the figure of a man, who had come out to see if the invaders were gone, was discerned on the top of the Sciur, against the sky line. The Macleods returned and by the foot-prints in the snow they tracked the man to his hiding place. They then heaped up the hearth and what timber they could procure, at the mouth of the cave, applied fire and suffocated all who had therein taken shelter. Is that not it?'

'The Macdonalds first burned the church at Trumpan down there. The bones of the Macdonalds are lying in the cave to this day, they say. I should like to see them.'

'But don't you think it was a dreadful revenge? Eigg was one of the safest places of the Macdonalds; and the people in the cave were chiefly old men, women and children. Don't you think it was a very barbarous act, Malcolm?'

'I don't know,' said Malcolm; 'I am a Macleod myself.'

By the time I had heard the story of Lady Grange, who sleeps in the Trumpan churchyard, we had toiled pretty well up the steep ascent. On our way we heard no fairy singing to the kine, nor did any unearthly figure accompany us. Perhaps the witchery of the setting sun was needed. By the time we reached the top of the hill the pyramidical forms of Macleod's Tables were distinctly visible and then Malcolm took his seat beside me in the dog-cart.

Macleod's Tables, two hills as high as Arthur's Seat, flat at the top as any dining table in the country, covered deep into spring by a tablecloth of snow; Macleod's Maidens, three spires of rock rising sheer out of the sea, shaped like women, around whose feet the foamy wreaths are continually forming, fleeting and disapearing – what magic in the names of rocky spire and flat-topped hill to him who bears the name of Macleod and who can call them his own! What is modern wealth compared to that old inheritance of land which bears your name, around which legends gather? The Tables and the Maidens remain for ever bearing the name, while the individual Macleod is a transitory as the mist wreath of the morning which melts on the one, on the momentary shape of the windblown foam which perishes on the base of the other.

'That's Orbost, sir, the house under the hill,' said Malcolm, pointing with his whip and obviously tired of the prolonged silence, 'and yonder on the left are the Cuchullins. The sea is down there, but you cannot see it from this. We'll be there in half an hour,' and exactly in half an hour, with Macleod's Tables behind us, we passed the garden and the offices and alighted on the daisied sward before the house.

After I had wandered about for an hour I made up my mind that, had I the choice, I should rather live at Orbost than at any other house in Skye. And yet, at Orbost, the house itself is the only thing that can reasonably be objected to. In the first place, it is one of those elegant expressionless houses in the Italian style which are found in the suburban districts of large cities and as such it is quite out of keeping with the scenery and the spiritual atmosphere of the island. It is too modern and villalike. It has a dandified look and, as it has not taken to the island, the island has not taken to it.

Around the trees have not grown well; they are mere stunted trunks, bare, hoary, wind-writhen. There is not a lichen or discoloration on its smoothly-chiselled walls; not a single chimney or gable has been shrouded with affectionate ivy. It looks like a house which has 'cut' the locality and which the locality has 'cut' in return.

In the second place, the house is stupidly situated. It turns a cold shoulder on the grand broken coast; on the ten miles of sparkling sea on which the sun is showering millions of silver coins, ever a new shower as the last one disappears; on Rum, with a veil of haze on its highest peak; on the lyrical Cuchullins – for although of the rigidest granite, they always give me the idea of passion and tumult; on the wild headlands of Bracadale, fading one after the other, dimmer and dimmer into distance; on all this the house turns a cold shoulder and on a meadow on which some dozen colts are feeding and on a low strip of moory hill beyond, from which the cotters draw their peats, it stares intently with all its doors and windows.

Right about face. Attention! That done, the most fastidious could object to nothing at Orbost, on the point of beauty at least. The faces of the Skye people, continually set like flints against assaults of wind and rain, are all lined and puckered about the eyes; and in Skye houses I naturally wish to see something of the same weather-beaten look. Orbost, with its smooth front and unwinking windows, outrages the fitness of things.

Of the interior no-one can complain; for on entering I was at once surrounded by a proper antiquity and venerableness. The dining-room is large and somewhat insufficiently lighted and on the walls hang two of Raeburn's half-lengths and several portraits of ladies with obsolete waists and head-dresses and military gentlemen in the uniform of the last century. The furniture is dark and massy; the mahogany drawing depth and colour from age and usage; the carpet has been worn so bare that the pattern had become nearly obliterated. The room was not tidy, I was pleased to see. A small table placed near the window was covered with a litter of papers; in one corner were guns and fishing rods and a fishing basket laid near them on the floor; and the round dusty mirror above the mantlepiece – which had the curious faculty of reducing my size, so that in its depth I saw myself as it were at a considerable distance – had spills of paper stuck between its gilded frame and the wall. From these spills of paper I concluded that the house was the abode of a bachelor who occasionally smoked after dinner – which, indeed, was the case, only the master of the house was from home at the time of my visit.

In the drawing room, across the lobby, hooped ladies of Queen Anne's time might have sat and drunk tea out of the tiniest china cups. The furniture was elegant, but it was the elegance of an ancient beau. The draperies were rich, but they had lost colour, like a spinster's cheek. In a corner stood a buffet with specimens of cracked china. Curious Indian ornaments and a volume of *Clarissa Harlowe* and another of the *Poetical Works* of Mr Alexander Pope, lay on the central table. Had the last reader left them there?

In a dusky corner a piano stood open, but the ivory keys had grown yellow and all richness of voice had been knocked out of them by the fingertips of dead girls. I touched them and heard the metallic complaint of ill-usage, of old age, of utter loneliness and neglect. I thought of Ossian and the flight of the dark-brown years. It was the first time they had spoken for long. The room, too, seemed to be pervaded by a scent of withered rose leaves, but whether this odour lived in the sense or the imagination, it would be useless to enquire.

Orbost lies pleasantly to the sun and in the garden I could almost fancy Malvolio walking cross-gartered – so trim it was, so sunnily sedate, so formal, so ancient-looking. The shadow on the dial told the age of the day, clipped boxwood ran along every walk. Trees, crucified to the warm brick walls, stretched out long arms on which fruit was ripening. The bee had stuck his head so deeply into a rose that he could hardly get it out again and so with the leaves he impatiently buzzed and fidgeted. And then I was not without sharp senses of contrast: out of the sunny warmth and floral odours I lifted my eyes and there were Macleod's Tables rising in an atmosphere of fable; and up in the wind above me, turning now and again its head in alert outlook, skimmed a snow-white gull, weary of dancing on the surges of sea.

Orbost stands high above the sea and if you wish thoroughly to enjoy yourself, you must walk down the avenue – as I did – to the stone seat placed on the road which winds along the brow of the broken cliffs and which, by many a curve and a bend, reaches the water level at about a quarter of a mile's distance, where there is a boathouse and boats lying keel uppermost or sideways and a stretch of yellow sand on which the tide flows, creamy line after creamy line.

From where I sat the ground breaks down first in a wall of cliff, then in huge boulders as big as churches, thereafter in bushy broken ground with huts perched in the coziest places, each hut swathed in the loveliest films of blue smoke; and all through this broken ground there are narrow winding paths along which a cow was being gingerly driven down and a wild Indian-looking girl was bringing water from some cool spring beneath. Here I quietly enjoyed the expanse of dazzling sea, a single sail breaking the restless scintillations; far Rum asleep on the silver floor; and, caught at a curious angle, the Cuchullin hills – reminding me of some stranded iceberg, splintered, riven, many-ridged, which the sun in all his centuries has been unable to melt. In midday light they had a curiously hoary look and I noticed that in the higher corries there were long streaks of snow.

On the right, beyond the boathouse, a great hill, dappled with brown and olive like a seal's back and traversed here and there by rocky terraces, breaks in precipices down to the sea line; and between it and the hill on which I was sitting and which slopes upward behind, I saw the beginning of a deep glen, in its softness and greenness suggesting images of pastoral peace, the bringing home of rich pails by milkmaids, the lowing of cattle in sober ruddy sunsets.

'What glen is that, Malcolm?'

'Oh, sir, it just belongs to the farm.'

'Is there a house in it?'

'No, but there's the ruins of a dozen.'

'How's that?'

'Ye see, the old Macleods liked to keep their cousins and second cousins about them; and so Captain Macleod lived at the mouth of the glen and Major Macleod at the top of it and Colonel Macleod over the hill yonder. If the last trumpet had been blown at the end of the French war, no-one but a Macleod would have risen out of the churchyard at Dunvegan. If you want to see a chief nowadays, you must go to London for him. Ay, sir, Dun Kenneth's prophecy has come to pass – "In the days of Norman, son of the third Norman, there will be a noise in the doors of the people and wailing in the house of the widow; and Macleod will not have so many gentlemen of his name as will row a five-oared boat around the Maidens!" The prophecy has come to pass and the Tables are no longer Macleod's – at least, one of them is not.'

After wandering about Orbost we resumed our seats in the dog-cart and drove to Dunvegan Castle.

As we drew near Dunvegan we came down on one of those sinuous sea-lochs which – hardly broader than a river – flow far inland and carry mysteriousness of sight and sound, the gliding sail, the seabird beating high against the wind, to the door of the shepherd, who is half a sailor among his bleating flocks. Across the sea and almost within hail of my voice, a farm and outhouses looked embattled against the sky. Along the shore, as we drove, were boats and nets and here and there little clumps and knots of houses. People were moving about on the roads intent on business. We passed a church, a merchant's store, a post office; we were plainly approaching some village of importance; and on the right hand the chestnuts, larches and ashes which filled every hollow and covered every rolling slope, gave sufficient indication that we were approaching the castle.

In the centre of these woods we turned up a narrow road to the right along which ran a wall and stopped at a narrow postern door. Here Malcolm rang a bell – the modern convenience grating somewhat on my preconceived notions of an approach to the old keep; if he had blown a horn I daresay I should have felt better satisfied – and in due time we were admitted by a trim damsel.

The bell was bad, but the brilliant garden into which we stepped was worse – soft level lawns, a huge star of geraniums, surrounded at proper distances by half-moons and crescents of calceolarias rimmed with lobelias. The garden was circled by a large wall, against which fruit trees were trained.

In thinking of Dunvegan my mind had unconsciously become filled with desolate and Ossianic images, piled and hoary rocks, the thistle waving its beard in the wind, flakes of sea-spray flying over all – and behold I rang a bell as if I were in Regent Street and by a neat damsel was admitted into a garden that would have done no disservice to Kensington!

After passing the garden we entered upon space of wild woodland, containing some finer timber and romance began to revive. Malcolm then led me to an outhouse and pointed out a carved stone above the doorway, on which were quartered the arms of the Macleods and the Macdonalds. 'Look there,' said he, 'Macleod has built the stone into his barn which should have been above his fireplace in his dining room.'

'I see the bull's head of Macleod and the galley of Macdonald – were the families in any way connected?'

'Oftener by a bloody dirk than by a gold marriage ring. But with all their quarrellings they intermarried more than once. Dunvegan was originally a stronghold of the Macdonalds.'

'Indeed! and how did the Macleods get possession?'

'I'll tell you that,' said Malcolm. 'Macdonald of Dunvegan had no son, but his only daughter was married to Macleod of Harris and a young chief was growing up in Macleod's castle. The Macdonalds, knowing that when the old man was dead, they would have no-one to lead them to battle, were pondering whom they should elect as chief; and at the same time, Macleod's lady was just as anxiously pondering by what means her son should sit in Dunvegan. Well, while all this thinking and scheming was going on secretly in Skye and Harris, Macdonald, wishing to visit Macleod, ordered his barge and rowers to be in readiness and pushed off. Macleod, hearing that his father-in-law was coming, went out in his barge to meet him halfway and to escort him to his castle with all honour.

'Macleod's barge was bigger and stronger than Macdonald's and held a greater number of rowers; and while his men were pulling, the chief sat in the stern steering and his wife sat by his side. When they got into mid-channel a heavy mist came down, but still the men pulled and still Macleod steered. All at once Macleod found that he was running straight on his father-in-law's barge and just when he had his hand on the helm to change the course and avoid striking, his wife gripped him hard and whispered in his ear, "Macleod, Macleod, there's only that barge betwixt you and Dunvegan." Macleod took the hint, steered straight on, struck and sunk Macdonald's barge in the mist and sailed for Dunvegan, which he claimed in the name of his son. That is the way, as the old people tell, that Macleod came into possession here.'

Then we strolled along the undulating paths and at a sudden turn there was the ancient keep on its rock, a stream brawling down close at hand, the tide far withdrawn, the long shore heaped with dulse and tangle and the seamews above the flagstaff, as the jackdaws fly above the cathedral towers in England. It was gray as the rock on which it stood – there were dark tapestries of ivy on the walls, but at first glance it was disappointingly modern looking towards the Bass and waving a matted beard of lichens in the sea wind and began to draw disadvantageous comparisons. The feeling was foolishness and on a better acquaintance with the building it wore off. Dunvegan is inhabited and you cannot have well-aired sheets, a well-cooked dinner and the venerableness of ruin. Comfort and decay are never companions.

Dunvegan is perhaps the oldest inhabited building in the country, but the ancient part is of small extent. One portion of it, it is said, was built in the ninth century. A tower was added in the fifteenth, another portion in the sixteenth and the remainder by different hands and at regular intervals since then. No inconsiderable portion is unquestionably modern. The old part of the castle looks toward the sea and entrance is obtained by a steep and narrow archway – up which, perhaps, came Macleod of Harris after he sunk the barge of his father-in-law in the misty Minch. In a crevice in the wall, which forms one side of this entrance, a well was recently discovered; it had been built up – no man knows for how long – and when tasted, the water was found perfectly sweet and pure. In the old days of strife and broil it may have cooled many a throat thirsty with siege.

The most modern portion of the building, I should fancy, is the present frontage which, as I approached it by the bridge which solidly fills up the ravine, was not without a certain grandeur and nobility of aspect. The rock on which the castle stands is surrounded on three sides by the sea; and fine as the old pile looked at ebb of tide, I could fancy how much its appearance would be improved with all that far-stretching ugliness of sand and tangle obliterated and the rock swathed with the azure and silence of ocean. To sleep in a bedroom at Dunvegan must be like sleeping in a bedroom in fairyland. I might hear a mermaid singing beneath my window and, looking out into the moonlight, behold, rising from the glistening swells, the perilous beauty of her breasts and hair.

After viewing the castle from various points, we boldly advanced across the bridge and rang the bell. After waiting some little time, we were admitted by a man who – the family at the time being from home – seemed the only person in possession. He was extremely polite, volunteered to show us all over the place and regretted that in the prolonged absence of his master the carpets and furniture in the 'drawing room' had been lifted. The familiar English *patois* sounded strange in the castle of a Macleod!

On his invitation we entered an unfurnished hall with galleries running to left and right and on the wooden balustrades of one of these galleries the great banner of Macleod was dispread – a huge white sheet on which the arms and legend of the house were worked in crimson. Going upstairs we passed through spacious suites of rooms, carpetless and with the furniture piled up in the centre and covered with an awning – through every window obtaining a glimpse of blue loch and wild Skye headland. In most cases the family pictures were left hanging, some fine, others sorry daubs enough, yet all interesting as suggesting the unbroken flow of generations. The rooms were spacious, but from their unfurnished and dismantled condition there arose a sort of Ossianic desolation, which, comfortless as it must have been to a permanent dweller, did not fail to yield a certain gloomy pleasure to the imagination of this visitor of an hour.

Passing up and down stairs in the more ancient portion of the castle, the man in possession showed us the dungeons in which the Macleods immured their prisoners. I had fancied that these would have been scooped out of the rock on which the castle stood. Whether such existed I cannot say; but by candlelight I peered into more than one stony closet let into the mighty wall – the entrance of which the garments of the lady must have swept every night as she went to bed – where the captured foemen of the family were confined. Perhaps the near contiguity of the prisoner, perhaps the sweeping of garments past the dungeon door, perhaps the chance-heard groan or clank of manacle, constituted the exquisite zest and flavour of revenge.

Men keep their dearest treasures near them; and it might be that the neighbourhood of the wretch he hated – so near that the sound of revel could reach him at times – was more grateful to Macleod than his burial in some faraway vault, perhaps to be forgotten. Who knows! It is difficult to creep into the hearts of those old sea-kings.

If I mistake not, one of the dungeons is at present used as a wine cellar. So the world and the fashion of it changes! Where the Macleod of three centuries ago kept his prisoner, the Macleod of today keeps his claret. From which of its uses the greatest amount of satisfaction has been derived would be a curious speculation.

By a narrow spiral stair we reached the most interesting apartment in Dunvegan – the Fairy Room, in which Sir Walter Scott slept once. This apartment is situated in the ancient portion of the building, it overlooks the sea and its walls are of enormous thickness. From its condition I should fancy that no-one has slept there since Sir Walter's time. In it there was neither bedspread nor chair and it seemed a general lumber room. The walls were hung with rusty broadswords, dirks, targes, pistols, Indian helmets; and tunics of knitted steel were suspended on frames, but so rotten with age and neglect that a touch frayed them as if they had been woven of worsted. There were also carved scimitars and curiously-hafted daggers and two tattered regimental flags – that no doubt plunged through battle-smoke in the front of charging lines. Moth-eaten volumes were scattered about amid a chaos of rusty weapons, cruses and lamps. In one corner lay a huge oaken chest with a chain wound round it, but the lid was barely closed and through the narrow aperture a roll of paper protruded, docketed in clerky hand and with faded ink – accounts from 1715 till some time at the close of the century – in which doubtless some curious items were embedded.

On everything lay dust and neglect of years. The room itself was steeped in a half twilight. The merriest sunbeam became grave as it slanted across the corroded weapons in which there was no answering gleam. Cobwebs floated from the corners of the walls – the spiders which wove them having died long ago of sheer age. To my feeling it would have been almost impossible to laugh in the haunted chamber and if I had done so I would likely have been startled by a strange echo, as if something mocked me. There was a grave-like odour in the apartment. I breathed dust and decay.

Seated on the wooden trunk round which the chain was wound, while Malcolm with his hand thrust in the hilt of a broadsword was examining the notches on its blade, I inquired, 'Is there not a magic flag kept at Dunvegan? The flag was the gift of a fairy, if I remember the story rightly.'

'Yes,' said Malcolm, making a cut at an imaginary foeman and then hanging the weapon up on the wall, 'but it is kept in a glass case and never shown to strangers at least when the family is from home.'

'How did Macleod come into possession of the flag, Malcolm?'

'Well, the old people say that one of the Macleods fell in love with a fairy and used to meet her at the green hill out there, Macleod promised to marry her; and one night the fairy gave him a green flag, telling him that, when either he or one of his race was in distress, the flag was to be waved and relief would be certain. Three times the flag might be waved; but after the third time it might be thrown into the fire, for the power would have gone all out of it. I don't know, indeed, how it was, but Macleod deserted the fairy and married a woman.

'Is there anything astonishing in that? Would you not rather marry a woman than a fairy yourself?'

'Maybe, if she was a rich one like the woman Macleod married,' said Malcolm with a grin. 'But when the fairy heard of the marriage she was in a great rage whatever. She cast a spell over Macleod's country and all the women brought forth dead sons and all the cows brought forth dead calves. Macleod was in great tribulation. He would soon have no young men to fight his battles and his tenants would soon have no milk or cheese wherewith to pay their rents. The cry of his people came to him as he sat in his castle and he waved the flag and next day over the country there were living sons and living calves. Another time, in the front of a battle, he was sorely pressed and nigh being beaten, but he waved the flag again and got the victory and a great slaying of his enemies.'

'Then the flag has not been waved for the third time and last time?'

'No. At the time of the potato failure, when the people were starving in their cabins, it was thought that he should have waved it and stopped the rot. But the flag stayed in its case. Macleod can only wave it once now; and I'm sure he's like the man with his last guinea in his pocket – he does not like to spend it. But maybe, sir, you would like to climb up to the flagstaff and see the view.'

We then left the haunted chamber, passed through the dismantled room in which the portraits hung and ascended the narrow spiral stair – the walls of which, whether from sea-damp, or from a peculiarity of the lime used in building, were covered with glistening scurf of salt – and finally emerged on the battlemented plateau from which the flagstaff sprang. The huge mast had fallen a month or two previously and was now spliced with rope and propped with billets of wood. A couple of days before the catastrophe, a young fellow from Cambridge, Malcolm told me, had climbed to the top – lucky for him it did not fall then, else he and Cambridge had parted company for ever.

From our airy perch the outlook was wonderfully magnificent. From the breast of the hill which shut out everything in one direction, there rolled down on the castle billow on billow of many-coloured foliage. The garden through which we had passed an hour before was but a speck of bright colour. The little toy village sent up its pillars of smoke. There was the brown stony beach, the boats, the ranges of nets, the sinuous snake-like loch and the dark far-stretching promontories asleep on the sleekness of summer sea. With what loveliness of shining blue the sea flowed in everywhere, carrying silence and the foreign-looking bird into inland solitudes, girdling with its glory the rock on which the chief's castle had stood for ten centuries and at the door of the shepherd's sheiling calling on the brown children with the voices of many wavelets, to come down and play with them on crescents of yellow sand!

Driving homeward, I enquired, 'Does the Laird live here much?'

'No, indeed,' said Malcolm. 'he lives mainly in London.'

And thereupon I thought how pleasant it must be for a man to escape from the hollow gusty castle with its fairy flag which has yet to be waved once, its dungeons, its haunted chambers, its large gaunt rooms, with portraits of men and women from whom he had drawn his blood, its traditions of revenge and crime – and take up his abode in some villa at breezy Hampstead, or classic Twickenham, or even in some half-suburban residence in the neighbourhood of Regent's Park. Were I the possessor of a haunted, worm-eaten castle, around which strange stories float, I should fly from it as I would from a guilty conscience and in the whirl of vivid life lose all thoughts of my ancestors. I should appeal to the present to protect me from the past. I should go into Parliament and study blue books and busy myself with the better regulation of alkali works and the drainage of Stoke Poges. No ancestor could touch me *then*.

'It's a strange old place, Dunvegan,' said Malcolm, as we drove down by the Fairy Bridge, 'and many strange things have happened in it. Did you ever hear, sir, how Macdonald of Sleat – Donald Gorm, or Blue Donald, as he was called – stayed a night with Macleod of Dunvegan at a time when there was a feud between them?'

'No; but I shall be glad to hear the story now.'

'Well,' Malcolm went on, 'on a stormy winter evening, when the walls of Dunvegan were wet with the rain of the cloud and the spray of the sea, Macleod, before he sat down to dinner, went out to have a look at the weather. "A giant's night is coming on, my men," he said when he came in, "and if Macdonald of Sleat were at the foot of my rock seeking a night's shelter, I don't think I could refuse it." He then sat down in the torchlight at the top of the long table, with his gentlemen around him. When they were half-through with their meal a man came in with the news that the barge of Macdonald of Sleat – which had been driven back by stress of weather on its way to Harris – was at the foot of the rock and that Macdonald asked shelter for the night for himself and his men.

"They are welcome," said Macleod; "tell them to come in." The man went away and in a short time Macdonald, his piper and his bodyguard of twelve came in, wet with spray and rain and weary with rowing. Now on the table there was a boar's head – which is always an omen of evil to a Macdonald – and noticing the dish, Donald Gorm with his men about him sat at the foot of the long table, beneath the salt and away from Macleod and the gentlemen. Seeing this, Macleod made a place beside himself and called out, "Macdonald of Sleat, come and sit up here!" "Thank you," said Donald Gorm, "I'll remain where I am; but remember that wherever Macdonald of Sleat sits, that's the head of the table."

'So when dinner was over, the gentlemen began to talk about their exploits in hunting and their deeds in battle and to show each other their dirks. Macleod showed his, which was very handsome and it passed down the long table from gentleman to gentleman, each one admiring it and handing it to the next one, till at last it came to Macdonald, who passed it on, saying nothing. Macleod noticed this and called out, "Why don't you show your dirk, Donald; I hear it's very fine?" Macdonald then drew his dirk and, holding it up in his right hand, called out, "Here it is, Macleod of Dunvegan and in the best hand for pushing it home in the four and twenty islands of the Hebrides."

'Now Macleod was a strong man, but Macdonald was stronger and so Macleod could not call him a liar; but thinking he would be mentioned next, he said. "And where is the next best hand for pushing a dirk home in the four and twenty islands?"

"*Here*," cried Donald Gorm, holding up his dirk in his left hand and brandishing it in Macleod's face, who sat amongst his gentlemen biting his lip with vexation.

'Now it so happened that one of the body guard of twelve had a sweetheart in the castle, but he had no opportunity of speaking to her. But once when she was passing the table with a dish she put her mouth to the man's ear and whispered, "Bid your master beware of Macleod. The barn you sleep in will be red flame at midnight and ashes in the morning." The words of the sweetheart passed the man's ear like a little breeze, but he kept the colour of his face and looked as if he had heard nothing. So when Macdonald and his men got into the barn, where fresh heather had been spread for them to sleep on, he told the words which had been whispered in his ear.

'Donald Gorm then saw the trick that was being played and led his men quietly out by the back door, down to a hollow rock which stood up against the wind and there they sheltered themselves. By midnight the sea was red with the reflection of the burning barn and the morning broke on gray ashes and smouldering embers. The Macleods thought they had killed their enemies; but fancy their astonishment when Donald Gorm with his bodyguard marched past the castle down to the foot of the rock, where his barge was moored, with his piper playing in front – 'Macleod, Macleod, Macleod of Dunvegan, I drove my dirk into your father's heart and in payment of last night's hospitality I'll drive it to the hilt in your son's yet." '

'Macleod of Dunvegan must have been a great rascal,' said I; 'and I hope he got his deserts.'

'I don't know, indeed,' said Malcolm; 'but if Donald Gorm caught him he could hardly miss.' He then added, as if in deprecation of the idea that any portion of ignominy was attachable to him, 'I am not one of the Dunvegan Macleods; I come from the Macleods of Raasay.'

Duntulm

THE LANDLORD'S HOUSE had been enveloped for several days in misty rain, which began just as Fellowes returned from his tramping. It did not pour straight down, it did not patter on door and window, it has no action as it has in the south. An immense quantity of moisture was held in the atmosphere and it descended in a soft, silent, imperceptible drizzle. It did not seem so very bad when looked out on from the window, but when I once ventured on the gravel I was wet to the skin in a trice. White damp vapours lay low on the rising grounds where the sheep fed: white damp vapours hid the tops of the larches which sheltered the house from the south-west winds. Heaven was a wet blanket and everything felt its influence.

During the whole day Maida lay dreaming on the rug before the fire. The melancholy parrot moped in its cage and at intervals attacked the lump of white sugar between the wires, or suspended itself, head downwards and eyed us askance. The horses stamped and pawed in their stables. The drenched peacock which, but a few days before was never weary displaying his starry tail, was a lesson on the instability of human glory. It sat on the garden seat, a mere lump of draggled feathers and as gray as a hedge-sparrow.

The Landlord shut himself up in his own room, writing letters against the departure of the Indian mail. We read novels and yawned and made each other miserable with attempts at conversation – and still the clouds hung low on hill and rising ground and large plantation, like surcharged sponges; and still the drizzle came down mercilessly, until the world was sodden and was rapidly becoming sponge-like too.

On the fourth day we went upstairs, threw ourselves on our beds, dead beat and fell asleep, till we were roused by the gong for dinner. Thrusting my face hurriedly into a basin of cold water, tidying dishevelled locks, I got down when the soup was being taken away and was a good deal laughed at. Somehow the spirits of the party seemed lighter; the despotism of rain did not weigh so heavily on them; I felt almost sportively inclined myself; and just at the conclusion of dessert, when wine had circulated once or twice, there was a flush of rosy light on the panes. I went at once to the window and there was the sun raying out great lances of splendour and armies of fiery mist lifting from the hills and streaming upwards. The westward-ebbing loch was sleek gold, the wet trees twinkled, every puddle was sun-gilt. I looked at the barometer and saw the mercury rising like hope in a man's breast when fortune smiles on him. The curtains were drawn back to let the red light fully into the room.

'I like to see that fiery smoke on the hills,' said the Landlord, 'it's always a sign of fine weather setting in. Now it won't do for you fellows to lie up here like beached boats doing nothing. You must be off after tiffin tomorrow. I'll give you letters of introduction, a dog-cart and a man and in a week or so come back and tell me what you think of Duntulm, and Quirang. You must rough it you know. You mustn't be afraid of a shower, or of getting your feet wetted in a bog.'

And so next day after tiffin, the Landlord sent us off into the wilds, as a falconer might toss his hawk into the air.

The day was fine, the heat was tempered by a pleasant breeze, great white clouds swam in the blue void and every now and again a shower came racing across our path with a sunbeam at its heel. We drove past the village, past the huts that ran along the top of the cultivated hillside, dropped down on Skeabost and the stream with the island of graves and in due time reached the solitary schoolhouse at the junction of the roads. Turning to the left here, we drove along the east shore of Loch Snizort, up stages of easy ascent and then, some four or five miles on, left the Parliamentary Road and descended on Kingsburgh.

I pointed out to Fellowes the ruins of the old house, spoke to him of the Prince, Flora Macdonald, Dr Johnson and Boswell. After sauntering there for a quarter of an hour, we walked down to the present house with its gables draped with ivies and its pleasant doors and windows scented with roses and honeysuckles. To the gentleman who then occupied the farm we bore a letter from the Landlord, but, on inquiring, found that he had gone south on business a couple of days previously. This gentleman was a bachelor, the house was tenanted by servants only and of course at Kingsburgh we could not remain.

This was a disappointment; and as we walked back to the dog-cart, I told my companion of a pleasant ten days I had wasted there three or four summers since. I spoke to him of the Kingsburgh of that time – the kindly, generous Christian Highland gentleman; of his open door and frank greeting, warm and hospitable; of the pleasant family, so numerous, so varied; the grandmother, made prisoner to an easy chair, yet never fretful, never morose his sisters, one a widow, one a spinster; his brave soldier nephew from India; his pretty nieces, with their English voices and their English wild-rose bloom; of his sons, deep in the *Gorilla Book* and to whose stories and the history of whose adventures and exploits grandmamma's ears were ever open. I spoke too of the guests that came and went during my stay; the games of croquet on the sunny lawn, the picnics and excursions, the books read in the cool twilight of the moss-house, the smoking parliament held in the stables on rainy days, of the quiet cigar in the open air before going to bed. 'Twas the pleasantest fortnight I ever remember to have spent; and before I had finished telling my companion all about it we had taken our seats in the dog-cart and were pretty well on the way to Uig.

Uig is distant from Kingsburgh about five miles; the road is high above the sea and, as we drove along, we beheld the northern headlands of Skye, the wide blue Minch and Harris, rising like a cloud on the horizon; and as the day was fine, we enjoyed the commerce of sea and sky, the innumerable tints thrown by the clouds on the watery mirror, the mat of glittering light spread beneath the sun, the gray lines of showers on the distant promontories, the tracks of air currents on the mobile element between. The clouds pass from shape to shape – what resembles a dragon one moment resembles something else the next; the promontory which was obscure ten minutes ago is now yellow-green in sunlight; the watery pavement is tesselated with hues, but with hues that continually shift and change. In the vast outlook there is utter silence, but no rest. What with swimming vapour, obscure showers that run, vagrant impulses of wind, sunbeams that gild and die in gilding, the vast impressionable floor outspread – the sight we beheld when we toiled up the steep road from Kingsburgh to Uig was full of motion.

Just when we reached the highest part of the road we came in view of the Bay of Uig. We were high above it as we drove along; the ground is equally high on the other side and, about a mile inland, on a great sandy beach, the tide was rolling in long white lines that chased each other. On the deep water outside the tidal lines a yacht was rocking. There is a mansion house with a flagstaff on the shore and at the top of the bay are several houses, a church and a schoolhouse, built of comfortable stone and lime. When the Minch is angry outside, washing the headlands with spray, Uig is the refuge which the fisherman and the coaster seek. When once they have entered its rocky portals they are safe.

The road now descends towards the shore; there is an inn midway, low-roofed, dimly-lighted, covered with thatch – on the whole perhaps the most unpromising edifice in the neighbourhood.

Here we pulled up. Already we had driven some twenty-five miles and as we wished to push on to Duntulm that evening, we were anxious to procure a fresh horse. The keen air has whetted our appetites and we were eager for dinner, or what substitute for dinner could be provided. Our driver unharnessed the horse and we entered a little room, spotlessly clean, however and knocked with our knuckles on the deal table.

When the red-haired handmaiden entered, we discovered that the Uig bill of fare consisted of bread and butter, cheese, whisky, milk and hard-boiled eggs – and a very satisfactory bill of fare we considered it too. There is no such condiment as hunger honourably earned by exercise in the open air. When the viands were placed before us we attacked them manfully. The bread and butter disappeared, the hard-boiled eggs disappeared, we flinched not before the slices of goats'-milk cheese; then we made equal division of the whisky, poured it into bowls of milk and drank with relish.

While in the middle of the feast the landlord entered – he wore the kilt, the only person almost whom I had seen wearing it in my sojourn in the island – to make arrangements relative to the fresh horse. He admitted that he possessed an animal, but as he possessed a gig and eke a driver, it was his opinion that the three should go together. To this we objected, stating that as we already had a vehicle and a driver and as they were in no wise tired, such a change as he suggested would be needless. We told him also that we meant to remain at Duntulm for one night only and that by noon of the following day we would be back at his hostelry with his horse.

The landlord seemed somewhat moved by our representations and just when victory was hanging in the balance the brilliant idea struck my companion that he should be bribed with his own whisky. At the rap on the deal table the red-haired wench appeared, the order was given and in a trice a jorum of mountain dew was produced. This decided matters, the landlord laid down the arms of argument and after we had solemnly drunk each other's health he went out for the fresh horse and in a quarter of an hour we were all right and slowly descending the steep hillroad to Uig.

We drove through the village, where a good deal of building seemed to be going on and then began to climb the hillroad that rose beyond it. Along the hillside this road zigzagged in such a curious manner, ran in such terraces and parallel lines, that the dog-cart immediately beneath us – our machine heading east, the other west – would take ten minutes before it reached the point at which we passed over it. At last we reached the top of the wavy ascent, passed through a mile or two of moory wilderness, in which we met a long string of women bringing home creels of peat and then in the early sunset descended the long hillside which led to Kilmuir.

Driving along we had Mugstot pointed out to us – a plain white dwelling on our left in which Macdonald lived after he had vacated Duntulm and while Armadale was yet building. About this place, too, the Parliamentary Road stopped. No longer could we drive along smoothly as on an English turnpike. The pathway now was narrow and stony and the dog-cart bumped and jolted in a most distressing manner. During the last hour, too, the scenery had changed its character. We were no longer descending a hillside on which the afternoon sun shone pleasantly. Our path still lay along the sea, but above us were high cliffs with great boulders lying at their feet; beneath us and sloping down to the sea level, boulders lay piled on each other and against these the making tide seethed and fretted.

The sun was setting on the Minch and the irregular purple outline of Harris was distinctly visible on the horizon. For some time back we had seen no house, nor had our path been crossed by a single human being. The solitariness and desolation of the scenery affected me. Everything around was unfamiliar and portentous. The road on which we drove was like a road in the *Faerie Queene*, along which a knight might prick in search of perilous adventure. The chin of the sun now rested on the Minch, the overhanging cliffs were rosy and the rocky road began to seem interminable. At last there was a sudden turn and there, on a little promontory, with shattered wall and loophole against the red light, stood Duntulm – the castle of all others that I most wished to see.

Going down the rocky road, the uncomfortable idea crept into our minds that Duntulm, to whom we bore a letter of introduction from the Landlord, might – like the owner of Kingsburgh – have gone south on business. We could hardly have returned to Uig that night and this thought made yet more rigid the wall of rosy cliff above us and yet more dreary the seethe of the Minch amongst the broken boulders beneath. As suspense was worse than certainty, we urged on the Uig horse and in a short time, with the broken castle behind us, drew up at the house.

Duntulm had seen us coming and when we alighted he was at the door, his face hospitable as a fire in wintertime and his outstretched hand the best evidence of good wishes. In a moment the bald red cliffs and the homeless seething of the Minch among the broken stones faded out of my memory. We mentioned our names and proffered the letter of introduction.

'There is no need,' said he, as he thrust the epistle into his pocket, 'civility before ceremony. Having come you are of course my guest. Come in. The letter will tell me who you are soon enough.' And so we were carried into the little parlour till our bedrooms were got ready and then we went upstairs, washed our hands and faces, changed our clothes and came down for tea. When we entered the parlour, the tea-urn was hissing on the table and with our host sat a photographer – bearded as all artists of the present day are – who had been engaged during the afternoon on Flora Macdonald's grave.

When tea was over we were carried into another room where were materials placed for the brewing of punch. Through the window I behold spectral castle, the sea on which the light was dying, the purple fringe of Harris on the horizon. And seated there, in the remotest corner of Skye, amongst people whom I had never seem, girt by walls of cliffs and the sounding sea, in a region, too, in which there was no proper night, I confess to have been conscious of a pleasant feeling of strangeness, of

removal from all customary conditions of thought and locality, which I like at times to recall and enjoy over again. Yet I
am almost certain that the strange feeling was heightened to
no inconsiderable extent by the peculiar spirit bottle on the
table. This bottle was pale green in colour, was composed of two
hollow hemispheres like a sand-glass, the mouthpiece surmounting the upper hemisphere to the lower sprang four hollow arms,
through which the liquid coursed, giving the bottle a curiously
square appearance. I had never seen such a bottle before and I
suppose till I go back to Duntulm I am not likely to see its like.
Its shape was peculiar and that peculiarity dovetailed into the
peculiarity of everything else. We sat there till the light had died
out on the sea and the cloud had come down on Harris and then
the candles were brought in.

But the broken tower of Duntulm still abode in my memory
and I began to make inquiries concerning it. I was told that it was
long the seat of the Macdonalds, but that after the family had been
driven out of it by the ghost of Donald Gorm, they removed to
Mugstot.

'Donald Gorm!' I said, 'were they driven out by the restless
spirit of the Donald who flouted Macleod at his own table at
Dunvegan – who, when he was asked to show his dirk, held it
up in the torchlight in the face of Macleod and of his gentlemen,
with the exclamation, "here it is, Macleod of Dunvegan and in
the best hand for pushing it home in the four and twenty islands
of the Hebrides?"!'

'They were driven away by the spirit of the same Donald,'
said our host. 'That chieftain had been stricken by a lingering
yet mortal illness and removed to Edinburgh and placed himself
under the care of the leeches there. His body lay on a sickbed in
Edinburgh, but his spirit roamed about the passages and galleries
of the castle. The people heard the noises and the slamming of
doors and the waving of tartans on the staircases and did not know
that it was the spirit of their sick master that troubled them. It was
found out, however. The servants were frightened out of their

wits and declared that they would no longer abide in the castle. At last a young man, from Kilmuir over there, said that if they would provide him with a sword and a Bible and plenty to eat and drink, he would sit up in the hall all night and speak to the apparition. His offer was accepted and he sat down to supper in the great hall with his sword drawn and his Bible open on the table before him. At midnight he heard doors open and close and the sound of footsteps on the stairs and before he knew where he was, there was Donald Gorm, dressed in tartan as if for feast or battle, standing on the floor and looking at him.

' "What do you want of me, Donald?" ' said the young man.

' "I was in Edinburgh last night,' said the spirit, "and I am in my own castle tonight. Don't be afraid, man; there is more force in the little pebble which you chuck away from you with your finger and thumb than there is in my entire body of strength. Tell Donald Gorm Og . . ." '

'Donald's son, you know,' interpolated the photographer.

' ". . . tell Donald Gorm Og to stand up for the right against might, to be generous to the multitude, to have a charitable hand stretched out to the poor. Woe's me! woe's me! I have spoken to a mortal and must leave the castle tonight," and so the ghost of Donald vanished and the young man was left sitting in the hall alone. Donald died in Edinburgh and was buried there; but after his death, as during his life, his spirit walked about here until the family was compelled to leave. It was a fine place once, but it has been crumbling away year by year and is now broken and hollow like a witch's tooth. The story I have told you is devoutly believed by all the fisherman, herdsmen and milkmaids in the neighbourhood. I think Mr Maciver, the clergyman at Kilmuir, is the only person in the neighbourhood who has no faith in it.'

This ghost story the photographer capped by another and when that was finished we went to bed.

Next morning we went out to inspect the old castle and found it a mere shell. Compared with its appearance the night before, when it stood in relief against the red sky, it was strangely unimpressive; a fragment of a tower and a portion of flanking wall stood erect; there were traces of building down on the slope near the sea, but all the rest was a mere rubble of fallen masonry. It had been despoiled in every way; the elements had worn and battered it, the people of the district had for years made it a quarry and built out of it dwellings, outhouses and dikes – making the past serve the purposes of the present. Sheep destined for the London market were cropping the herbage around its base. While we were loitering about the ruins the photographer came up and, under his guidance, we went to visit Kilmuir churchyard, in which Flora Macdonald rests. We went along the stony road down which we had driven the night previously – the cliffs lately so rosy, gray enough now and the seethe of the fresh sea amongst the boulders and shingle beneath rather exhilarating than otherwise. After a walk of about a couple of miles we left the road, climbed up a grassy ascent and found the churchyard there, enclosed by a low stone wall.

Everything was in hideous disrepair. The gate was open, the tombstones were broken and defaced and above the grave of the heroine nettles were growing more luxuriously than any crop I had yet the good fortune to behold in the island. Skye has only one historical grave to dress – and she leaves it *so*.

On expressing our surprise to the photographer, he told us that a London sculptor passing that way and whose heart burned within him at the sight, had offered at several dinner tables in the district to execute a bronze medallion of the famous lady, gratis, provided his guests would undertake to have it properly placed and to have a fitting inscription carved upon the pedestal.

'The proposal was made, I know,' said the photographer, 'for the sculptor told me about it himself. His proposal had not been taken up, nor is it likely to be taken up now. The country which treats the grave of a heroine after that fashion is not worthy to have a heroine. Still,' he went eyeing the place critically, with his head a little to one side, 'it makes a picturesque photograph as it stands – perhaps better than if it were neat and tidy.' We plucked a nettle from the grave and then returned to Duntulm to breakfast.

Shortly after breakfast our dog-cart was at the door and, followed by Duntulm and the photographer in a similar machine, we were on our way to Quirang. A drive of a couple of hours brought us to the base of the singular mountain. Tilting our vehicles, leaving the horses to roam about picking the short grass and carrying with us materials for luncheon on the crest, we began the ascent. The day was fine, the sky cloudless and in an hour we were toiling past the rocky spire of the needle and in fifteen minutes thereafter, we reached the flat green plateau on the top. Here we lunched and sang songs and made mock heroic speeches in proposing each other's health. I had ascended the Quirang before, but could hardly recognise it now under such different atmospherical conditions. Then every stone was slippery, every runnel a torrent, the top of the needle lost in flying mist, everything looking spectral, weird and abnormal. On the present occasion, we saw it in fair sunlight; and what the shattered precipices lost in terror they gained in beauty.

Reclining on the soft green grass – strange to find grass so girdled by fantastic crags – we had, through fissures and the rents of ancient earthquake, the loveliest peeps of the map-like underworld swathed in faint sea azure. An hour, perhaps, we lay there; and then began the long descent. When we reached the dog-carts we exchanged a parting cup and then Duntulm and the photographer returned home and we hied on to Uig.

Arriving at Uig we dined – the bill of fare identical with that on the preceding day; the hard-boiled eggs only a shade harder boiled perhaps; and then having settled with the kilted landlord – the charge wonderously moderate – we got out our own horse and, with the setting sun making splendid the Minch behind us, we started for Portree. It was eleven p.m. before we reached the little town, the moon was shining clearly, a stray candle or two twinkling in the houses and when we reached the hotel door, the building was lighted up – it had been a fair day, the prices for cattle were good and, over whisky punch, farmer and drover were fraternising.

M'Ian Again

NEXT MORNING, IN the soft sky was the wild outline of the Cuchullins, with which we were again to make acquaintance. Somehow these hills never weary, I never become familiar with them, intimacy can no more stale them than it could the beauty of Cleopatra. From the hotel door I regarded them with as much interest as when, from the deck of the steamer off Ardnamurchan ten years ago, I first beheld them with their clouds on the horizon.

While at breakfast in the public room, farmer and drover dropped in – the more fiery-throated drinking pale ale instead of tea. After breakfast we were again in the dog-cart driving leisurely toward Sligachan – the wonderful mountains beyond gradually losing tenderness of morning hue and growing worn and hoary, standing with sharper edges against the light, becoming rough with rocky knob and buttress and grayly wrinkled with ravines. When we reached the inn we found it full of company, bells continually jangling, half a dozen machines at the door and a party of men in knickerbockers starting with rods and fishing baskets. Here we returned the dog-cart to the Landlord and began to address ourselves to the desolate glen stretching between the inn and Camasunary.

In Glen Sligachan, although sight of the Cuchullins proper was lost, we were surrounded by their outlying and far-radiating spurs. The glen is some eight miles in length and is wild and desolate beyond conception. Walking along, too, the reticulations of the hills are picked out with that pale greenish tint, which I had noted as characteristic of the hills seen from Lord

Macdonald's deer forest. There is no proper path and we walked in the loose debris of torrents; and in Glen Sligachan, as in many other parts of Skye, the scenery curiously repelled me and drove me in on myself. I had a quickened sense of my own individuality. The enormous bulks, their gradual recedings to invisible crests, their utter movelessness, their austere silence, daunted me. I was conscious of their presence, and I hardly dared speak lest I be overheard. I couldn't laugh. I would not crack a joke for the world. Glen Sligachan would be the place to do a little bit of self-examination in.

I do not know what effect mountains have on the people who live in them continually, but this stranger they make serious and grave at heart. Through this glen we trudged silently enough and when two-thirds of the distance had been accomplished, it was with a feeling of relief that a lake was descried ahead. The sight of anything mobile, of an element that could glitter and dimple and dance, took away from the sense of the stony eternities, gray and wrinkled as with the traces of long-forgotten passion, listening forever, dumb forever.

After rounding the lake, which splashed merrily on its margin and clambering over a long waste of boulder, we saw as we ascended a low flank of Blaavin, the Bay of Camasunary, the house and the very boat which M'Ian had borrowed on the day we went to visit Loch Coruisk, below us. The tobacco-less man was nowhere visible and I marvelled whether his messenger had yet returned from Broadford.

When we got to the top of the hill we had to descend the slope to Kilmaree; and as on my return from Loch Coruisk I had come down pleasantly under the guidance of M'Ian, I fancied, naturally enough, that I could act as a guide on the present occasion. But there is a knack in descending hills as there is in everything else. First of all, I lost the narrow footpath at the top; then as we were bound to reach Loch Eishart and as Loch Eishart lay below us distinctly visible, I led directly for it; but somehow we were getting continually on the wrong bank of a pestilent stream which, through chasm and ravine, found its way to the sea by apparently the most circuitous of courses.

This stream we forded a dozen times at the least and sometimes in imminent danger of a ducking. It was now late in the afternoon and the weather had changed. The tops of the hills began to be lost in mist and long lines of sea fog to creep along the lower grounds. There was at intervals a slow drizzle of rain. Fetching a cunning circuit, as I supposed, we found the inevitable stream again in our front and got across it with difficulty – happily for the last time. After we had proceeded about a hundred yards we came upon the lost pathway and in fifteen minutes thereafter we were standing upon the shore of the loch watching the flying scud of the Atlantic mist and the green waves rolling underneath with their white caps on.

The question now arose – by what means could we reach Mr M'Ian? There was no ferry at Kilmaree, but sundry boats were drawn up on the shore and a couple were bobbing on the restless water at the stony pier. There were the boats certainly enough, but where were the boatmen? In the neighbourhood men could surely be obtained who, for a consideration, would take us across. We directed our steps to the lodge at Kilmaree, which seemed untenanted and after some little trouble penetrated into the region of the offices and outhouses. Here we found a couple of men chopping sticks and to them my companion – who as a man of business and learned in the law was the spokesman on such occasions – addressed himself.

'You want to go over to Mr M'Ian's tonight?' said the elder, desisting from his task and standing up with his axe in his hand.

'Yes, we are particularly anxious to get across. Can you take us?'

'I don't know; you see we are no' ferrymen an' if we take you across we must leave our work.'

'Of course you must; but we'll pay you for your trouble.'

Here the two men exchanged a sentence or two of Gaelic and then the elder wood-chopper asked, 'Do you know Mr M'Ian?'

'Oh yes, we know him very well.'

'Does he expect you this night?'

'No; but we are anxious to see him and he will be glad to see us.'

'I'm no sure we can take you across,' said the man hesitatingly; 'you see the master is from home an' the wind is rising an' we're no' ferrymen an' we'll need to borrow a boat an' . . .' here he hesitated still more, '. . . it would cost you something.'

'Of course it will. What will you expect?'

'Wad you think ten shillings too much?'

'No, we'll give you ten shillings,' said Fellowes, clinching the bargain.

'And,' said I, coming in like a swift charge of lancers on a half-disorganised battalion and making victory complete, 'we'll give you a glass of spirits at the house, too, when you get across.'

The men threw down their axes, put on their jackets, which hung on the walls and, talking busily in Gaelic, led the way to the little stony pier where the boats were moored.

'There's a gale rising,' said one of the men, as he pulled in a boat to the pier by a rope, 'an' it'll no' be easy taking you across and still harder to get back ourselves.'

As, however, to this expression of opinion we made no response, the men busied themselves with getting the boat to rights, testing the rollock pins, rolling in stones for ballast, examining the sail and ropes and suchlike matters. In a short time we took our seats and then the men pulled slowly out to sea in the opposite direction from Mr M'Ian's house in order to catch the wind, which was blowing freshly inland. The course of the boat was then changed, the oars shipped, the sail shaken out and away we went through the green seas with long lurches, the foam gathering up high at the bows, hissing along the sides and forming a long white wake behind. The elder man sat with the rope of the sail in his hand and taking a shrewd squint at the weather at intervals. When not so engaged, he was disposed to be talkative.

'He's a fine gentleman, Mr M'Ian, a vera fine gentleman; an' vera good to the poor.'

'I understand,' I said, 'that he is the most generous of mankind.'

'He is that; he never lets a poor man go past his door without a meal. Maybe sir, ye'll be a friend o' his?'

'Yes, both of us are friends of his and friends of his son's too.'

'Maybe ye'll be a relation of his? He has many relations in the south country.'

'No,' I said, 'no relation, only a friend. Do you smoke?'

'Oh, yes, but I forgot my spleuchan.'

'I can provide you with tobacco,' I said and so, when his pipe was lighted, he became silent.

We were now two-thirds across and the white watery mists hung low on the familiar coast as we approached. Gradually the well-known objects became defined in the evening light – the clumps of birchwood, the huts seated on the shore, the house, the cliffs behind on which the clouds lay halfway down. When we drew near the stony quay we noticed that we were the subjects of considerable speculation. It was but seldom that a boat stood across from the Strathaird coast and by our glass we could see a group of the menservants standing at the corner of the black kitchen watching our movements and Mr M'Ian himself coming out with his telescope. When the keel grated on the peebles we got out.

'Now, my men,' said Fellowes, 'come up to the house and have your promised glass of spirits!'

To our astonishment the men declined; they could not wait, they were to go back immediately.

'But you must come,' said my companion, who acted as purser, 'for before I can pay you I must get Mr M'Ian to change me a sovereign. Come along.'

'We climbed up to the house and were welcomed by Mr M'Ian, father and son, in the ivy-coloured porch. 'By the way,' said Fellowes, 'I wish you to change me a sovereign, as we have ten shillings to pay these men.'

'Did the scoundrels charge that sum for bringing you over? It's extortion! Five shillings is quite enough. Let me go and speak to them.'

'But,' remonstrated Fellowes, 'we don't consider the charge immoderate; we made the bargain with them; and so anxious were we to be here that we would willingly have paid them double.'

'Don't talk to me,' cried M'Ian, as he put on his hat and seized his stick. 'Why, you rascals, did you charge these gentlemen ten shillings for taking them across the Loch? You know you are well enough paid if you get half.'

'Sir,' said the elder man respectfully, while both touched their bonnets, 'we'll just take what you please; just anything you like Mr M'Ian.'

'Don't you see the mischief you do and the discredit you bring on the country by this sort of thing? Every summer the big lying blackguard *Times* is crammed with complaints of tourists who have been cheated by you and the like of you – although I don't believe half the stories. These fools,' here the old gentleman made reference to us by a rapid backward chuck of his thumb, 'may go home to the south and write to the newspapers about you.'

'The bargain the gentlemen made was ten shillings,' said the man, 'but if you think we have asked too much we'll take six. But it's for your sake we'll take it, not for theirs.'

'They're honest fellows these,' cried the old gentleman, as he poured the coins into the palm of the elder man; 'Alick, bring out a dram.'

The dram, prefaced by a word or two of Gaelic, to which Mr M'Ian nodded, was duly swallowed and the men, touching their bonnets, descended to their boat. The old gentlemen led the way into the house and we had no sooner reached the porch than my companion remembered that he had left something and ran down to fetch it. He returned in a little while and in the course of the evening he gave me to understand that he had seen the boatmen and fully implemented his promise.

M'Ian Again

The wind had changed during the night and next morning broke forth gloriously – not a speck of vapour on the Cuchullins; the long stretch of Strathaird wonderfully distinct; the loch bright in sunlight. When we got down to breakfast we found Mr M'Ian alone. His son, he said, had been on the hill since four o'clock in the morning gathering the lambs together and that about noon he and his assistants would be branding them at the fank.

When breakfast was over – Fellowes having letters to write remained indoors – I and the old gentleman went out. We went up the glen and as we drew near the fank we saw a number of men standing about, their plaids thrown on the turfen walls, with sheepdogs couched thereupon; a thick column of peat smoke rising up, smelt easily at the distance of half a mile; no sheep were visible, but the air was filled with bleatings – undulating with the clear plaintive trebles of innumerable ewes and the hoarser *baa* of tups. When we arrived we found the narrow chambers and compartments at one end of the fank crowded with lambs, so closely wedged together that they could hardly move and between these chambers and compartments, temporary barriers erected, so that no animal could pass from one to the other.

The shepherds must have had severe work of it that morning. It was as yet only eleven o'clock and since early dawn they and their dogs had coursed over an area of ten miles, sweeping every hill face, visiting every glen and driving down rills of sheep toward this central spot. Having got the animals down, the business of assortment began. The most perfect ewes – destined to be mothers of the next brood of lambs on the farm – were placed in one chamber; the second best, whose fate it was to be sold at Inverness, were placed in a congeries of compartments, the one opening into the other; the inferior qualities – *shots*, as they are technically called – occupied a place by themselves: these also to be sold at Inverness, but at lower prices than the others.

The fank is a large square enclosure; the compartments into which the bleating flocks were huddled occupied about one half of the walled-in space, the remainder being perfectly vacant.

One of the compartments opened into this space, but a temporary barrier prevented all egress. Just at the mouth of this barrier we could see the white ashes and the dull orange glow of the peat fire in which some half-dozen branding irons were heating. When everything was prepared, two or three men entered into this open space. One took his seat on a large smooth stone by the side of the peat fire, a second vaulted into the struggling mass of heads and fleeces, a third opened the barrier slightly, lugged out a struggling lamb by the horns and consigned it to the care of the man seated on the smooth stone. This worthy got the animal dexterously between his legs, so that it was unable to struggle, laid its head down on his thigh, seized from the orange glow one of the red-hot heating irons and with a hiss and a slight curl of smoke, drew it in a diagonal direction across its nose. Before the animal was sufficiently branded the iron had to be applied twice or thrice. It was then released and trotted bleating into the open space, perhaps making a curious bound on the way as if in bravado, or shaking its head hurriedly as if snuff had been thrown into its eyes.

All day this branding goes on. The peat fire is replenished when needed; another man takes his seat on the smooth stone; by two o'clock a string of women bring up dinner from the house and all the while young M'Ian sits on the turfen wall, notebook in hand, setting down the number of the lambs and their respective qualities. Every farmer has his own peculiar brand and by it he can identify a member of his stock if it should go astray. The brand is to the farmer what a trademark is to a manufacturer. These brands are familiar to the drovers even as brands of wine and cigars are familiar to the connoisseurs in these articles. The operation looks a cruel one, but it is not perfectly clear that the sheep suffer much under it. While under the iron they are perfectly quiet – they neither bleat nor struggle – and when they get off they make no sign of discomfort save the high bound or the restless shake of the head. In a minute or so they are cropping herbage in the open space of the fank, or if the day is warm, lying down in the cool shadows of the walls as composedly as if nothing had happened.

Leaning against the fank walls we looked on for about an hour, by which time a couple of hundred lambs had been branded and then we went up the glen to inspect a mare and foal of which Mr M'Ian was specially proud. Returning in the direction of the house, the old gentleman pointed out what trenching had been done, what walls had been built in my absence and showed me on the other side of the stream what brushwood he meant to clear next spring for potatoes, what fields he would give to the people for their crops, what fields he would reserve for his own use. Flowing on in this way with scheme and petty detail of farm work, he suddenly turned round on me with a queer look in his face.

'Isn't it odd that a fellow like me, standing on the brink of the grave, should go pottering about day after day thinking of turnips and oats, tups and ewes, cows and foals? The chances are that the oats I sow I shall never reap – that I shall be gone before the blossom comes on my potatoes.'

The strangeness of it had often struck me before, but I said nothing.

'I suppose it is best that I should take an interest in these things,' went on the old gentleman. 'Death is so near me that I can hear him as if it were through a crazy partition. I know he is there. I can hear him moving about continually. My interest in the farm is the partition that divides us. If it were away I should be with him face to face.'

Mr M'Ian was perhaps the oldest man in the island and he did not dislike talking about his advanced age. A man at fifty-five, perhaps, wishes to be considered younger than he really is. The man above ninety has outlived that vanity. He is proud of the years he has numbered and in respect of his great age is singular amongst his fellows. After a little pause Mr M'Ian flowed on:

'I remember very well the night the century came in. My regiment was then lying in the town of Galway in Ireland. We were all at supper that evening at the quarters of Major M'Manus, our commanding officer. Very merry we were, singing songs and toasting the belles we knew. Well, when twelve o'clock struck the major rose and proposed in a flowing bowl the health of the stranger – the nineteenth century – coupled with the hope that it would be a better century than the other. I'm not sure that it has been a whit better, so far at least as it has gone. For thirty years I have been the sole survivor of that merry table.'

'Sixty-five years is a long time to look back, Mr M'Ian.'

The old gentleman walked on laughing to himself. 'What fools men are – doctors especially! I was very ill shortly after with a liver complaint and was sent to Edinburgh to consult the great doctors and professors there. They told me I was dying; that I had not many months to live. The fools! They are dead, their sons are dead and here I am, able to go about yet. I suppose they thought that I would take their stuffs.'

By this time we had reached the house. Mr M'Ian left his white hat and staff in the porch: he then went to the cupboard and took out a small spirit case in which he kept bitters cunningly compounded. He gave Fellowes and myself – Fellowes had finished his letters by this time – a tiny glassful, took the same amount himself. We then all went out and sat on a rocky knoll near the house which looked seaward and talked about Sir John Moore and Wellington till dinner time.

We stayed with the M'Ians for a couple of days and on the third we drove to Ardvasar to catch the steamer there that afternoon on its way to Portree.

When we reached the top of the glen and dropped down on the Parliamentary Road near the lake of waterlillies, we held our way to the right, toward the Point of Sleat. We passed the farm of Knock, the white outhouses, the church and schoolhouse, the old castle on the shore and, driving along, we could pleasantly depasture our eyes on the cultivated ground, with a picturesque hut perched here and there; the towering masses of the Knoydart hills and the Sound of Sleat between. Sleat is the best wooded, the sunniest and most carefully cultivated portion of the island; and passing along the road the traveller is struck with signs of blithe industry and contentment. As we drew near Armadale Castle it was hard to believe that we were in Skye at all. The hedges are as trim as English hedges, the larch plantations which cover the faces of the low hills that look towards the sea are not to be surpassed by any in the country. The Armadale home farm is a model of neatness, the Armadale porter lodges are neat and white; and when, through openings of really noble trees, we obtained a glimpse of the castle itself, a handsome modern-looking building rising from sweeps of closely-shaven lawn, I found it hard to believe that I was within a few miles of the moory desolation that stretches between Isle Oronsay and Broadford.

From far Duntulm Macdonald has come here and settled and around him to their very tops the stony hills laugh in green. Great is the power of gold. Bestow on land what gold can purchase, labour and of the stoniest aridity you make an emerald.

Ardvasar is situated about the distance of a mile from the Armadale plantations and counts perhaps some twenty houses. A plain inn stands by the wayside, where refreshments may be procured; there is a merchant's shop filled with goods of the most miscellaneous description; in this little place also resides a most important personage – the agent of the Messrs Hutcheson, who is learned in the goings and comings of the steamers. On our arrival we learned from the agent that the steamer on the present occasion would be unusually late, as she had not yet been sighted between Ardnamurchan and Eigg. In all probability she would not be off Ardvasar till ten p.m.

It is difficult to kill time anywhere; but at this little Skye clachan it is more difficult than almost anywhere else. We fed the horse and returned it and the dog-cart to Mr M'Ian. We sat in the inn and looked aimlessly out of the window; we walked along the ravine and saw the stream sleeping in brown pools and then hurrying on in tiny waterfalls; we watched the young barbarians at play in the wide green in front of the houses; we lounged in the merchant's shop; we climbed to the top of eminencies and looked seaward and imagined fondly that we beheld a streak of steamer smoke on the horizon. The afternoon wore away and then we had tea at the inn. By this time the steamer had been visible for some little time and had gone in to Eigg. After tea we carried our traps down to the stony pier and placed them in the boat which would convey us to the steamer when she lay to in the bay. Thereafter we spent an hour in watching men blasting a huge rock in a quarry close at hand. We saw the train laid and lighted, the men scuttling off and then there was a dull report and the huge rock tumbled quietly over in ruins.

When we got back to the pier, passengers were gathering: drovers with their dogs; ancient women in scarlet plaids and white caps, going on to Balmacara of Kyle; a sailor, fresh from China, dressed in his best clothes, with a slate-coloured parrot in a wicker cage, which he was conveying to some young people at Broadford. On the stony pier we waited for a considerable time and then Mr Hutcheson's agent, accompanied by some half-dozen men, came down in a hurry; into the boat we were all bundled – drovers, dogs, women, sailor, parrot and all, the boat shoved off, the agent stood up in the bow, the men bent to their oars and by the time we were twenty boat-lengths from the pier the *Clansman* had slid into the bay opposite the castle and lay to, letting off volumes of noisy steam.

When the summer night was closing the *Clansman* steamed out of Armadale Bay. Two or three ladies were yet visible on the deck. Wrapped in their plaids and with their dogs around them, drovers were smoking amidships; sportsmen in knickerbockers were smoking on the hurricane deck and from the steerage came at intervals a burst of canine thunder from the leashes of pointers and setters congregated there. As the night fell the air grew cold, the last lady disappeared, the sportsmen withdrew from their airy perches, amidships the pipe of the drover became a point of intense red. In the lighted cabin gentlemen were drinking whisky punch and discussing, as their moods went, politics, the weather, the fluctuations in the price of stock and the condition of grouse.

Among these we sat; and my companion fell into conversation with a young man of an excited manner and a restless eye. I could see at a glance that he belonged to the same class as my tobacco-less friend of Glen Sligachan. On Fellowes he bestowed his entire biography, made known to him the name of his family – which was, by the way, a noble one – volunteered the information that he had served in the Mediterranean squadron, that he had been tried by a court martial for a misdemeanour of which he was entirely guiltless and had, through the testimony of nefarious witnesses, been dismissed the service.

While all this talk was going on the steward and his assistants had swept away the glasses from the saloon table and from the oddest corners and receptacles were now drawing out pillows, sheets and blankets. In a trice everything became something else; the sofas of the saloon became beds, the tables of the saloon became beds, beds were spread on the saloon floor, beds were extemporised near the cabin windows. When the transformation had been completed and several of the passengers had coiled themselves comfortably in their blankets, the remainder struggling with their boots, or in various stages of dishabille, the ex-naval man suddenly called out 'Steward!'

That functionary looked in at the saloon door in an instant.

'Bring me a glass of brandy and water.'

'It's quite impossible, sir,' said the steward; 'the spirit room is shut for the night. Besides, you have had a dozen glasses of brandy and water today already. You had better go to bed, sir.'

'Didn't I tell you,' said the ex-naval man, addressing Fellowes, who by this time had got his coat and vest off; 'didn't I tell you what the whole world is in a conspiracy against me? It makes a dead set at me. That fellow now is great as great a foe of mine as was the commodore at Malta.'

Fellowes made no reply and got into bed. I followed his example. The ex-naval man sat gloomily alone for a while and then with the assistance of the steward he undressed and clambered into a cool berth beside one of the cabin windows. Thereafter the lights were turned low.

I could not sleep, however; the stifling air of the place, in which there lived a faint odour of brandy and hot water and the constant throb of the engines, kept me awake. I turned from one side to the other, till at last my attention was attracted by the movements of my strange friend opposite. He raised his head stealthily and took covert survey of the saloon; then he leant on his elbow; then he sat upright in his berth. That feat accomplished, he began to pour forth to some imaginary auditor the story of his wrongs.

He had not gone on long when a white-nightcapped head bounced up in a far corner of the dim saloon. 'Will you be good enough,' said the pale apparition in a severe voice, 'to go to sleep? It's monstrous, sir, that you should disturb gentlemen at this hour of the night by your nonsensical speeches.'

At the sight and the voice, the ex-naval man sank into his berth as suddenly as an alarmed beaver sinks into his dam and there was silence for a time.

Shortly, from the berth, I saw the ex-naval man's head rising as stealthily as the head of a blackcock above a bunch of rushes. Again he sat up in bed and again enumerated his peculiar griefs.

'Confound you, sir!'

'What do you mean, sir!'

And at the half-dozen white apparitions confronting him, the ex-naval man again dived. But in about ten minutes his head began again to stir. Never from ambush did Indian warrior rise more noiselessly than did the ex-naval man from his blankets. He paused for a little on his elbow, looked about him cautiously, got into a sitting position and began a third harangue.

'What the devil!'

'This is intolerable!'

'Steward, steward!'

'Send the madman on deck!'

M'Ian Again

And the saloon rose *en masse* against the disturber of its rest. The steward came running in at the outcry, but the ex-naval man ducked under like a shot and was snoring away in simulated slumber as if he had been all of the Seven Sleepers rolled into one. That night he disturbed our rest no more and shortly after I fell asleep.

A fierce trampling on deck and the noise of the crane hoisting the cargo from the deep recesses of the hold awoke me. I dressed and went above. The punctual sun was up and at his work. We were off a strip of sandy beach, with a row of white houses stretching along it and with low rocky hills behind the houses. Some half-dozen deeply-laden shore boats were leaving the side of the steamer. Then a cow was brought forward, a door was opened in the bulwarks and the animal quietly shoved out. Crummie disappeared with a considerable plunge and came to the surface somewhat scant of breath and with her mind in a state of utter bewilderment. A boat was in readiness; by a deft hand a coil of rope was fastened around the horns, the rowers bent to their task and crummie was towed ashore in triumph and on reaching it seemed nothing the worse of her unexpected plunge.

The noisy steam was then shut off; from the moving paddles great belts of pale-green foam rushed out and died away far astern; the strip of beach, the white houses with the low rocky hills behind, began to disappear and the steamer stood directly for Portree, which place was reached in time for breakfast. We then drove to the Landlord's and, on alighting, I found my friend John Penruddock marching up and down on the gravel in front of the house.

John Penruddock

PENRUDDOCK WAS RATHER a hero of mine. He was as tall, muscular and broad-shouldered as the men whom Kingsley delights to paint and his heart was as tender as his head was shrewd. He was the healthiest-minded man I have ever met in my walk through life – strong yet gentle, pious yet without the slightest tincture of cant or dogmatism. He was loyal and affectionate to his backbone: he stuck to his friends to the last. Pen was like the run of ordinary mortals while your day of prosperity remained, but when your night of difficulty fell, he came out like a lighthouse and sent you rays of encouragement and help.

Pen had farms in Ireland as well as in Skye and it was when on a visit to him in Ulster some years since that I became acquainted with his homely but enduring merits. For years I had not seen such a man. There was a reality and honest stuff in him, which in living with him and watching his daily goings-on revealed itself hour by hour, quite new to me. The people I had been accustomed to meet, talk with, live with, were different and tended towards art in one form or another. And there was a certain sadness somehow in the contemplation of them. Common to all their efforts was failure – in their pictures, in their books, in their own lives.

With Penruddock all was different. What he strove after he accomplished. He had a cheery mastery over circumstances. All things went well with him. His horses ploughed for him, his servants reaped for him, his mills ground for him, successfully. The very winds and dews of heaven were to him helps and aids. Year after year his crops grew, yellowed, were cut down and gathered into barns and men fed thereupon; and year after year there lay an increasing balance at his banker's. This continual, ever-victorious activity seemed strange to me – a new thing under the sun. We usually think that poets, painters and the like are finer, more heroical, than cultivators of the ground. But does the production of a questionable book really surpass in merit the production of a field of unquestionable turnips?

I like to recall my six weeks' sojourn in sunny Ulster with my friend. I like to recall the rows of white-green willows that bordered the slow streams; the yellow flax fields with their azure flowers, reminding me of the maidens in German ballads; the flax tanks and windmills; the dark-haired girls embroidering muslins before the doors and stealing the while the hearts of sheepish sweethearts leaning against the cottage walls, by soft blarney and quick glances; the field in which a cow, a donkey, half a dozen long-legged porkers – looking for all the world like pigs on stilts – cocks and hens, ducks and geese promiscuously fed; and, above all, I like to recall the somnolent Sunday afternoon in the little uncomfortably-seated Presbyterian church, when – two-thirds of the congregation asleep, the precentor soundest of all and the good clergyman illustrating the doctrine of the Perseverance of the Saints by a toddler at its mother's knee attempting to walk, falling and bumping its forehead, getting picked up and, in a little while, spurring and struggling to get to the floor again – my eye wandering to the open church door and in the sunshine saw a feeding bee fold its wings on a flower and swing there in the wind and I forgot for a while drawling shepherd and slumbering flock. These are trifles, but they are pleasant trifles. Staying with Pen, however, an event of importance did occur.

It was arranged that we should go to the fair at Keady; but Pen was obliged on the day preceding to leave his farm at Arranmore on matter of important business. It was a wretched day of rain and I began to tremble for the morrow. After dinner the storm abated and the dull dripping afternoon set in. While a distempered sunset flushed the west the heavy carts from the fields came rolling into the courtyard the horses fetlock-deep in clay and steaming like ovens. Then, at the sound of the bell, the labourers came, wet, weary, sickles hanging over their arms, yet with spirits merry enough.

These the capacious kitchen received, where they found supper spread. It grew dark earlier than usual and more silent. The mill-wheel rushed louder in the swollen stream and lights began to glimmer here and there in the dusty windows. Penruddock had not yet come; he was not due for a couple of hours. Time began to hang heavily; so slipping to bed I solved every difficulty by falling soundly asleep.

The lowing cattle, the bleating sheep, the barking of dogs and loud voices of men in the courtyard beneath, awoke me shortly after dawn. In the silence that followed I again fell asleep and was roused at last by the clangour of the breakfast bell. When I got up the sun was streaming gloriously through the latticed window; heaven was all the gayer and brighter for yesterday's gloom and sulky tears and the rooks were cawing and flapping cheerfully in the trees above. When I entered the breakfast room Pen was already there and the tea-urn was bubbling on the table.

At the close of the meal Tim brought the dog-cart to the door. Pen glanced at his watch. 'We have hit the time exactly and will arrive as soon as Mick and the cattle.' There was an encouraging chir-r-r, a flick of the whip and in a trice we were across the bridge and pegging along the highway at a great pace.

After proceeding about a mile, we turned into a narrow path which gradually led us into a wild irregular country. Cornfields, flax-tanks and sunny pasture lands, dotted with sheep, were left behind as uphill we tugged and reached at last a level stretch of pale moor and black peat bog. Sometimes for a mile the ground was black with pyramids of peat; other times the road wriggled before us through a dark olive morass, enlivened here and there with patches of treacherous green; the sound of our wheels startling into flight the shy and solitary birds native to the region.

Ever and anon, too, when we gained sufficient elevation, we could see the great waves of the landscape rolling in clear morning light away to the horizon; each wave crested with farms and belts of woodland and here and there wreaths of smoke rising up from hollows where towns and villages lay hid.

After a while the road grew smoother and afar the little town of Keady sparkled in the sun, backed by a range of smelting furnaces, the flames tamed by the sunlight, making a restless shimmer in the air and blotting out everything beyond. Beneath, the high road was covered with sheep and cows and vehicles of every description, pushing forward to one point; the hillpaths also which led down to it were moving threads of life.

On the brow of the hill, just before we began to descend, John pulled up for a moment. It was a pretty sight. A few minutes' drive brought us into Keady and such a busy scene I had never before witnessed. The narrow streets and open spaces were crowded with stalls, cattle and people and the press and confusion was so great that our passage to the inn where our machine was to be put up was a matter of considerable difficulty. Men, stripped to trousers and shirt, with red hair streaming in the wind, rushed backwards and forwards with horses, giving vent at the same time to the wildest vociferations, while clumps of sporting gentlemen, with straws in their mouths, were inspecting, with critical eyes, the points of animals.

Travelling auctioneers set up their little carts in the streets and with astonishing effrontery and power of lung harangued the crowd on the worth and cheapness of the articles which they held in their hands. Beggars were very plentiful – disease and deformity their stock-in-trade. Fragments of humanity crawled about on crutches. Women stretched out shrunken arms. Blind men rolled sightless eyeballs, blessing the passenger when a copper tinkled in their iron jugs – cursing yet more fervently when disappointed in their expectation. In one place a melancholy acrobat in dirty tights and faded tinsel was performing revolutions with a crazy chair on a bit of ragged carpet; he threw somersaults over it; he embraced it firmly and began spinning along the ground like a wheel, in which performance man and chair seemed to lose their individuality and become one as it were; and at the close of every feat he stood erect with that indescribable curve of the right hand which should always be followed by thunders of applause, the clown meanwhile rolling in ecstasies of admiration in the sawdust. Alas! No applause followed the exertions of the artist. The tights were getting more threadbare and dingy. His hollow face was covered with perspiration and there was but the sparsest sprinkling of halfpence. I threw him a shilling, but it rolled among the spectators' feet and was lost in the dust. He groped about in search of it for some little time and then came back to his carpet and his crazy chair. Poor fellow! He looked as if he were used to that kind of thing.

There were many pretty faces among the girls and scores of them were walking about in holiday dresses – rosy-faced lasses, with black hair and blue eyes shadowed by long dark eyelashes. How they laughed and how sweetly the brogue melted from their lips in reply to the ardent blarney of their sweethearts.

At last we reached an open square, or cross, as it would be called in Scotland, more crowded, if possible than the narrow streets. Hordes of cattle bellowed here. Here were sheep from the large farms standing in clusters of fifties and hundreds; there a clump of five or six, with the widow in her clean cap sitting beside them. Many an hour ago she and they started from the turf hut and the pasture beyond the hills. Heaven send her a steady sale and good prices! In the centre of this open space great benches were erected, heaped with eggs, butter, cheeses, the proprietors standing behind anxiously awaiting the advances of customers. One section was crowded with sweetmeat stalls, much frequented by girls and their sweethearts. Many a rustic compliment there had for reply a quick glance or a scarlet cheek. Another was devoted to poultry; geese stood about in flocks; bunches of hens were scattered on the ground, their legs tied together; and turkeys, enclosed in wicker baskets, surveyed the scene with quick eyes, their wattles all the while burning with indignation.

On reaching the inn which displayed for ensign a swan with two heads afloat on an azure stream, we ordered dinner at three o'clock and thereafter started on foot to where Penruddock's stock was stationed. It was no easy matter to force a path; cows and sheep were always getting in the way. Now and then an escaped hen would come clucking and flapping among our feet and once a huge bull, with horns levelled to the charge, came dashing down the street, scattering everything before him. Finally, we reached the spot where Mick and his dogs were keeping watch over the cows and sheep.

'Got here all safe, Mick, I see.'

'All safe, sir, not a quarter o' an hour ago.'

'Well, I have opened my shop. We'll see how we get on.'

By this time the dealers had gathered about and were closely examining the sheep and holding whispered consultations. At length an excited-looking man came running forward; plunging his hand into his breeches pocket, he produced therefrom half-a-crown, which he slapped into Penruddock's hand, at the same time crying out, 'Ten-and-six a head.' 'Fifteen,' said John returning the coin.

'Twelve shillings.' said the man, bringing down the coin with tremendous energy; 'an' may I niver stir if I'll give another farthin' for the best sheep in Keady.'

'Fifteen,' said John, flinging the half-crown on the ground; 'and I don't care whether you stir again or not.'

By this time a crowd had gathered and the chorus began.

'There isn't a dacenter man than Mr Penruddock in the market. I've know him iver since he came to the counthry,' said one man.

213

'Shure an' he is,' began another; 'He's a jintleman ivery inch. He always gives to the poor a bit o' baccy, or a glass. Ach, Mr Loney, *he's* not one to ax you too high a price. Shure, Mr, Penruddock, you'll come down a six-pence jist to make a bargain.'

'Is't Mr Loney that's goin' to buy?' cried a lame man from the opposite side and in the opposite interest.

'There isn't sich a dealer in County Monaghan as Mr Loney,' averred the second spectator. 'Of coorse you'll come down some-thing, Mr Penruddock.'

'He's a rich one, too, is Mr Loney,' said the lame man, sidling up to John and winking in a knowing manner, 'an' a power o' notes he has in his pocketbook.'

Mr Loney, who has been whispering with his group a little apart and who had again made an inspection of the stock, returned the second time to the charge. 'Twelve-an'-six,' cried he and again the half-crown was slapped into Penruddock's palm. 'Twelve-an'-six an' not another farthin' to save my soul.'

'Fifteen,' said John, returning the half-crown with equal emphasis; 'you know my price and if you won't take it you can let it stand.'

The dealer disappeared in huge wrath and the chorus broke out in praises of both. By this time Mr Loney was again among the sheep; it was plain his heart was set upon the purchase. Every now and then he caught one, got it between his legs, examined the markings on its face and tested the depth and quality of its wool. He appeared for the third time, while the lame man and the leader of the opposing chorus seemed coming to blows, so zeal-ous were they in the praises of their respective heroes.

'Fourteen,' said Mr Loney, again producing the half-crown, spitting into his hand at the same time as much as to say, he would do the business now. 'Fourteen,' he cried, crushing the half-crown into Penruddock's hand and holding it there. 'Fourteen, an' divil a rap more I'll give.'

'Fourteen,' said John, as if considering then throwing back the coin, 'Fourteen-and-six and let it be a bargain.'

'Didn't I say,' quoth John's chorus leader, looking round him with an air of triumph, 'didn't I say that Mr Penruddock's a jintleman? Ye see how he drops the sixpence. I niver saw him do a mane thing yet. Ach, he's the jintleman ivery inch, an'that's a dale, considerin' his size.'

'Fourteen-and-six be it then,' said the dealer, bringing down the coin for the last time. 'An'if I take the lot you'll give me two pounds in t'myself?'

'Well, Loney, I don't care although I do,' said Penruddock, pocketing the coin at last. A roll of notes was produced, the sum counted out and the bargain concluded. The next moment Loney was among the sheep, scoring some mark or other on their backs with a piece of red chalk. Penruddock scattered what spare coppers he possessed among the bystanders and away they went to sing the praises of the next bargain-maker.

Pen returned to me laughing. 'This is a nice occupation for a gentleman of respectable birth and liberal education, is it not?'

'Odd. It is amusing to watch the process by which your sheep are converted into banknotes. Does your friend, Mr Loney, buy the animals for himself?'

'Oh, dear, no. We must have middlemen of one kind or another in this country. Loney is commissioned to purchase and is allowed so much on the transaction.'

By this time a young handsome fellow pushed his horse through the crowd and approached us. 'Good morning,' cried he to Penruddock. 'Any business doing?'

'I have just sold my sheep.'

'Good price?'

'Fair. Fourteen and six.'

'Ah, not bad. These cattle, I suppose, are yours? We must try if we can't come to a bargain about them.' Dismounting, he gave his horse in keeping to a lad and he and John went off to inspect the stock.

Business was proceeding briskly on all sides. There was great haggling as to prices and shillings and half-crowns were tossed in a wonderful manner from palm to palm. Apparently, nothing could be transacted without that ceremony, what ever it might mean. Idlers were everywhere celebrating the merits and 'dacency' of the various buyers and sellers. Huge greasy, leather pocketbooks, of undoubted antiquity, were to be seen in many a hand and rolls of banknotes were deftly changing owners. The ground, too, was beginning to clear and purchasers were driving off their cattle. Many of the dealers who had disposed of stock were taking their ease in the inns. I could see them looking out of the open windows; and occasionally a man whose potations had been early and excessive went whooping through the crowd. In a short time John returned with his friend.

'Captain Broster,' said John, presenting him, 'has promised to dine with us at three. Sharp at the hour, mind, for we wish to leave early.'

'I'll be punctual as clockwork,' said the captain, turning to look after his purchases.

We strolled up and down till three o'clock and then bent our steps to the inn, where we found Broster waiting. In honour to his guests the landlord himself brought in dinner and waited with great diligence. When the table was cleared we had punch and cigars and sat chatting at the open window. The space in front was tolerably clear of cattle now, but dealers were hovering about, standing in clumps, or promenading in parties of twos and threes. But at this point a new element had entered into the scene.

It was dinner hour and many of the forgemen from the furnaces above had come down to see what was going on. Huge, hulking, swarthy-featured fellows they were. Welshmen chiefly, as I was afterwards told, who, confident in their strength, were at no pains to conceal their contempt for the natives. They, too, mingled in the crowd, but the greater number leaned lazily against the houses, smoking their short pipes and indulging in the dangerous luxury of 'chaffing' the farmers.

Many a rude wit-combat was going on, accompanied by roars of laughter, snatches of which we occasionally heard.

Broster had been in the Crimea, wounded at Alma, recovered, went through the first winter of the siege, got knocked up, came home on sick leave and, having had enough of it, as he frankly confessed, took the opportunity on his father's death, which happened then, to sell out and settle as a farmer on a small property to which he fell heir. As he was telling us all this, voices rose in one of the apartments below; the noise became altercation and immediately a kind of struggling or dragging was heard in the flagged passage and then a tipsy forgeman was unceremoniously shot out into the square and the inn door closed with an angry bang. The individual seemed to take the indignity in good part; along he staggered, his hands in his pockets, heedless of the satirical gibes and remarks of his companions, who were smoking beneath our windows. Looking out, we could see that his eyes were closed, as if he scorned the outer world, possessing one so much more satisfactory within himself.

'I hope that fellow won't come to grief,' said Broster, as the forgeman lurched through a group of countrymen intent on a bargain and passed on without notice or apology, his eyes closed and sighing happily.

'By Jove, he's down at last and there'll be the devil to pay!' We looked out, the forgeman was prone in the dust, singing and apparently unconscious that he had changed his position. A party of farmers were standing around laughing; one of them had put out his foot and tripped the forgeman as he passed. The next moment a bare-armed black-browed hammersmith strode out from the wall and, without so much as taking the pipe from his mouth, felled the dealer at a blow and then looked at his companions as if wishing to be informed if he could do anything in the same way for them.

The blow was a match dropped in a powder magazine. Alelu! To the combat! There were shouts and yells. Insult had been rankling long in the breasts of both parties. Old scores had to be paid off. From every quarter, out of the inns, down the streets from among the cattle, the dealers came rushing to the fray. The forgemen mustered with alacrity, as if battle were the breath of their nostrils. In a few seconds the square was the scene of a grand *melee*.

The dealers fought with their short heavy sticks; the forgemen had but the weapons nature gave, but their arms were sinewed with iron and every blow told like a hammer. They were overpowered for a while, but the alarm had already spread to the furnaces above and parties of twos and threes came at a run and flung themselves in to the assistance of their companions. Just at this moment a couple of constables pressed forward into the yelling crowd. A hammersmith came behind one and, seizing his arms, held him, despite his struggles, firmly as in a vice. The other was knocked over and trampled under foot.

'Good heavens, murder will be done,' cried Broster, lifting his heavy whip from the table; 'we must try and put an end to this disgraceful scene. Will you join me?'

'With heart and soul,' said Penruddock, 'and there is no time to be lost. Come along.'

At the foot of the stair we found the landlord shaking in every limb. He had locked the door and was standing in the passage with the key in his hand.

'M'Queen, we want out; open the door.'

'Shure, jintlemen, you're no goin' just now. You'll be torn to paces if you go.'

'If you won't open the door, give me the key and I'll open it myself.'

The landlord passively yielded. Broster unlocked the door and flung the key down on the flagged passage. 'Now, my lads,' cried he to half-a-dozen countrymen who were hanging-on spectators on the skirts of the combat and at the same time twisting his whiplash tightly round his right hand till the heavy leaded head became a formidable weapon; 'Now, my lads, we are resolved to put an end to this; will you assist us?'

The captain's family had been long resident in the country, he was personally known to all of them and a cheerful 'Ay, ay,' was the response.

'Penruddock, separate them when you can, knock them over when you can't. Welshman or Irishman, it's quite the same.' So saying, in we drove. Broster clove a way for himself, distributing his blows with great impartiality and knocking over the combatants like ninepins. We soon reached the middle of the square, where the fight was hottest. The captain was swept away in an eddy for a moment and right in front of Penruddock and myself two men were grappling on the ground. As they rolled over, we saw that one was the hammersmith who had caused the whole affray. We flung ourselves upon them and dragged them up. The dealer, with whom I was more particularly engaged, had got the worst of it and plainly wasn't sorry to be released from the clutches of his antagonist. With his foe it was different. His slow sullen blood was fairly in a blaze and when Pen pushed him aside, he dashed at him and struck him a severe blow on the face. In a twinkling Penruddock's coat was off, while the faintest stream of blood trickled from his upper lip.

'Well, my man,' said he, as he stood up ready for action, 'if that's the game you mean to play at, I hope to give you a bellyful before I've done.'

'Seize that man, knock him over,' said Broster; 'you're surely not going to fight *him*, Penruddock, it's sheer madness; knock him over.'

'I tell you what it is,' said Penruddock, turning savagely, 'you shan't deprive me of the luxury of giving this fellow a sound hiding.'

Broster shrugged his shoulders, as if giving up the case. By this time the cry arose, 'Black Jem's goin' to fight the gentleman;' and a wide enough ring was formed. Many who were prosecuting small combats of their own desisted, that they might behold a greater one.

Broster stood beside John. 'He's an ugly mass of strength,' whispered he, 'and will hug you like a bear; keep him well off and remain cool for Heaven's sake.'

'Ready?' said John, stepping forward.

'As the lark i' the mornin',' growled Jem, as he took up his ground.

The men were very wary – Jem retreating round and round, John advancing. Now and then one or the other darted a blow, but it was generally stopped and no harm done. At last the blows went home; the blood began to rise. The men drew closer and struck with greater rapidity. They are at it at last, hammer and tongs. No shirking of flinching now. Jem's blood was flowing. He was evidently getting severely punished. He couldn't last long at that rate. He fought desperately for a close, when a blinding blow full in the face brought him to earth. He got up again like a madman, the whole bulldog nature of him possessed and mastered by brutal rage. He cursed and struggled in the arms of his supporters to get back at his enemy, but by main force they held him back till he recovered himself.

'He'll be worked off in another round,' I heard Broster whisper in my ear. 'Ah! here they come!'

I glanced at Pen for a moment as he stood with his eye on his foe. There was that in his face that boded no good. The features had hardened into iron somehow; the pitiless mouth was clenched, the eye cruel. A hitherto unknown part of his nature revealed itself to me as he stood there – perhaps unknown to himself. God help us, what strangers we are to ourselves!

But they are at it again; Jem still fights for a close and every time his rush is stopped by a damaging blow. They are telling rapidly; his countenance, by no means charming at the best, is rapidly transforming. Look at that hideously gashed lip! But he has dodged Penruddock's left this time and clutched him in his brawny arms. Now comes the tug of war, skill pitted against skill, strength against strength. They breathe for a little in each other's grip, as if summoning every energy. They are at it now, broad chest to chest. Now they are motionless, but by the quiver of their frames I can guess the terrific strain going on. Now one has the better, now the other, as they twine round each other, lithe and supple as serpents. Penruddock yields! No! That's a bad dodge of Jem's. By Jove he loses his grip. All is over with him. Pen's brow grows dark; the veins start out on it; and the next moment Black Jem, the hero of fifty fights, slung over his shoulder, falls heavily to the ground.

At his fall a cheer rose from the dealers. 'You blacksmith fellows had better make off,' cried Broster; 'your man has got the thrashing he deserves and you can carry him home with you. I am resolved to put a stop to these disturbances – there have been too many of late.'

The furnacemen hung for a moment irresolute, seemingly half-inclined to renew the combat, but a formidable array of cattle-dealers pressed forward and turned the scale. They decided on a retreat. Black Jem, who had by now come to himself, was lifted up and, supported by two men, retired toward the works and dwellings on the upper grounds, accompanied by his companions, who muttered many a surly oath and vow of vengeance.

When we got back to the inn, Pen was very anxious about his face. He washed and carefully perused his features in the little looking-glass. Luckily, with the exception of the upper lip slightly cut by Jem's first blow, no mark of the combat presented itself. At this happy result of his investigations he expressed great satis-faction – Broster laughing the meanwhile and telling him that he was as careful of his face as a young lady.

The captain came down to see us off. The fair was over now and the little streets were almost deserted. The dealers – apprehensive of another descent from the furnaces – had hurried off as soon as their transactions could in any way permit. Groups of villagers, however, were standing about the doors discussing the event of the day; and when Penruddock appeared he became, for a quarter of an hour, an object of public interest for the first time in his life and, so far as he has yet lived, for the last; an honour to which he did not seem to attach any particular value.

We shook hands with the captain; then, at a touch of the whip, the horse started at a gallant pace, scattering a brood of ducks in all directions; and in a few minutes Keady – with its white-washed houses and dark row of furnaces, tipped with tongues of flame, pale and shrunken yet in the lustre of the afternoon, but which would rush out wild and lurid when the evening fell – lay a rapidly dwindling speck behind.

I am induced to set down this business of the Irish market and market fight in order that the reader may gather some idea of the kind of man Penruddock was. He was not particularly witty; on no subject was he profoundly read; he did not care for art. He had his limitations, you see: but as a man I have seldom met his equal – he was sagacious, kindly, affectionate, docile, patient and unthinking of self. Above all things, he was sincere and I trusted Pen when I came to know him as implicitly as I would a law of nature.

It was Pen's business 'to make good sheep,' as the Skye people say and magnificent sheep he did make. He had an ideal sheep in his mind and to reach that ideal he was continually striving. At the yearly winnowings of his stock he selected his breeding ewes with the utmost care and these ewes, without spot or blem-ish, he crossed with wonderfully-horned and far-brought rams, for which he sometimes paid enormous prices – so at least his neighbours said. His sheep he bred in Skye for the most part and then he sent them over to Ulster to fatten. There, on pasture and turnips, they throve amazingly, all their good points coming into prominence, all their bad points stealing modestly into the shade. At markets, Penruddock's sheep always brought excellent prices and his lot was certain to be about the best shown.

Pen and the Landlord had business relations. In partnership, they brought over meal from Ireland, they speculated in turnips, they dealt in curious manures which were to the sour Skye soil what plum-pudding is to a charity boy: above all he was confederate in a scheme of emigration which the Landlord had concocted and was in the course of carrying out. Pen's visit at this time was purely a business one: he wished to see me, but that was far from his sole motive in coming – so he frankly said. But I did not care for that; I was quite able to bear the truth and was glad to have him on any conditions.

Emigration

ONE MORNING AFTER our return, when breakfast was over, the Landlord, followed by Maida, carried the parrot into the sunshine in front of the house and, sitting down on one of the iron seats, lighted a cheroot. As there was nothing on the cards that special morning, we all followed him and, lifting his cheroot case, helped ourselves. The morning was warm and pleasant; and as no-one had anything particular to say, we smoked in silence and were happy. The only one who was occupied was Fellowes. A newspaper had reached him by post the evening before and with its pages he was now busy. Suddenly he burst out laughing and read out from a half-column of *facetiae* an anecdote about an Irishman in search of the other side of the street who kept crossing, only to be told it was 'over there.' We all laughed and Fellowes, shutting up the paper, maintained that the hunt after the opposite side of the street was no bad image of the hunt after the truth.

'Truth is always "over there," ' he said, 'and when you get "over there" you find it has gone back to the place from which you started. No man has ever yet reached truth, or the opposite side of the street.'

'What creatures those Irish are, to be sure!' said the Landlord, as he knocked a feather of white ash from the tip of his cheroot. 'It would be a dull world without them. In India, a single Irishman at a station is enough to banish blue devils. The presence of an Irishman anywhere keeps away low spirits, just as a cat in the house keeps away rats and mice.'

'I have lived a good deal both in Ireland and the Highlands,' said Pen, 'and the intellectual differences between the two races have often struck me as not a little curious. They are of the same stock originally, antiquaries say; and yet Ireland is a land over-flowing with the milk and honey of humour, whereas in every quality of humour the Highlands are as dry as a desert. Jokes don't usually come farther north than the Grampians; one of two are occasionally found in Ross-shire over there; but no joke has yet been found strong-winged enough to cross the Kyles. That's odd, is it not?'

'But have not the Highlanders wit?' I asked.

'Oh yes, plenty of it,' replied Pen, 'but rather of the strenuous than the playful kind; their wit is born for the most part of anger or contempt – a rapid retort, a blow returned swiftly and with interest. But the Highlander differs from the Irishman in that he has no eye for the pleasantly droll side of things; he has no fun in him, no sense of the genially comic. He laughs, but there is generally a touch of scorn in his laughter and it is almost always directed *against* a man or a thing. The Irishman's humour puts a stitch on the torn coat, ekes the scanty purse, boils the peas with which he is to limp graveward. The two races dine often scantily enough, but it is only the Irishman that can sweeten his potatoes with *point*. "They talk of hardships," said the poor Irish soldier as he lay down to sleep on the deck of the transport, "They talk of hardships; but bedad this is the hardest ship I ever was in in me life." No Highlander would have said *that*. And I believe that the joke made the hard plank all the softer to the joker.'

'And how do you account for this difference,' inquired Fellowes.

'I can't account for it. The two races springing from the same stock, I rather think it is *un*accountable; unless, indeed, it be trace-able to climatic influence – the soft, green, rainy Erin producing luxuriant and ebullient natures; the bare, flinty Highlands, hard and austere ones. The light-hearted Irishman delights to "chaff" and to be "chaffed;" the intense and more serious-hearted Highlander can neither do the one nor endure the other. The bit of badinage which an Irishman will laugh at and brush carelessly aside stings the Highlander like a gadfly. If you enter into a gay wit-combat with a Highlander, it is almost certain to have a serious ending – just as the old Highland wedding-feasts, beginning with pledged healths and universal three-times-three, ended in a brawl and half-a-dozen men dirked.'

'Chaff,' I suggested, 'is the offspring of impudence and loquacity. I am not astonished that the Highlander cannot endure it, nor do it and I don't think the worse of him for that. It is out of his way altogether. A London cabman would slang Socrates into silence in a quarter of an hour.'

'I suppose,' said the Landlord, turning the talk to a subject which had been favourite on the Island this summer and the last, 'when the Skye railway is finished we poor Highlanders will get our jokes from the South, as we get our tea and sugar. It's a pity the Board of Directors did not mention that special import in their prospectus. The shares might have gone off more rapidly, Pen!'

'You are a great friend of the railway, are you not?' asked Fellowes.

'Of course I am,' said the Landlord. 'I consider the locomotive the good wizard of our modern day. Its whistle scares away filth, mendicancy and unthrift; ignorance and laziness perish in the glare of its red eyes. I have seen what it has done for the Hindu and I know that it will do for the Islesman. We hold India by our railways today rather than by our laws or our armies. The swart face of the stoker is the first sign of the golden age that has become visible in my time.'

'What benefits do you expect the railway will bring with it to Skye?'

'It will bring us in closer contact with the South. By the aid of the railway we shall be enabled to send out stock to the southern markets more rapidly, more cheaply and in better condition and, as a consequence, we will obtain better prices. By aid of the railway the Islands will be opened up, our mineral treasures will be laid bare, our marbles will find a market, the Skye apple and the Skye strawberry will be known in Covent Garden, our fisheries will flourish as they have never flourished before. The railway will bring southern capital to us and humane southern influences. The railway will send an electric shock throughout the entire Island. Everybody's pulse will be quickened; the turf hut will disappear; and the Skyeman will no longer be considered a lazy creature: which he is not – he only seems so because he has never found a proper field for the display of his activities. There are ten chances to one that your Skye lad, if left *in* Skye, will remain a fisherman or a shepherd; but transplant him to Glasgow, Liverpool or London and he not unfrequently blossoms into a merchant prince. There were quick and nimble brains under the shock heads of the lads you saw at my school the other day and to each of these lads the railway will open a career great or small or, at all events, the chance of one.'

When the Landlord had ceased speaking, a boy brought the postbag and laid it on the gravel. It was opened and we got our letters – the Landlord a number of Indian ones. These he put into his coat pocket. One he tore open and read.

'Hello, Pen!' he cried, when he got to the end, 'my emigrants are to be at Skeabost on Thursday; we must go over to see them.'

Then he marched into the house and in a little time thereafter our smoking parliament dissolved, but I sat alone, musing on emigration and how it is viewed.

The English emigrant is prosaic; Highland and Irish emigrants are poetical. How is this? The wild-rose lanes of England, I would think, are as bitter to part from and as worthy to be remembered at the antipodes, as the wild coasts of Skye or the green hills of Ireland. Yet poet and painter turn a cold shoulder on the English emigrant, while they expend infinite pathos on the emigrants from Erin or the Highlands. The Highlander has his *Lochaber-no-more* and the Irishman has the Countess of Gifford's pretty song. The ship in the offing and the parting of Highland emigrants on the seashore, have been made the subject of innumerable paint-ings; and yet there is a sufficient reason for it all.

Rightly or wrongly, it is popularly understood that the English emigrant is not mightily moved by regret when he beholds the shores that gave him birth withdrawing themselves into the dimness of the far horizon – although, if true, why should it be so? and, if false, how has it crept into the common belief? are questions not easy to answer. If the Englishman is obtuse and indifferent in this respect, the Highlander is not. He finds it as difficult to part from the faces of the familiar hills as from the faces of his neighbours. In the land of his adoption he cherishes the language, the games and the songs of his childhood; and he thinks with a continual sadness of the gray-green slopes of Lochaber and the thousand leagues of dim, heartbreaking sea tossing between them and him.

The Celt clings to his birthplace, as the ivy nestles lovingly to its wall; the Saxon is like the arrowy seeds of the dandelion, that travel on the wind and strike root afar. Emigration *is* more pain-ful to the Highlander than it is to the Englishman – this, poet and painter have instinctively felt – and in wandering up and down Skye I come into contact with this pain, either fresh or in remi-niscence, not unfrequently. Although the member of his family be years removed, the Skyeman lives in him imaginatively – just as the man who has endured an operation is for ever conscious of the removed limb.

And his horror of emigration – common to the entire Highlands – has been increased by the fact that it has not unfrequently been a forceful matter, that potent landlords have torn down houses and turned out the inhabitants, have authorised evictions, have deported the dwellers of entire glens. That the landlords so acting have not been without grounds of justification may, in all prob-ability, be true. The deported villagers may have been cumberers of the ground, they may have been unable to pay rent, they may have been slowly but surely sinking into pauperism, their pros-pect of securing a comfortable subsistence in the colonies may be considerable, while in their own glens it may be *nil* – all this may be true; but to have your house unroofed before your eyes and made to go on board a ship bound for Canada, even although the passage money be paid for you, is not pleasant. An obscure sense of wrong is kindled in the heart and brain. It is just possible that what is for the landlord's interest may be for yours also in the long run; but you feel that the landlord has looked after his own interest in the first place. He wished you away and he has got you away; whether you will succeed in Canada is a matter of dubiety. The human gorge rises at this kind of forceful banishment – more particularly the gorge of the banished!

When Thursday came, the Landlord drove us over to Skeabost, at which place, at noon, the emigrants were to assemble. He told me on the way that some of the more sterile portions of his property were overpopulated and that the people there could no more prosper than trees that have been too closely planted. He was consequently a great advocate of emigration. He maintained that force should never be used, but advice and persuasion only; that when consent was obtained, there should be held out a helping hand.

It was his idea that if a man went all the way to Canada to oblige him, it was but fair that he should make that man's journey as pleasant as possible and provide him employment, or, at all events, put him in the way of obtaining it when he got there. In Canada, consequently, he purchased lands, made these lands over to a resident relative and, to the charge of that relative – who had erected houses and who had trees to fell and fields to plough and cattle to look after – he consigned his emigrants. He took care that they were safely placed on shipboard at Glasgow or Liverpool and his relative was in waiting when they arrived. When the friendly face died on this side of the Atlantic, a new friendly face dawned on them on the other.

With only one class of tenant was he inclined to be peremptory. He had no wish to disturb in their turf hut the old man and woman who had brought up a family; but when the grown-up son brought home a wife to the same hut, he was down upon them, like a severing knife, at once. The young people could not remain there; they might go where they pleased; he would rather they go to Canada than anywhere, but out of the old dwelling they must march. And the young people frequently jumped at the Landlord's offer – labour and good wages calling sweetly to them from across the sea. The Landlord had already sent out a troop of emigrants, of whose conditions and prospects he had the most encouraging accounts, both from themselves and others and the second troop were that day to meet him at Skeabost.

When we got to Skeabost there were the emigrants, to the number perhaps of fifty or sixty, seated on the lawn. They were dressed as was their wont on Sundays, when prepared for church. The men wore suits of blue or gray felt, the women were wrapped for the most part in tartan plaids. They were decent, orderly, intelligent and on the faces of most was a certain resolved look, as if they had carefully considered the matter and they had made up their minds to go through with it. They were of every variety of age too; the greater proportion young men who had long years of vigorous work in them, who would fell many a tree and reap many a field before their joints stiffened: women, fresh, comely and strong, not yet mother, but who would be grandmothers before their term of activity was past. In the party, too, was a sprinkling of middle-aged people, with whom the world had gone hardly and who were hoping that Canada would prove kinder than Skye.

They all rose and saluted the Landlord respectfully as we drove down towards the house. The porch was immediately made a hall of audience. The landlord sat in a chair, Pen took his seat at the table and opened a large scroll-book in which the names of the emigrants were inscribed. One by one the people came from the lawn to the porch and made known their requirements:- a man had not yet made up his passage money and required an advance; a woman desired a pair of blankets; an old man wished the Landlord to buy his cow, which was about to calve and warranted an excellent milker.

With each of these the Landlord talked, sometimes in Gaelic, more frequently in English: entered into the circumstances of each and commended, rebuked, expostulated, as occasion required. When an emigrant had finished his story and made his bargain with the Landlord, Pen wrote the conditions thereof against his or her name in the large scroll-book. The giving of audience began about noon and it was evening before it was concluded. By that time every emigrant had been seen, talked with and disposed of. For each the way to Canada was smoothed and the terms set down by Pen in his scroll-book; and each, as he went away, was instructed to hold himself in readiness on the 15th of the following month, for on that day they were to depart.

When the emigrants were gone we smoked on the lawn, with the moon rising behind us. Next morning our party broke up. Fellowes and the Landlord went off in the mail to Inverness; the one to resume his legal reading there, the other to catch the train for London. Pen went to Bracadale, where he had some business to transact preparatory to going to Ireland and I drove in to Portree to meet the southward-going steamer, for vacation was over and my Summer in Skye had come to an end.

Homewards

LIFE IS PLEASANT, but unfortunately we have got to die; vacation is delightful, but unfortunately vacations come to an end. Mine has come to an end; and sitting in the inn at Portree waiting for the southward-going steamer, I began to count up my practical and ideal gains, just as in dirty shillings and half-crowns a cobbler counts up his of a Saturday night.

In the first place, I was a gainer in health. When I came up here a month ago I was tired, jaded, ill at ease. I put spots in the sun, I flecked the loveliest blue of summer sky with bars of darkness. I felt the weight of the weary hours. Each morning called me as a slavedriver calls a slave. In sleep there was no refreshment, for in dream the weary day repeated itself yet more wearily. I was nervous, apprehensive of evil, irritable – ill, in fact.

Now I had the appetite of an ostrich, I laughed at dyspepsia; I could have regulated my watch by my pulse; and all the dusty, book-lettered and be-cobwebbed chambers of my brain had been tidied and put to rights by the fairies Wonder, Admiration, Beauty, Freshness. Soul and body were braced alike – into them had gone something of the peace of the hills and the strength of the sea. I had work to do and I was able to enjoy work. Here there was one gain, very palpable and appreciable.

Then by my wanderings up and down, I had made solitude forever less irksome, because I had covered the walls of my mind with a variety of new pictures. The poorest man may have a picture gallery in his memory which he would not exchange for the Louvre. In the picture gallery of my memory there hung Blaavin, the Cuchullins, Loch Coruisk, Dunsciach, Duntulm, Lord Macdonald's deer-forest, Glen Sligachan and many another place and scene besides. Here was a gain quite as palpable and appreciable as the other.

Then, again, I had been brought into contact with peculiar individuals, which is in itself an intellectual stimulus, insofar as I am continually urged to enter, explore and understand them. What a new variety of insect is to an entomologist, that a new variety of man is to one curious in men, who delights to brood over them, to comprehend them, to distinguish the shades of difference that exist between them and, if possible, sympathetically to *be* them. This sympathy enables a man in his lifetime to lead fifty lives. I don't think in the south I shall ever find the counterparts of John Kelly, Lachlan Roy, or Angus-with-the-dogs. I am certain I shall never encounter a nobler heart than that which has beat for so long a term in the frame of Mr M'Ian, nor a wiser or humaner brain than the Landlord's.

Even to have met the tobacco-less man was something on which speculation could settle.

Then, in the matter of gain, I may fairly count up being brought into contact with songs, stories and superstitions; for through means of these I obtain access into the awe and terror that lie at the heart of that ancient Celtic life which is fast disappearing now. Old songs illustrate the spiritual moods of a people, just as old weapons, agricultural implements, furniture and domestic dishes, illustrate the material conditions.

All these things were gains: and waiting at Portree for the steamer and thinking over them all, I concluded that my Summer in Skye had not been misspent; and that no summer can be misspent anywhere, provided that the wanderer brings with him a quick eye, an open ear and a sympathetic spirit. It is the cunningest harper that draws the sweetest music from the harp string; but no musician that ever played had exhausted all the capacities of his instrument – there is more to take for him who can take.

The *Clansman* reached Portree Bay at eleven p.m., and I went on board at once and went to bed. When I awoke next morning, the engines were in full action and I could hear the rush of the water past my berth. When I got on deck we were steaming down the Sound of Raasay; and when breakfast time arrived, it needed but a glance to discover that autumn had come and that the sporting season was well-nigh over.

A lot of sheep were penned up near the bows, amidships were piles of wool, groups of pointers and setters were scattered about and at the breakfast table were numerous sportsmen returning to the south, whose conversation ran on grouse-shooting, salmon fishing and deerstalking. While breakfast was proceeding I saw everywhere sun-browned faces, heard cheery voices and witnessed the staying of prodigious appetites. Before these stalwart fellows steaks, chops, platefuls of ham and eggs disappeared as if by magic. The breakfast party, too, consisted of all orders and degrees of men. There were drovers going to, or returning from markets; merchants from Stornoway going south; a couple of Hebridean clergymen, one of whom said grace; several military men of frank and hearty bearing; an extensive brewer; three members of Parliament who had entirely recovered from the fatigues of legislation; and a tall and handsome English Earl of some repute on the turf. Several ladies, too, dropped in before the meal was over. We were all hungry and fed like Homer's heroes. The commissariat on board the Highland steamers is plentiful and of quality beyond suspicion; and the conjunction of good viands and appetites whetted by the sea breeze, results in a play of knife and fork perfectly wonderful to behold.

When breakfast was over we all went upstairs; the smoking men resorted to the hurricane deck, the two clergyman read, the merchants from Stornoway wandered uneasily about us as if seeking someone to whom they could attach themselves and the drovers smoked short pipes amidships and talked to the passengers there and, when their pipes were out, went forward to examine the sheep.

The morning and forenoon wore away pleasantly – the great ceremony of dinner was ahead and drawing nearer every moment – that was something – and then there were frequent stoppages and the villages on the shore, the coming and going of boats with cargo and passengers, the throwing out of empty barrels here, the getting in of wool there, were incidents quite worthy of the regard of idle men leading for the time being a mere life of the senses.

We stopped for a couple of hours in Broadford Bay – we stopped at Kyleakin – we stopped at Balmacara; and the long-looked-for dinner was served after we had passed Kylerhea and were gliding down into Glenelg. For some little time previously, savoury steams had assailed our nostrils. We saw the stewards descending into the cabin with covered dishes and at first sound of the bell the hurricane deck, crowded a moment before, was left entirely empty.

The captain took his seat at the head of the table with a mighty roast before him, the clergyman said grace – somewhat lengthily, I fear, in the opinion of most – the covers were lifted away by deft waiters and we dined that day at four as if we had not previously breakfasted at eight and lunched at one. Dinner was somewhat protracted; for as we had nothing to do after the ladies went, we sat over cheese and wine and then talk grew animated over whisky-punch. When I went on deck again we had passed Knock and were steaming straight for Armadale. The Knoydart hills were on the one side, the low shores of Sleat, patched here and there by strips of cultivation, on the other; and in a little we saw the larch plantations of Armadale and the castle becoming visible through the trees on the lawn.

In autumn the voyage to the south is lengthened by stop-pages and frequently the steamer has to leave her direct course and thread along inland running lochs to take wool on board. These stoppages and wanderings out of the direct route would be annoying if I were hurrying south to be married, or if I were summoned to the deathbed of a friend from whom I had expectations; but as it is a holiday for me and as every divergence brings me into unexpected scenery, then I regard them rather as a pleasure than anything else.

At Armadale we stayed for perhaps half an hour and then struck directly across the Sound of Sleat and sailed up the windings of Loch Nevis. When we reached the top there was an immense to-do on the beach; some three or four boats laden with wool were already pulling out towards the steamer, which immediately lay to and let off noisy steam; men were tumbling bales of wool into the empty boats that lay at the stony pier and to the pier laden carts were hurrying down from the farmhouse that stood remote. The wool boats came on either side of the steamer; doors were opened in the bulwarks, to these doors steam cranes were wheeled and with many a shock of crank and rattle of loosened chain, the bales were hoisted on deck and consigned to the gloomy recesses of the hold.

As soon as a boat was emptied, a laden one pulled out to take its place; the steam cranes were kept continually jolting and rattling and in the space of a couple of hours a considerable amount of business had been done. On the present occasion the transference of wool from the boats to the hold of the steamer occupied a longer time than was usual; sunset had come in crimson and died away to pale gold and rose; and still the laden boats came slowly on, still storms of Gaelic execration surged along the sides of the ship and still the steam cranes were at their noisy work. The whole affair, having by this time lost all sense of novelty, was in danger of becoming tiresome, but in the fading light the steward had lighted up the saloon into hospitable warmth and glow and then the bell rang for tea.

In a moment all interest in the wool boats had come to an end, the passengers hurried below and, before the tinklings of cup and saucer had ceased, the last bale of wool had been transferred from the boats along side to the hold and the *Clansman* had turned round and was softly gliding down Loch Nevis.

A lovely, transparent autumn night arched above us, a young moon and single star by her side, when we reached Arisaig. By this time the ladies had retired and those of the gentlemen who remained on deck were wrapped in plaids, each shadowy figure brought out more keenly by the red tip of a cigar. The entrance into Arisaig is difficult and the *Clansman* was put on half steam. The gentlemen were requested to leave the hurricane deck and there the captain stationed himself, while a couple of men were sent to the bows and three or four stationed at the wheel.

Slowly the large vessel moved onward, with low black reefs of rocks on either side, like smears of dark colour, but perfectly soft and tender in outline; and every here and there we could see the dark top of a rock peering out of the dim sea like a beaver's head. From these shadowy reefs, as the vessel moved on, the sea-birds were awakened from their slumbers and strangely sweet and liquid as flute notes were their cries and signals of alarm. Every now and again, too, with a sort of weary sigh, a big wave came heaving in and broke over the dark reefs in cataracts of ghostly silver; and in the watery trouble and movement that followed, the moon became a well of moving light and the star a quivering swordblade.

The captain stood alone on the hurricane-deck and the passengers leaned against the bulwarks watching rock and sea and listening to the call and re-call of disturbed mews, when suddenly there was a muffled shout from the out-look at the bows, the captain shouted 'Port! Port! *Hard*!' and away went the wheel spinning, the stalwart fellows toiling at the spokes and the ship slowly falling off. After a little while there was another noise at the bows, the captain shouted 'Starboard!' and the wheel was rapidly reversed. We were now well up the difficult channel; and looking back we could see a perfect intricacy of reefs and dim single rocks behind and a fading belt of pallor wandering amongst them, which told the track of the ship – a dreadful place to be driven upon on a stormy night, when the whole coast would be like the mouth of a wounded boar – black tusks and churning foam.

After a while, however, a low line of coast became visible, then a light broke upon it; and after a few impatient turns of the paddles we beheld a dozen boats approaching, with lights at their bows. These were the Arisaig boats, laden with cargo. At sight of them the captain left the hurricane deck, the anchor went away with a thundering chain, the passengers went to bed and, between asleep and awake, I could hear half the night the trampling of feet, the sound of voices and the jolt of the steam cranes, as the Arisaig goods were being hoisted on deck and stowed away.

I was up early next morning. The sky was clear, the wind blowing on shore and the bright, living, rejoicing sea came seething in on the rocky intricacies through which we slowly sailed. Skye was perfectly visible, the nearer shores dark and green; farther back the dim Cuchullins, standing in the clouds. Eigg rose opposite, with its curiously-shaped sgurr; Muck lay ahead. The *Clansman* soon reached the open sea and we began to feel the impulse of the Atlantic. By the time the passengers began to appear on deck the ship was lurching heavily along towards the far-stretching headland of Ardnamurchan. It was difficult to keep my feet steady – more difficult to keep steady my brain.

Great glittering watery mounds came heaving on, to wash with unavailing foam the rocky coast; and amongst these the steamer rolled and tossed and groaned, its long dark pennon of smoke streaming with the impulse of the sea. The greater proportion of the passengers crawled amidships – beside the engines and the cook's quarters, which were redolent with the scent of herrings frying for a most unnecessary breakfast – for there the motion was least felt. To this unhappy landsman that morning, the whole world seemed topsy-turvy. There was no straight line to be discovered anywhere; everything seemed to have changed places. Now I beheld the steersman against the sky on the crest of an airy acclivity, now one bulwark was buried in surge, now the other and anon the sheep at the bows were brought out against a foamy cataract.

But with all this turmoil and dancing and rolling, the *Clansman* went swiftly on and in due time we were off the Ardnamurchan lighthouse. Here we rolled and tossed in an unpleasant manner – the smitten foam springing to the top of the rocks and falling back in snowy sheets – and seemed to make but little progress. Gradually, however, the lighthouse began to draw slowly behind us, slowly we rounded the rocky buttress, slowly the dark shores of Mull drew out to sea and in a quarter of an hour, with dripping decks and giddy brains, we had passed from the great bright heave and energy of the Atlantic to the quiet waters of Loch Sunart; and, sheltered by Mull, were steaming towards Tobermory.

The first appearance of Tobermory is prepossessing: but further acquaintance is, if possible, to be eschewed. As the *Clansman* stems into the bay, the little town, with its half circle of white houses, backed by hill terraces on which pretty villas are perched and flanked by sombre pine plantations, is a pleasant picture and takes heart and eye at once. As you approach, however, your admiration will be lessened and when you go ashore it will be quite obliterated. It has a 'most ancient and fish-like smell,' and all kinds of refuse float in the harbour. Old ocean is a scavenger at Tobermory and is as dirty in his habits as Father Thames himself.

The houses look pretty and clean when seen from the steamer's deck, but on a nearer view they deteriorate and become squalid and several transform themselves into small inns, suggestive of the worst accommodation and the fiercest alcohol. The steamer is usually detained at Tobermory for a couple of hours and during all that time there is a constant noise of lading and unlading. I became tired of the noise and tumult and experienced a sense of relief when steam was got up again and with much backing and turning and churning of dirty harbour water into questionable foam, the large vessel worked its way through the difficult channel and slid calmly down the Sound of Mull.

Gliding down that magnificent Sound, *The Lord of the Isles* is in my memory, just as *The Lady of the Lake* is in my memory at Loch Katrine. The hours float past in music. All the scenes of the noble poem rise in vision before me. I pass the entrance to the beautiful Loch Aline; I pass Ardtornish Castle on the Morven shore, where the Lords of the Isles held their rude parliaments and discussed ways and means; while opposite, Mull draws itself grandly back into lofty mountains. Further down I see Duart Castle, with the rock peering above the tide, on which Maclean exposed his wife – a daughter of Argyll's – to the throttling of waves. After passing Duart, Mull trends away to the right, giving a space of open sun-bright sea, while on the left the Linnhe Loch stretches toward Fort William and Ben Nevis. Straight ahead is the green Lismore – long a home of Highland learning – and, passing it, while the autumn day is wearing towards afternoon, we reached Oban, sheltered from western waves by the island Kerrera.

The longest delay during the passage is at Oban, but then we had dinner there, which helped to kill the time in a pleasant way. The *Clansman* had received a quantity of cargo at Tobermory, at Loch Aline a flock of sheep were driven on board, goods were taken in plentifully at other places in the Sound at which we touched and when we received all the stuffs waiting for us at Oban, the vessel was heavily laden.

The entire steerage was a bellowing and bleating mass of black cattle and sheep, each 'parcel' divided from the other by temporary barriers. The space amidships was a chaos of barrels and trunks and bales of one kind or another and amongst these the steerage passengers were forced to dispose themselves. Great piles of wooden boxes containing herring were laid along the cabin deck, so that if a man were disposed to walk about it behoved him to take care of his footsteps. But who cared! We were away from Oban now, the wind was light, the sun setting behind us and the bell ringing for tea. It was the last meal we were to have together and, through some consciousness of this, the ice of reserve seemed to melt and the passengers to draw closer to each other.

The Hebridean clergymen unbent; the handsome Earl chatted to his neighbours as if his forehead had never known the golden clasp of the coronet; the sporting men stalked their stags over again; the members of Parliament discussed every subject except the affairs of the nation; the rich brewer joked; the merchants from Stornoway laughed immoderately; while the cattle dealers listened with awe. Tea was prolonged after this pleasant fashion and then, while the Stornoway merchants and the cattle dealers solaced themselves with a tumbler of punch, the majority of the other passengers went upstairs to the hurricane deck to smoke.

What a boon is tobacco to the modern Englishman! It stands in place of wife, child, profession and the interchange of ideas. With a pipe in your mouth indifference to your neighbour is no longer churlish and silent rumination becomes the most excellent companionship. The English were never very great talkers, but since Sir Walter Raleigh introduced the Virginian weed they have talked less than ever.

Slowly the night fell around the smokers, the stars came out in the soft sky, as the air grew chill and, one by one, they went below. Then there was more toddy drinking, some playing at chess, one or two attempts at letter writing and at eleven o'clock the waiters cleared the tables and began to transform the saloon into a large sleeping apartment.

I climbed up to my berth and fell comfortably asleep. I must have been asleep for several hours, although of the lapse of time I was of course unconscious, when gradually the horror of nightmare fell upon me. This horror was vague and formless at first, but gradually it assumed a definite shape. I was Mazeppa, they had bound me to the back of a camel and the mighty brute maddened with pain and terror, was tearing along the wilderness, crashing through forests, plunging into streams, with the howling of wolves close behind and coming ever nearer. At last, when the animal cleared a ravine at a bound, I burst the bondage of my dream.

For a moment I could not understand where I was. The sleeping apartment seemed to have fallen on one side, then it righted itself, but only to fall over on the other, then it made a wild plunge forward as if it were a living thing and had received a lash. The ship was labouring heavily, I heard the voices of the sailors flying in the wind, I felt the shock of solid and the swish of broken seas. In such circumstances sleep, for me at least, was impossible, so I slipped out of bed and, steadying myself for a favourable moment, made a grab at my clothes. With much difficulty I dressed, with greater difficulty I got into my boots and then I staggered on deck.

Holding on by the first support, I was almost blinded by the glare of broken seas. From a high coast against which the great waves rushed came the steady glare of a lighthouse and by that token I knew we were 'on' the Mull of Kintyre. The ship was fuming through a mighty battle of tides. Shadowy figures of steerage passengers were to be seen clinging here and there. One – a young woman going to Glasgow as a housemaid, as she afterwards told me – was in great distress, was under the impression that we were all going to the bottom and came to me for comfort. I quieted her as best I could and procured her a seat. Once, when the ship made a wild lurch and a cloud of spray came flying over the deck, she exclaimed to a sailor who was shuffling past wearing a sou'-wester and canvas overalls, 'O sailor, is't ever sae bad as this?'

'As bad as this,' said the worthy, poising himself on the unsteady deck, 'as bad as this! Lord, ye sud jist a seen oor last vi'age. There was only three besides mysel o' the ship's crew able to haud on by a rape.' Delivering himself of this scrap of dubious comfort, the sailor shuffled onward.

Happily the turmoil was not of long duration. In an hour we

had rounded the formidable Mull, had reached comparatively smooth water and, with the lights of Campbeltown behind, the pallid glare of furnaces seen afar on the Ayrshire coast and the morning beginning to pencil softly the east, I went below again and slept till we reached Greenock.

Paisley, Glasgow and Home

THE TOURIST WHO travels by train from Greenock to Glasgow must pass the town of Paisley. If he glances out of the carriage window he will see beneath him a third-rate Scotch town, through which flows the foulest and shallowest of rivers. The principal building in the town and the one which first attracts the eye of a stranger, is the jail; then follow the church spires in their order of merit. Unfortunately, the train passes not through Paisley, but over; and from this 'coign of vantage' the tourist beholds much that is invisible to the passenger in the streets. All the back-greens, piggeries, filthy courts and unmentionable abominations of the place are revealed to him for a moment as the express flashes darkly across the railway bridge.

For the seeing of Scotch towns, a bird's-eye view is plainly the worst point of view. In all likelihood the tourist, as he passes, will consider Paisley the ugliest town he has ever beheld and feel inwardly grateful that his lot had not been cast therein. But in this the tourist may be very much mistaken. Paisley is a remarkable place – one of the most remarkable in Scotland. At this moment – and the same might have been said of any moment since the century came in – there is perhaps a greater number of poets living and breathing in this little town than in the whole of England! Whether this may arise from the poverty of the place, on the principle that the sweetness of the nightingale's song is connected in some subtle way with the thorn against which she leans her breast, it may be useless to inquire. Proceed from what cause it may, Paisley has been for the last fifty years or more, an aviary of singing birds.

Well, it is from this town that I propose taking a walk, for behind Paisley lie Gleniffer Braes, the scene of Tannahill's songs. One can think of Burns apart from Ayrshire, of Wordsworth apart from Cumberland, but hardly of Tannahill apart from the Braes of Gleniffer. The district, too, is of but little extent; in a walk of three hours you can see every spot mentioned by the poet – his birthplace in the little straggling street, where the sound of the shuttle is continually heard; the green hills where he delighted to wander and whose charms he has celebrated; the canal where, when the spirit 'finely touched to fine issues,' was disordered and unstrung, he sought repose. Birth, life and death lie side by side.

'But who is Tannahill?' the southerner reader asks with some wonder. Tannahill was a weaver, who wrote songs, became crazed and committed suicide before he reached middle life. His was a weak, tremulous nature. He was wretched by reason of over-sensitiveness. 'He lived retired as noon-tide dew.' He wanted strength, self-assertion, humour and rough sagacity. He knew nothing of Love, Scorn, Despair – those wild beasts that roam the tropics of the heart. But, limited as was his genius, it was in its quality perhaps more exquisite than that of ever Burns and Hogg. He was only a songwriter; he knew nothing of the mysteries of life; he looked upon nature with a pensive, yet loving eye. But anyone wishing to prove the *truth* of Tannahill's verse, could not do better than bring out his songbook here and read and ramble, ramble and read again.

Leaving the suburbs of Paisley, I pass into a rough and undulating country with masses of gray crag interspersed with whinny knolls where, in the evenings, the linnet sings; with narrow sandy roads wandering through it hither and thither, passing now a clump of gloomy firs, now a house where some wealthy townsman resides, now a pleasant cornfield. A pretty bit of country enough, with larks singing above it from dawn to sunset and where, in the gloaming, the wanderer not unfrequently can mark the limping hare.

A little further on are the ruins of Stanley Castle. This castle, in the days of the poet, before the wilderness of the country had been tamed by the plough, must have lent a singular charm to the landscape. It stands at the base of the hills which rise above it with belt of wood, rocky chasm, white streak of waterfall – higher up into heath and silence, silence deep as the heaven that overhangs it; where nothing moves save the vast cloud-shadows, where nothing is heard save the cry of the moorland bird.

Tannahill was familiar with the castle in its every aspect – when sunset burned on the walls, when the moon steeped it in silver and silence and when it rose up before him shadowy and vast through the marshy mists. He had his loom to attend during the day and he knew the place best in its evening aspect. Twilight, with its quietude and stillness, seemed to have peculiar charms for his sensitive nature and many of his happiest lines are descriptive of its phenomena. But the glory is in a great measure departed from Stanley Tower; the place has been turned into a reservoir by the Water Company and the ruin is frequently surrounded by water.

This intrusion of water has spoiled the scene. The tower is hoary and broken, the lake looks a thing of yesterday and there are traces of quite recent masonry about. The lake's shallow extent, its glitter and brightness, are impertinences. Only during times of severe frost, when its surface is iced over, when the sun is sinking in the purple vapours like a globe of red-hot iron – when the skaters are skimming about like swallows and the curlers are boisterous – only in such circumstances does the landscape regain some kind of keeping and homogeneousness.

There is no season like winter for improving country; he tones it down to one colour; he breathes over its waters and in the course of a single night they become gleaming floors, on which youth may disport itself. He powders his black forest boughs with the pearling of his frosts; and the fissures which spring tries in vain to hide with her flowers and autumn with fallen leaves, he fills up at once with a snow-wreath.

But I must be getting forward, up that winding road, progress marked by gray crag, tuft of heather, bunch of mountain violets, the country beneath stretching out farther and farther. Lo! A strip of emeralds steals down the gray of the hill and there, by the wayside, is an ample well, with the 'netted sunbeam' dancing in it. Those who know Tannahill's 'Gloomy Winter's noo awa' ' must admire its curious felicity of touch and colour.

Turn round, I am in the very scene of the song. In front is 'Gleniffer's dewy dell,' to the east 'Glenkelloch's sunny brae,' afar the woods of Newton, over which at this moment laverocks fan the 'snaw-white cluds;' below, the 'burnie' leaps in sparkle and foam over many a rocky shelf, till its course is lost in that gorge of gloomy firs and I can only hear the music of its joy.

But why go farther today? The Peesweep Inn, where the rambler baits, is yet afar on the heath; Kilbarchan, queerest of villages, is basking its straggling length on the hillsides in the sun, peopled by botanical and bird-nesting weavers, its cross adorned by the statue of Habbie Simpson, 'with his pipes across the wrong shoulder.' Westward is Elderslie, where Wallace was born and there, too, till within the last few years, stood the oak amongst whose branches, as tradition tells, the hero, when hard-pressed by the Southrons, found shelter with all his men. From afar came many a pilgrim to behold the sylvan giant. Before its fall it was sorely mutilated by time and tourists. Of its timber were many snuffboxes made. Surviving the tempests of centuries, it continued to flourish green atop, although its heart was hollow as a ruined tower. At last a gale, which heaped our coasts with shipwreck, struck it down with many of its meaner brethren. 'To this complexion must we come at last.'

At our feet lies Paisley with its poets. Seven miles off, Glasgow peers, with church spire and factory stalk, through a smoky cloud; the country between gray with distance and specked here and there with the vapours of the trains. How silent the vast expanse! Not a sound reaches the ear on the height. Gleniffer Braes are clear in summer light, beautiful as when the poet walked across them.

Enough, their beauty and his memory. I am in no mood to look even at the unsightly place beside the canal which was sought when to the poor disordered brain the world was black and fellow men ravening wolves. Here he walked happy in his genius; not a man to wonder at and bow the knee to, but one fairly to appreciate and acknowledge. For the twitter of the wren is music as well the lark's lyrical up-burst; the sigh of the reed shaken by the wind as well as the roaring of a league of pines.

The idea of Glasgow in the ordinary British minds is probably something like the following.

Glasgow, believed by the natives to be the second city of the empire, is covered by a smoky canopy through which rain penetrates, but which is impervious to sunbeam.

It is celebrated for every kind of industrial activity: it is fervent in business six days of the week and spends the seventh in hearing sermon and drinking toddy.

Its population consists of a great variety of classes.

The *operative*, quiet and orderly enough while plentifully supplied with provisions, becomes a Chartist when hungry and extracts great satisfaction in listening to orators – mainly from the Emerald Isle – declaring against a bloated aristocracy. The *merchant prince*, known to all ends of the earth and subject sometimes to strange vagaries; at one moment he is glittering away cheerily in the commercial heaven, the next he has disappeared, like a lost Pleiad, swallowed up of night for ever.

The history of Glasgow may be summed up in one word – cotton; its deity – gold; its river, besung by poets – a sewer; its environs – dust and ashes; the *gamin* of its wynds and closes less tinctured by education than a Bosjesman; a creature that has never heard a lark sing save perhaps in a cage outside a window in the sixth storey, where a consumptive seamstress is rehearsing *The Song of the Shirt*, 'the swallows with their sunny backs' omitted.

Now this idea of Glasgow is entirely wrong. It contains many cultivated men and women. It is the seat of an ancient university. Its cathedral is the noblest in Scotland; and its statue of Sir John Moore the finest statue in the empire. It is not in itself an ugly city and it has many historical associations. Few cities are surrounded by prettier scenery and the environs of Glasgow have been amply and justly sung by Hugh Macdonald who, in his *Rambles around Glasgow*, visits, stick in hand, every spot of interest to be found for miles around, knows every ruin and its legend, can tell where each unknown poet has lived and died and has the martyrology of the district at his fingers' ends.

In his eyes, Scotland was the fairest portion of the planet; Glasgow, the fairest portion of Scotland; and Bridgeton – the district of the city in which he dwelt – the fairest portion of Glasgow. He would have shrieked like a mandrake at uprootal. He never would pass a night away from home. But he loved nature – and the snowdrop called him out of the smoke to Castlemilk, the lucken-gowan to Kenmure, the craw-flower to Gleniffer. His heart clung to every ruin in the neighbourhood like the ivy. He was learned in epitaphs and spent many an hour in the village churchyards in extracting sweet and bitter thoughts from the half-obliterated inscriptions. He knew Lanarkshire, Renfrewshire and Ayrshire by heart. Keenly sensible to natural beauty, full of anti-quarian knowledge and in possession of a prose style singularly quaint, picturesque and humorous, he began, week by week, in the columns of the *Glasgow Citizen*, the publication of his 'Rambles around Glasgow.'

City people were astonished to learn that the country beyond the smoke was far from prosaic – that it had its traditions, its glens and waterfalls worthy of special excursions. These sketches were afterwards collected and ran, in their separate and more conven-ient form, through two editions. No sooner were the 'Rambles' completed than he projected a new series of sketches entitled 'Days at the Coast,' which also appeared in the newspaper's columns. Also collected into a book, *Days at the Coast* contains

Macdonald's best writing – several of the descriptive passages being really notable in their way.

As we read, the Firth of Clyde glitters before us, with white villages sitting in the green shores: Bute and the twin Cumbraes are asleep in sunshine; while beyond, a stream of lustrous vapour is melting in the grisly Arran peaks.

Glasgow, as most British readers are aware, is situated on both sides of the Clyde, some twenty or thirty miles above its junction with the sea. Its rapidity of growth is perhaps without a parallel in the kingdom. There are persons yet alive who remember when the river, now laden with shipping, was an angler's stream, in whose gravelly pools the trout played and up whose rapids the salmon from the sea flashed like a sunbeam; and when the banks, now lined with warehouses and covered with merchandise of every description, really merited the name of the Broomy Law.

Science and industry have worked wonders here. The stream, which a century ago hardly allowed the passage of a herring boat or a coal gabbert, bears on its bosom today ships from every clime and mighty ocean steamers which have wrestled with the hurricanes of the Atlantic.

Before reaching Glasgow, the Clyde traverses one of the richest portions of Scotland, for in summer Clydesdale is one continued orchard – although, away to the north-east lie the mineral districts of Gartsherrie and Monkland, where everything is grimed with coal dust, where spring comes with a sooty face, where the soil seems calcined, where by night innumerable furnaces and ironworks will rush out into vaster volume and wilder colour and for miles the country will be illuminated, restless with mighty lights and shades; it is the Scottish Staffordshire. On the other hand, away to the south-west, stretch the dark and sterile moors of the Covenant, with wild moss-haggs, treacherous marshes green as emerald and dark mossy lochs, on whose margins the water-hen breeds; a land of plovers and curlews, in whose recesses and in the hearts of whose mists, the hunted people lay while the men of blood were hovering near.

Approaching the city and immediately to the left, are the Cathkin Braes: and close by the village of Cathcart, past which the stream runs murmuring in its rocky bed, is the hill on which Mary stood and saw Moray shiver her army like a potsherd. Below Glasgow and westward, stretches the great valley of the Clyde. On the left is the ancient burgh of Renfrew; farther back Paisley and Johnstone, covered with smoke; above all, Gleniffer Braes, greenly fair in sunlight; afar Neilston Pad, raising its flat summit to the sky, like a table spread for a feast of giants. On the right are the Kilpatrick Hills, terminating in the abrupt peak of Dumbuck; and beyond, the rock of Dumbarton, the ancient fortress, the rock of Ossian's songs. It rises before me out of another world and state of things, with years of lamentation and battle wailing around it like sea-mews. By this time the river has widened to an estuary. Port Glasgow, with its deserted piers and Greenock, populous with ships, lie on the left. Mid-channel, Rosneath is gloomy with its woods; on the farther shore Helensburgh glitters like a silver thread; in front, a battlement of hills. Once past the point of Gourock, you are in the Highlands. From the opposite coast Loch Long stretches up into yon dark world of mountains. Yonder is the Holy Loch, smallest and loveliest of them all. A league of sea is glittering like a frosted silver between me and Dunoon.

The mighty city, twenty miles away, loud with traffic, dingy with smoke, is the working Glasgow; here; nestling at the foot of the mountains, stretching along the sunny crescents of bays, clothing beaked promontories with romantic villas, is another Glasgow keeping holiday the whole summer long. These villages are the pure wheat; the great city, with its strife and toil, its harass and heartbreak – the chaff and husks from which it is winnowed. The city is the soil, this region the bright consummate flower.

The merchant leaves behind him in the roar and vapour his manifold vexations and appears here with his best face and happiest smile. Here no bills intrude, the fluctuations of stock appear not, commercial anxieties are unknown. In their places are donkey

rides, the waving of light summer dresses, merry picnics and boat-
ing parties at sunset on the splendid sea.

Hugging the left shore, we have Largs before us, where long
ago Haco and his berserkers found dishonourable graves. On the
other side is Bute, fairest, most melancholy of all the islands of the
Clyde. From its sheltered position it has an atmosphere soft as that
of Italy and is one huge hospital now. Turn out in the dog days,
your head surmounted with a straw hat ample enough to throw a
shadow round you, your nether man encased in linen ducks and
you will see invalids sitting everywhere in the sunniest spots like
autumn flies, or wandering feebly about, wrapt in greatcoats, their
faces shawled to the nose. If you are half-broiled, they shiver as if
in an icy wind. Their bent figures take the splendour out of the sea
and the glory out of the sunshine. They fill the summer air as with
the earthy horror of a new-made grave. You will feel that they
hang on life feebly and will drop with the yellow leaf.

Beyond Bute are the Cumbraes, twin sisters born in one fiery
hour; and afar Arran, with his precipices, purple-frowning on the
level sea.

In one of his earliest rambles, Mr Macdonald follows the river
for some miles above the city. The beauty of the Clyde below
Glasgow is well known to the civilised world; but it is not only
in her maturity that the Clyde is fair. Beauty attends her from her
birth on Rodger Law until she is wedded with ocean – Bute and
the twin Cumbraes, bridesmaids of the stream; Arran, grooms-
man to the main. With Mr Macdonald's book in my pocket to
be a companion at intervals – for I require no guide, having years
before learned every curve and bend of the river – I start along
its banks towards Carmyle and Kenmure wood. Past Dalmarnock
Bridge and leave the city, with its windowed factories and driving wheels and everlasting canopy of smoke behind. The stream
comes glittering down between green banks, one of which rises
high on the left, so that further vision in that quarter is inter-
cepted. On the right are villages and farms; afar, the Cathkin
Braes, the moving cloud shadows mottling their sunny slopes;

and straight ahead and closing the view, the spire of Cambuslang Church, etched on the pallid azure of the sky.

I am but two miles from the city and everything is bright and green. The butterfly flutters past; the dragonfly darts hither and thither. See, he poises himself on his winnowing wings, about half a yard from my nose, which he curiously inspects; that done, off darts the winged tenpenny-nail, his rings gleaming like steel. There are troops of swallows about. Watch one. Now he is high in the air – now he skims the Clyde. I can hear his sharp querulous twitter as he jerks and turns. Nay, it is said that the kingfisher himself has been seen gleaming along these sandy banks, illuminating them like a meteor.

At some little distance a white house is pleasantly situated amongst trees – it is Dalbeth Convent. As I pass, one of the frequent bells summoning the inmates to devotion is stirring the sunny Presbyterian air. A little on this side of the convent, a rapid brook comes rushing to the Clyde, crossed by a rude bridge of planks, which has been worn by the feet of three generations at the very least. The brook, which is rather huffy and boisterous in its way, particularly after rain, had, a few days before, demolished and broken up these wooden planks and carried one of them off. Arriving, I find a woman and boy anxious to cross, yet afraid to venture. Service is proffered and after a little trouble, both are landed in safety on the farther bank. The woman is plainly, yet neatly dressed and may be about forty-five years of age or thereby. The boy has turned eleven, has long yellow hair hanging down his back and looks thin and slender for his years. With them they have something wrapped up in canvas cloth, which, to the touch as they are handed across, seem to be poles of about equal length. For the slight service the woman returns thanks in a tone which smacks of the southern English countries. 'Good-bye' is given and returned and I proceed, puzzling myself a good deal as to what kind of people they are and what their business may be in these parts, but can come to no conclusion.

However, it does not matter much, for the ironworks are passed now and the riverbanks are beautiful. They are thickly wooded and at a turn the river flows straight down upon me for a mile, with dusty meal mills on one side, a dilapidated wheelhouse on the other and, stretching from bank to bank a half-natural, half-artificial shallow horseshoe fall, over which the water tumbles in indolent foam – a sight which a man who has no pressing engagements and is fond of exercise, may walk fifty miles to see and be amply rewarded for his pains. In front is a ferry – a rope extended across the river by which the boat is propelled – and lo! a woman in a scarlet cloak on the opposite side hails the ferryman and that functionary comes running to his duty.

Just within the din of the shallow horseshoe fall lies the village of Carmyle, an old, quiet, sleepy place, where nothing has happened for the last fifty years and where nothing will happen for fifty years to come. Ivy has been the busiest thing here; it has crept up the walls of the houses and in some instances fairly 'put out the light' of the windows. The thatched roofs are covered with emerald moss. The plum tree which blossomed some months ago blossomed just the same in the spring which witnessed the birth of the oldest inhabitant. For half a century not one stone has been placed upon another here – there are only a few more green mounds in the churchyard. It is the centre of the world. All else is change: this alone is stable. There is a repose deeper than sleep in this little, antiquated village – ivy-muffled, emerald-mossed, lullabied for ever by the fall of waters. The meal mills, dusty and white as the clothes of the miller himself, whir industriously; the waters of the lade come boiling out from beneath the wheel and reach the Clyde by a channel dug by the hand of man long ago, but like a work of nature's now, so covered with furze as it is. Look down through the clear amber of the current and see the 'long green gleet of the slippery stones' in which the silver-bellied eel delights.

Leaving the village, I proceed onward. The banks come closer, the stream is shallower and whirls in eddy and circle over a rocky bed. There is a woodland loneliness about the river which is aided by the solitary angler standing up to his middle in the water and waiting patiently for that bite that never comes, or by the water-ousel flitting from stone to stone. In a quarter of an hour I reach Kenmuir Bank, which rises some seventy feet or so, filled with trees, their trunks rising bare for a space and then spreading out with branch and foliage into matted shade, permitting the passage only of a few flakes of sunlight at noon, resembling in the green twilight, a flock of visionary butterflies alighted and asleep. Within, the wood is jungle; I wade to the knees in brushwood and bracken. The trunks are clothed with ivy and snakes of ivy creep from tree to tree, some green with life, some tarnished with decay.

At the end of the Bank there is a clear well, in which, my face meeting its shadow, I quench my thirst. Seated here, I have the full feeling of solitude. An angler wades out into mid-channel – a bird darts out of a thicket and slides away on noiseless wing – the shallow wash and murmur of the Clyde flows through a silence as deep as that of an American wilderness – and yet, by tomorrow, the water which mirrors as it passes the beauty of the lucken-gowan hanging asleep, will have received the pollutions of a hundred sewers and be bobbing up and down among the crowds of vessels at the Broomielaw.

Returning homeward by the top of Kenmuir Bank, I gaze westward. Out of a world of smoke the stalk of St Rollox rises like a banner-staff, its vapoury streamer floating on the wind; and afar, through the gap between the Campsie and Kilpatrick hills, Ben Lomond himself, with a streak of snow upon his shoulder. Could I but linger here for a couple of hours, I would of a verity behold a sight – the sun setting in yonder lurid, smoke-ocean. The wreaths of vapour which seem so commonplace and vulgar now, so suggestive of trade and swollen purses and rude manners, would then become a glory such as never shepherd beheld at sunrise on his pastoral hills. Beneath a roof of scarlet flame, I would see the rolling edges of the smoke change into a brassy brightness, as with intense heat; the dense mass and volume of it dark as midnight, or glowing with the solemn purple of thunder; while right in the

centre of all, where it has burned a clear way for itself, the broad
fluctuating orb, paining my eye with concentrated splendours and
sinking gradually down, a black spire cutting his disk in two.

But for this I cannot wait and the apparition will be unbeheld
but by the rustic stalking across the field in company with his
prodigious shadow and who, turning his face to the flame, will
conceive it the most ordinary thing to do in the world.

I keep the upper road on my return and in a short time am
again at Carmyle; I have no intention of tracing the river bank
a second time and so turn up the narrow street. But what is to
do? The children are gathered in a circle and the wives are standing at the open doors. There is a performance going on. The
tambourine is sounding and a tiny acrobat, with a fillet round
his brow, tights covered with tinsel lozenges and flesh-coloured
shoes, is striding about on a pair of stilts, to the small amazement
and delight of the juveniles. He turns his head and – why, it's the
little boy I assisted across the brook at Dalbeth three hours ago
and of course, that's the old lady who is thumping and jingling
the tambourine and gathering in the halfpennies! God bless her
jolly old face! Who would have thought of meeting her here? I
am recognised, the boy waves me farewell, the old lady smiles
and curtsies, thumps her tambourine and rattles the little bells of
it with greater vigour than ever.

The road to Glasgow is now comparatively uninteresting. The
trees wear a dingy colour; I pass farmhouses, with sooty stacks
standing in the yard. 'Tis a coaly, dusty district, which has characteristics worth nothing. For, as the twilight falls dewily on far-off
lea and mountain, folding up daisy and buttercup, putting the
linnet to sleep beside his nest of young in the bunch of broom,
here the circle of the horizon becomes like red-hot steel; the
furnaces of the Clyde ironworks lift up their mighty towers of
flame, throwing 'large and angry lustres o'er the sky/ and shifting lights across the long dark roads;' and so, through chase of
light and shade, through glimmer of glare and gloom, I find my
way back to Glasgow – its low hum breaking into separate and

recognisable sounds, its nebulous brightness into far-stretching street lamps, as I draw near.

When of an autumn evening the train brought me into Edinburgh, the scales of familiarity having to some extent fallen from my eyes, I thought I had never before seen it so beautiful. Its brilliancy was dazzling and fairy-like. It was like a city of Chinese lanterns. It was illuminated as if for a great victory, or the marriage of a king.

Princes Street blazed with street lamps and gay shop windows. The Old Town was a maze of twinkling lights. The Mound lifted up its starry coil. The North Bridge leaping the chasm, held lamps high in the air. There were lights on the Calton Hill, lights on the crest of the Castle. The city was in a full blossom of lights – to wither by midnight, to be all dead ere dawn.

And then to an ear accustomed to silence there arose on every side the potent hum of moving multitudes, more august in itself, infinitely more suggestive to the imagination than the noise of the Atlantic on the Skye shores. The sound with which I have been for some time familiar was the voice of many billows; the sound which was in my ears was the noise of men.

And in driving home, too, I was conscious of a curious oppugnancy between the Skye life which I had for some time been leading and the old Edinburgh life which had been dropped for a little and which had now to be resumed. The two experiences met like sheets of metal, but they were still separate sheets – I could not solder them together and make them one. I knew that a very few days would do that for me; but it was odd to attempt by mental effort to unite the experiences and to discover how futile was all such effort. Coming back to Edinburgh was like taking up abode in a house to which I had been for a while a stranger, in which I knew all the rooms and all the articles of furniture in the rooms, but with which knowledge there was mingled a feeling of strangeness. I had changed my clothes of habit and for the moment I did not feel so much at ease in the strange Edinburgh, as the familiar Skye, suit.

It was fated, however, that the two modes of life should, in my consciousness, melt into each other imperceptibly. When I reached home I found that my friend the Rev. Macpherson of Inverary had sent me a packet of Ossianic translations. These translations, breathing the very soul of the wilderness I had lately left, I next day perused in my Edinburgh surroundings and through their agency the two experiences coalesced. Something of Edinburgh melted into my remembrance of Skye – something of Skye was projected into actual Edinburgh. Thus is life enriched by ideal contrast and interchange.

And should the shadows in my book have impressed the reader to any extent, as the realities have impressed me – if I have in any way kindled the feeling of Skye in your imagination as it lives in mine – I will lay down my pen satisfied.